MW01293692

Encounters
Finding God
in All Walks of Life

JOHN F. COVERDALE

Scepter

Encounters: Finding God in All Walks of Life © 2023 John F. Coverdale

The total or partial reproduction of this book is not permitted, nor its informatic treatment, or the transmission of any form or by any means, either electronic, mechanic, photocopy, or other methods without the prior written permission of the owners of the copyright.

Unless otherwise noted, Scripture texts from the New and Old Testaments are taken from The Holy Bible Revised Standard Version Catholic Edition © 1965 and 1966 by the Division of Christian Education of the National Council of the Churches of Christ in the United States. All rights reserved. All copyrighted material is used by permission of the copyright owner. No part of it may be reproduced without permission in writing from the copyright owner.

Published by Scepter Publishers, Inc.
info@scepterpublishers.org
www.scepterpublishers.org
800-322-8773
New York

All rights reserved.

Images throughout this book are used with permission from the Prelature of the Holy Cross and Opus Dei, and from the relatives of Ruth Pakaluk, Pepe Serret, and Ed Dillette. Many thanks.

Cover Image: Pixabay illustration by Duke678
Text and cover design by Rose Design

Library of Congress Control Number: 2023944226
ISBN: (pbk.) 978-1-59417-511-4
ISBN: (eBook) 978-1-59417-512-1

CONTENTS

INTRODUCTION

St. Josemaría Escrivá was fond of saying that by founding Opus Dei the Lord had "opened up all the divine paths of the earth." By this, he meant that for those who try to live the spirit of Opus Dei, all walks of life—the many ways in which men and women earn a living and live out their lives—can be divine paths that lead to holiness and heaven. To express both the unity of Opus Dei and the variety of its members, St. Josemaría liked to compare it to fractions with varied numerators, reflecting the diverse circumstances, temperaments, and activities of the members, and a small common denominator representing the Catholic faith and the spirit of Opus Dei.

Today, Opus Dei, which is often referred to as the Work, is made up of some ninety thousand men and women spread throughout the world. Some members are single. Most are married. Some are young, others middle-aged, and some old. A large majority are laypeople, but some are priests. They work in a vast array of professions and hold diverse political, social, and cultural opinions. Even a very long book could only begin to catalog how they differ. This book undertakes something much less ambitious. It offers brief biographical sketches of fourteen members of the Work who lived out their vocation to Opus Dei in various circumstances.

What unites the members of Opus Dei is their adherence to the Catholic faith and their effort to incorporate the spirit of Opus Dei into their own lives and spread it to others. This book will take for granted that readers are familiar with the basic teaching and practice of the Catholic Church. Rather than repeating in each of the biographical essays the main features of the spirit Opus Dei members try to live, we summarize it in this introduction. Readers who are already well acquainted with Opus Dei may want to skip to chapter one.

Children of God

The spirit of Opus Dei is based on a vivid awareness of being children of God, who is our loving Father. This joyful reality fosters members' cheerful, simple confidence in both God and other people, who are also children of God. It leads to a desire to live in the presence of God, and to maintain a loving dialogue with him throughout the day. Awareness of being a child of God, also known as *divine filiation*, gives peace, confidence, and happiness, along with a desire to improve one's life to serve our Father God better and more faithfully.

As God's sons and daughters, Opus Dei members come to know and value the gift of freedom he has given them. Opus Dei inculcates in its members great esteem for what St. Josemaría describes as "this inexhaustible treasure that belongs to Christianity: 'The glorious freedom of the children of God!' (Rom. 8:21)." In a 1956 homily, the Founder said:

> I like to speak of the adventure of freedom because that is how your lives
> and mine unfold. I insist that it is freely, as children and not as slaves, that
> we follow the paths which Our Lord has marked out for each one of us.
> We relish our freedom of action as a gift from God. I opt for God because I
> want to, freely, without compulsion of any kind.

Holiness in Ordinary Life

Opus Dei emphasizes the call to holiness in daily life. As the Vatican Congregation for Bishops stated in a 1982 declaration: "In the aims and spirit of Opus Dei, stress is laid on the sanctifying value of ordinary work; that is to say, on the obligation to sanctify work, to sanctify oneself in one's work, and to turn it into an instrument of apostolate."

Christ's life as a craftsman in Nazareth inspires the members of Opus Dei. For thirty years, Jesus's life did not call attention to itself. He loved God above all things and dedicated all his energies to doing the will of his Father at each moment, but this did not involve doing anything unusual. He earned his living as a village craftsman, dressed like other people in his village, spoke like them, and shared their interests and concerns. To the casual observer, he seemed to be simply one more village artisan. Nothing in his behavior during the first thirty years of his life prepared his relatives, neighbors, and friends for his preaching and miracles. That is why, when he began his public life, they asked themselves in amazement "Is not this Jesus, the son of Joseph, whose father and mother we know? How then does he say that 'I have come down from heaven?'" (Jn 6:24).

Anyone acquainted with a member of Opus Dei will recognize that he or she takes the faith seriously and tries to put it into practice. Those who are closer to them—their relatives, friends, and colleagues—will know they belong to Opus Dei. But since they are called to imitate Christ's life in Nazareth and to live a normal, ordinary life in the world, they prefer not to announce publicly their personal commitment to God. The vocation of Opus Dei members is quiet and unobtrusive, like Christ's hidden life. It shows in a father's interest in the education of his children, a nurse's stopping to listen to an elderly patient, a college student's willingness to help a classmate understand a difficult math problem, and a neighbor's effort to help the person next door solve a family problem in a Christian manner. These, of course, are things that all good Christians try to do, but that is precisely the point. Members of Opus Dei try to sanctify themselves and others by doing as well as they can, out of love for God and others, the things that God asks all Christians living in the world to do.

Sanctification of Work

Opus Dei's statutes stress that

> the Lord created man "to work" Cf. Gen. 2:15. The law of work belongs, then, to the general human condition. The spirit of Opus Dei leads its faithful not only to work but to love deeply their daily work. They see in work an outstanding human value and an essential means for the dignity of the human person and social progress. Above all they consider it a marvelous opportunity and means for personal union with Christ, imitating his hidden life that was full of work and generous service to others. Through their ordinary work, the members of Opus Dei cooperate in God's loving work of creation and redemption of the world.

Because we cannot offer God shoddy, defective work, anyone who wants to sanctify their work must try to work as well as they can. So, doctors motivated by this spirit attempt to develop their technical skills, keep up-to-date with the most recent developments in their field, and give each of their patients the attention and the time they require. Similarly, house painters who belong to Opus Dei try to complete their work neatly and carefully and do an honest day's work for their pay.

The faithful of the Prelature of Opus Dei strive for excellence not merely to get ahead or from a sense of professionalism, but primarily because they see their work as part of God's plan for them, something God wants them to do as well as possible out of love for him and for those whom their work affects. For a Christian, and concretely for a member of Opus Dei, working well means, among other things, working unselfishly. A Christian sees the just rewards of work, including the income it produces, as something to be administered prudently according to God's purposes. Members of Opus Dei try to live sober and austere personal lives. They don't use their earnings to satisfy their whims but to support their families, assist apostolic works, carry their share of society's burdens, and help those in need.

Opus Dei helps its members form their consciences in accordance with Catholic social teaching. The Work urges them to be acutely aware of the demands of justice and to be magnanimous and generous in attempting to improve the situation of less fortunate members of society. Numerous social centers founded and run by Opus Dei members all over the world are one result of this. Even more important, however, are the efforts of individual members to implement the Church's social teaching in their work and other activities.

Work offers concrete daily opportunities to practice many virtues, including concern for others, order, punctuality, justice, and humility. Above all, work is a way to practice charity through service. As St. Josemaría wrote: "I undertake to serve, to convert my whole life into a means of serving others, out of love for my Lord Jesus." This spirit leads members of Opus Dei to undertake their work in such a way that it constitutes a real service to others. The lives of the members portrayed in this book testify to this principle and manifest charity through service. The holiness of their lives did not consist of extraordinary deeds but of practicing Christian virtue in everyday circumstances.

Work and Prayer

Work and the social contact it involves can become an occasion for raising one's heart to God and conversing with him. People whose lives are inspired by the spirit of Opus Dei try, therefore, to take advantage of the natural breaks in their work to offer it to God, to ask for his help, or simply to tell him that they love him. To the extent that people succeed in incorporating the spirit of Opus Dei into the fabric of their lives, they find that their work, along with the other aspects of their daily lives, brings them closer to God and helps them to carry on a loving conversation with him during the day. They become, in the words of Opus Dei's founder, "contemplatives in the midst of the world"; that is, people who live in loving conversation with God precisely through work that is externally no different from that of millions of other people.

Without dedicating some time exclusively to God, it would be impossible to turn daily work and other daily activities into an occasion of conversation with him. To live in the presence of God and in loving dialogue with him throughout the day, a Catholic needs the sacraments and a certain amount of time set aside each day expressly for prayer. Opus Dei, therefore, stresses the importance of daily Mass, Gospel reading, and personal prayer. These periods dedicated exclusively to personal contact with God are not meant to be isolated moments nor religious interludes in an otherwise mundane existence. They enable a person to convert work, recreation, and all of life into ways of loving God as the fruit of a friendship that seeks to share everything with him. The prayer life of Opus Dei members is centered on Jesus Christ and concretely on the Mass. In the words of St. Josemaría, the Mass forms the "center and root of the interior life" of the members of Opus Dei. In the Mass, work and other daily activities take on their full meaning as part of the sacrifice which Jesus Christ offers to God the Father. The sacrament of penance also plays a central role in the spiritual life of Opus Dei members as an opportunity to "put on the Lord Jesus Christ" (Gal 3:27), receiving not only God's forgiveness but also the grace needed to overcome their defects and grow in virtue.

The prayer life of people in Opus Dei varies from member to member. Even the way an individual prays varies from one time and set of circumstances to another. All the members, however, try to attend daily Mass, spend some time each day in mental prayer, say the Rosary, and read from the Gospels and some other spiritual book. In addition, they also try to have a spirit of examination of conscience, to be habitually aware of God's presence, and to sanctify their work. All of this, St. Josemaría called the "norms" or "plan of life" of the members.

Children of Mary

Besides cultivating a strong sense of being children of God and maintaining lively personal contact with Jesus Christ in Scripture and the sacraments, members of Opus Dei cultivate devotion to the Blessed Virgin Mary. St. Josemaría encouraged his spiritual sons and daughters to "go to her with a son's love and joy." In a book written a few years after the foundation of the Work, he said: "The beginning of the way, at the end of which you will find yourself completely carried away by love for Jesus, is a trusting love for Mary."

Devotion to Mary reinforces the spirit of service that arises from an awareness that all men and women are children of God. In a homily on the Blessed Virgin, the Founder said:

> If we have this filial contact with Mary, we won't be able to think just about ourselves and our problems. Selfish personal problems will find no place in our minds. Mary brings us to Jesus, and Jesus is the "firstborn among many brothers" (Rom 8:29). And so, if we know Jesus, we realize that we can live only by giving ourselves to the service of others. . . . Concern for one's own spiritual improvement is not really a personal thing, for sanctification is completely bound up with apostolate.

Devotion to Saint Josemaría Escrivá

Pope St. John Paul II described St. Josemaría Escrivá as occupying "an eminent place among the men and women faithful to Christ who throughout the centuries have illuminated different epochs of history with their lives and with their message." In an audience he granted to members and friends of Opus Dei the day after the beatification of its founder, John Paul II expressed his hope that they would be "illuminated by the example and teaching of

Blessed Josemaría Escrivá," whom the Pope described as a "model of sanctity" and as an "eminent testimony of Christian heroism in the exercise of everyday human activities."

As the Pope urged them to do, members of Opus Dei find in the writings of St. Josemaría the spirit which they attempt to put into practice. The Founder's life constitutes a concrete example of how that spirit can be lived day-to-day. Like many other people, members of Opus Dei have learned by experience that St. Josemaría is a powerful intercessor before God, and they turn to him for help in their spiritual lives and apostolates as well as for other daily needs. For all these reasons, the members of Opus Dei make an effort to become familiar with the life and writings of the Founder and seek his intercession. Naturally, they encourage other people to do the same.

Spirit of Sacrifice

Even on the purely natural plane, self-discipline and self-sacrifice are necessary. Athletes subject themselves to rigorous training. Many people diet to improve their health or appearance. Men and women in all walks of life put in long hours to excel in their professions or to achieve some other personal goal. Similarly, St. Paul insisted to the early Christians at Corinth that following Christ requires personal sacrifice. "Every athlete must keep all his appetites under control; and he does it to win a crown that fades, whereas ours is imperishable. . . . I buffet my own body, and make it my slave; or I, who have preached to others, might be rejected as worthless" (1 Cor 9:25, 27). Mortification helps Christians to grow in virtue, control their appetites, fulfill the duties of their state in life, and live charity toward others.

Above all, however, Christians embrace sacrifice to imitate Christ and to share in his life. Jesus invites everyone who wants to follow him to renounce himself and take up his cross each day (cf. Lk 9:23). He warns that "he who does not take up his cross and follow me is not worthy of me" (Mt 10:39). Members of Opus Dei strive to share Christ's life until they can say with St. Paul, "I live, now not I, but Christ lives in me" (Gal 2:20). But for this to become a reality, a Christian must also be able to say, "With Christ, I hang upon the cross" (Gal 2:19).

In addition to uniting us personally with Christ, sacrifice helps bring others closer to him. When the apostles asked Jesus why they had been unable to cast out a devil, he told them, "There is no way of casting out such spirits as this except by prayer and fasting" (Mt 17:20). St. Paul told the early faithful at Colossae, "I am glad of my sufferings on your behalf, as, in this mortal frame of mine, I help to pay off the debt which the afflictions of Christ leave still to be paid, for the sake of his body, the Church" (Col 1:24).

In the spirit of Opus Dei, sacrifice finds expression primarily in the effort required to fulfill, as perfectly as possible, professional, family, and social duties. Work and the other aspects of daily life offer numerous opportunities for living an authentic spirit of self-denial and sacrifice manifested in constancy, order, punctuality, and cheerful acceptance of the setbacks and difficulties of life.

Members of Opus Dei also attempt to respond generously to Christ's invitation to share in the Cross by traditional Christian practices of self-denial. In some cases, this includes the use of the disciplines and the cilice.[1] These practices of Christian asceticism are no more harmful to health than are the rigors of athletic training or the diets followed by many to improve their health or appearance. Corporal mortifications are a way of sharing voluntarily, to a small degree, in the suffering of Jesus Christ, as many saints and holy people down through the centuries have done, including St. Dominic, St. Francis of Assisi, St. Ignatius of Loyola, St. Thomas More, St. Francis de Sales, St. John Henry Newman, and in our own time, St. Teresa of Calcutta (Mother Teresa), Thomas Merton, St. Paul VI, and St. John Paul II.

The asceticism and penance practiced by Opus Dei members are fully compatible with a cheerful, contented life, and contribute to it. St. Josemaría said: "If things go well, let's rejoice, blessing God, who makes them prosper. And if they go wrong? Let's rejoice, blessing God, who allows us to share the sweetness of his cross." "I want you always to be happy," he added, "for cheerfulness is an essential part of your way." Anyone who visits a center of Opus Dei finds a "bright and cheerful Christian home," where people are "peaceful and brimming over with joy," as the Founder intended.

---

1. The Opus Dei website has an excellent explanation of corporal mortification, its use, and pupose. "Opus Dei and Corporal Mortification," January 20, 2005. https://opusdei.org/en/article/opus-dei-and-corporal-mortification.

Bringing Others Closer to Christ

Besides being worthwhile in themselves, work, social life, recreation, and the other activities of ordinary daily life offer members of Opus Dei the opportunity and means for bringing others to know and love Christ better. The apostolate of Opus Dei members primarily rests on the friendships that naturally arise in the course of work and the rest of ordinary life, as well as on the example of work well done, completed with cheerfulness and a spirit of service. In this setting of ordinary life, members try to carry out their mission of spreading the message that God calls all men and women to the fullness of holiness. In their awareness of God's fatherly love, Opus Dei members find a source of peace and happiness. Naturally, they want to share that peace and joy with others. And so they seek to bring their friends, colleagues, family members, and neighbors closer to God. In addition to giving good example, members of Opus Dei pray for their friends and offer sacrifices for them. Through their conversation, they also try to help their friends get to know Christ better, love him more, and answer his call to holiness. Frequently, an encouraging word, an assurance that they will pray for the solution of a particular problem, or a bit of friendly advice will reflect this deeply Christian friendship. At other times, friendship will inspire a serious heart-to-heart talk about some aspect of Christ's teaching, the demands of Christian life, or a friend's possible vocation to Opus Dei.

Some members of Opus Dei join together with their fellow citizens to promote schools, medical clinics, clubs, agricultural training centers, and other similar activities that help meet the needs of society and provide an opportunity to spread Christ's teaching to larger groups of people. Some members find their professional work in these settings. The majority, however, have jobs in factories, law firms, offices, educational institutions, hospitals, and so forth, where they try to work as well as they can for the love of God and in service to their fellow men and women.

Different Modes of Living the Same Vocation

St. Josemaría often stressed that all members of Opus Dei have the same vocation. Whether clergy or laity, married or single, young or old, all are called by God to dedicate themselves entirely to him in daily life, to sanctify their work, to sanctify themselves in their work, and to sanctify others through their work. All are called to the fullness of holiness in their personal circumstance.

If the vocation is the same for all members, the circumstances in which they are called to respond to it are very different. Those circumstances influence the details of how God wants each individual to respond to his call—and the degree to which they are available to assist with Opus Dei's formation and apostolic activities. This is reflected in the existence of the various groups of members that will be mentioned in this book.

Supernumeraries constitute the majority of members. Not called by God to apostolic celibacy, they are usually married and live with their families. A large part of their apostolate is caring for their spouses and children and their efforts to bring others closer to God through their professional work which they try to carry out with love for God and a spirit of service. Ordinarily, this means that they do not direct apostolic activities of Opus Dei nor do they work in its governing structures. Examples in this book are Tomás and Paquita Alvira, Ernesto Cofiño, Ed Dillett, Eduardo Ortiz de Landázuri, Ruth Pakaluk, and Pepe Serrett.

Numeraries and *associates* have responded to God's call to apostolic celibacy. Among other things, this tends to make them available to direct apostolic activities and, in the case of numeraries, to work in Opus Dei's governmental structures. Most numeraries live in centers of the Work, where they often meet with other members and friends to explain the spirit of Opus Dei and provide individual guidance on how to put it into practice. Most associates do not live in centers of the Work. Numeraries in this book are Montserrat Grases, Ana Gonzalo, Guadulupe Ortiz de Landázuri, Isidoro Zorzano, and Toni Zweifel. Carlos Martínez was an associate.

Some numeraries and associates are asked by the Prelate if they would be willing to become priests. If they are, they are ordained for Opus Dei and become part of its presbyterium. They dedicate themselves primarily to the pastoral care of the Work's members and other people who take part in Opus Dei's formational activities.

All the members of Opus Dei's presbyterium are automatically members of the Priestly Society of the Holy Cross, an association of secular priests inextricably linked to Opus Dei. Priests of Opus Dei are not, however, the only members of the Priestly Society; diocesan priests can also belong to it. They remain priests of their diocese and carry out the pastoral tasks assigned to them by their bishop. The Work provides them the spiritual support and assistance they need to live its spirit by sanctifying themselves in their work, which is their priestly ministry. An example of a member of the Priestly Society of the Holy Cross in this book is Fr. Joseph Múzquiz.

Numerary assistants are numerary members of Opus Dei's women's branch who work professionally to provide housekeeping services in both the women's and the men's centers. St. Josemaría often described their work as "the apostolate of the apostolate." An example of a numerary assistant in this book is Dora del Hoyo.

CHAPTER ONE

~

Ruth Pakaluk:
Wife, Mother, Friend, Activist

Ruth Pakaluk converted from atheism to Christianity at Harvard and became a Catholic the year after her graduation. The mother of seven children, she was deeply involved in the Right to Life movement and played an active role in the life of her parish and in organizing the apostolic activities of Opus Dei. She was diagnosed with breast cancer at thirty-four years of age but continued to live a normal life until a month before her death, seven years later in September 1998 at the age of forty-one.

From Atheist to Catholic, Passing through Evangelical

Ruth was born Ruth Elizabeth Van Kooy on March 19, 1957, in South Orange, New Jersey, a suburban town on the outskirts of New York City. Her father was an electrical engineer. Rather than practicing engineering,

1

he taught in a vocational high school as a way of contributing to society. Her mother stayed at home while the children were very young but later worked as an executive secretary. In high school Ruth produced, directed, and acted in numerous plays and musicals under the auspices of a theater group founded and managed by students. She was an excellent singer, chosen for the All-Eastern choir. She was also an accomplished pianist and played the oboe, flute, violin, and bass drum in various musical groups. Ruth was a good athlete and played on the field hockey team. In her childhood, she attended a Presbyterian church with her family, but as an adolescent, she rejected her parents' liberal Christianity and became a pro-choice atheist.

During her senior year in high school, Ruth considered attending stewardess school because "all you need to do is smile, and you can see the world." She also thought about going to McGill University, where the boy with whom she was having what she described toward the end of her life as "an almost fairytale romance" planned to go. At the suggestion of a local Radcliffe College alum, she applied to Harvard University. She could not turn down its offer because if she had, "I would never have known if I could compete with the best."

Ruth did so well in her freshman year that she was asked to serve as a teaching assistant the next year for the course Space, Time, Motion. In her sophomore year, her assigned reading included Governor Bradford's account of how the Pilgrims survived their first bitterly cold winter in America. She was struck by the heroism and sacrifice with which they cared for each other during the illness which swept through the colony and contrasted it with her own hedonistic and self-centered life. "I want to live like them," she thought to herself. "I don't even care if what these people believed is true. I want to live like them." Despite her avowal that she didn't care whether Christianity was true, she soon resolved to search for a truth in which she could believe.

A few years later, Ruth wrote to a friend:

As soon as I came (or rather, returned) to the conviction that God exists, it seemed obvious that the only rational thing to do was to find out more about Him and what He wanted, since by definition God is infinitely more worthwhile and important than anything else. It's now hard for me to remember or imagine how a person can have a belief in God and yet not think that it's imperative that he strive to put God at the center of his consciousness. Doing that may sound terribly exhausting to you but consider this—the church has always taught that God made man in such a way that he cannot help desiring happiness, yet we can only be happy (truly happy, as opposed to momentarily amused or distracted) by being united with Him. So then, constantly turning one's attention to God would be the most natural thing for a man to do.

Among the students in Ruth's section of the course on Space, Time, Motion, was Michael Pakaluk, a lapsed Catholic who entered Harvard as a religious skeptic. After a narrow escape from death by drowning during the summer between freshman and sophomore year, he had set out on a search to determine whether Christianity was true. Michael and Ruth began dating and soon fell passionately in love. According to Michael, their "falling in love looked inseparable from being faithful to a common yearning to investigate whether Christianity might possibly be true." Neither of them knew a single student or professor who was a Christian, so their determination to figure out if Christianity was true immediately became a bond between them.

Both Ruth and Michael were convinced that the key factor was how one lived. By the end of sophomore year, they concluded that to live a Christian life one had to belong to a Christian community, so they began attending United Church Congregational located on the Cambridge Common. As time went on, they became increasingly frustrated with the church's exclusive focus on social and political issues and its lack of interest in theology or spirituality. Although they continued to attend services there, they joined the Evangelical InterVarsity Christian Fellowship (IVCF) at Harvard. They expected to find frequent intellectual debates about philosophical and theological topics. Instead, they found emotional enthusiasm and an emphasis on maintaining an upbeat mood.

In fall 1978, Ruth and Michael were married at her parents' Presbyterian church. At the time, only a handful of other Harvard undergraduates were married. The Pakaluks rented a small apartment and lived a very frugal life. They budgeted twenty dollars per week for food, a very small sum of money even then. They could get by on so little because they had become deeply concerned about world hunger and consequently had become vegetarians. Buying in bulk and shunning prepared foods allowed them to eat for less than seventy-five cents per day. They tithed, giving ten percent of their after-tax income, including financial aid, to their church, the InterVarsity Fellowship, and their two favorite charities, Oxfam and Bread for the World, an advocacy group.

At first, both Ruth and Michael firmly rejected Catholicism—Ruth because of the anti-Catholicism of the Reformed church she had grown up in, and Michael because he considered the nominal Catholicism of his childhood a false religion that prevented forming a personal relationship with Christ. They both were appalled when Curt, a friend in the InterVarsity small group that Michael was leading, announced that he was taking instruction to become a Catholic. The couple argued with him at length but found themselves unable to refute his reasons for becoming Catholic.

An important factor in their approach to the Catholic Church was Malcolm Muggeridge's book on Mother Teresa. As Michael recalls:

> Mother Teresa was clearly a deeply prayerful woman, a true follower of Christ, who was, moreover, holy. And this posed a problem for us. How could it be that a false and apostate form of Christianity would be the place where one alone found what seemed to us a true appraisal of suffering, prayerfulness, and holiness? There was an argument in the early Church about Christ: either he was a bad man, or he was God, but there was no intermediate. He couldn't be simply a good moral teacher. We vaguely sensed that we were encountering a similar dilemma here. The Catholic Church was either very bad or very good. Yet Mother Teresa was making the first option appear untenable.

They read many books about the Catholic Church and the early history of Christianity, especially the writings of Fr. John Hardon, SJ. Gradually, they came to accept the Church's positions on both abortion and contraception and admire its courage in defending them. Around Christmas 1978, they decided to stop using contraception. Michael explains their decision:

> The attitudes fostered by contraception (the "contraceptive" mentality) are contrary to the attitudes a Christian ought to have. Christians for centuries had always rejected contraception. It was easy to believe that the change in the teaching of most Christian churches on this matter was an example of the same sort of "secularization"—swimming with the tide—that

was apparent in churches as regards abortion, which was unquestionably wrong and unchristian. At the same time, we thought, it would hardly be surprising if rejection of contraception were a kind of "test" of real fidelity to Christ in the modern world. The way we saw it, each generation had its test—for each generation of Christians there was some practice that the world embraced and Christians had to reject, or which the world rejected and Christians had to embrace—a practice which would require sacrifice; a practice which to "the world" made no sense but which to Christians was evidently the way of true discipleship to Christ. Given that there was likely to be such a test, it seemed to us that contraception was a likely candidate for that sort of thing. Therefore, we decided that as followers of Christ, we should stop using contraceptives. . . . Yet the bigger question of whether we should try to conceive a child was not one that we engaged. We were students and simply presumed that we should not have a baby.

By Spring 1980, both Ruth and Michael were leaning toward the Catholic Church. Since Michael had won a Marshall Fellowship to study in Edinburgh, however, and they were going to move to Scotland for two years in the fall, they did not want to make an immediate decision. By the time they arrived in Scotland, Ruth had made up her mind, although Michael still had some doubts. In Edinburgh, they both began taking instruction in the Catholic faith at the Catholic chaplaincy of the university. Ruth wrote to her in-laws: "Life is going along so well for us—I am often amazed at the quantity and quality of our blessing. Harder times may very well come—this is always in God's almighty hands—but I do not worry. How few people receive in a lifetime all the joys I've had in just two years!" On Christmas Eve, Michael made a general confession and received Communion, and Ruth was received into the Church and confirmed.

Soon, they began to attend daily Mass. Michael explains their decision:

We insisted that our conversion to Catholicism did not change the fact that we were evangelical Christians. We were now evangelicals who were Catholics, who believed that what we loved and were looking for in evangelical Christianity was safeguarded and found in its most intense form in the saints of the Catholic Church. As evangelicals, we believed that we should have a daily "quiet time," when we conversed with Christ, developing a personal relationship with him. We wanted to get as close as possible to Christ—that's why we wanted to be like the early Christians as much as possible. . . . We came to see the Mass as the Lord's Supper transcending time. To go to Mass was to be at the table of the Lord's Supper, alongside the apostles, and completely on a par with them as far as our nearness to Christ was concerned. The early Christians enjoyed no priority which was not also enjoyed by someone who simply attended Mass. But given that that is so, then, we reasoned, what better prayer could there be, and what better way to grow in the personal relationship with Christ which we sought than to attend Mass and pray there? Thus, our practice of the daily "quiet time" led naturally to daily Mass. Not that we didn't also aim to pray silently and "in secret" at other times in the day; but it seemed to us that the very first time free for prayer, the "first fruits" of our time, as it were, should be given to the Mass.

Ruth and Michael found it hard to keep their resolution to attend Mass every day. They would succeed for a few days or a week and then let things slip for a week or two. Both felt this was unacceptable. They recognized they needed some help, but did not know what this could be, or what form it might take. Years later, when they first learned about Opus Dei, they recognized that it was exactly what they had been looking for.

Their first child, Michael, was born on November 27, 1981. According to her husband, his birth made Ruth much more selfless. He recalls that

twice during the night [Michael] made some slight fussy sounds, and Ruth immediately got up in the dark to pick him up and nurse him. This dedication astonished me. Of course, it makes sense: when a baby cries at night you have to feed him. . . . But I had never seen that kind of straightforward, spontaneous selflessness in Ruth. She didn't grumble or tarry in bed for a moment. The baby made a sound, and she sprung to her feet to tend to him.

Michael's birth also transformed Ruth's attitude toward abortion. During the previous year, she had studied the issue in depth and had become intellectually convinced that abortion involved the taking of an innocent human life. That conviction was bolstered by her acceptance of the

Church's teaching on the subject. She was deeply convinced, but was not viscerally committed to the pro-life cause. Her husband noticed that with Michael's birth, she began

> to look at the abortion controversy in a new and more urgent light. She observed this change in herself, writing at that time, in connection with the miscarriage suffered by a friend, that she was no longer capable of being "philosophical about the deaths of other people's children" and that "what seemed sad and tragic before is now plain terrible to contemplate." Her opposition to abortion was now rooted in her own motherhood and was not simply the cool, intellectual conclusion of the philosophical argument.

In the summer of 1982, after two years in Scotland, the Pakaluks returned to Harvard, where Michael began studying for a doctorate in philosophy. During the six years they would remain at Harvard, they had two more boys, Max (June 1983) and John Henry (March 1986), and a daughter, Maria (October 1987). They briefly considered daycare, but Ruth decided she didn't want her children raised by people who, while they might be competent and even kind, did not love them.

To supplement Michael's meager stipend, Ruth took a part-time job doing bookkeeping and general office work for their landlord. The work would have struck most people of her intelligence and education as extremely dull, but she focused on its good side and wrote to a friend, "It's fun work, very convenient, and adequately lucrative."

Member of Opus Dei

In Scotland, a friend had given the Pakaluks a copy of St. Josemaría's book *The Way*, but their first contact with Opus Dei came when a Harvard graduate student saw Michael at daily Mass and invited him to an evening of recollection preached at the Opus Dei Center near Harvard by Fr. Sal Ferigle. Michael was deeply impressed by what he heard. As he recalls, he thought, "This is the Catholic faith that I converted to. This is what I have read in books written by saints and in the documents of the early Church." He immediately arranged to begin spiritual direction with Fr. Sal and to attend his classes on Catholic doctrine.

When Michael explained to Ruth what he had learned about Opus Dei, she concurred that it seemed to be exactly what they had been looking for:

> Since we converted to Catholicism, we were aware that we need some kind of help, some "external structure" (as we would explain it to ourselves), in practicing the interior life. We were aware, first of all, that we needed a spiritual director. . . . The priests of Opus Dei were evidently holy and knowledgeable men of the church who were available to give such direction. Secondly, we realized that we weren't successful at consistently going to Mass and saying our prayers. We would be better or worse at this depending upon the difficulty of the circumstances, or our subjective feelings; and yet apparently there were many members of Opus Dei who had been consistently living a demanding life of devotion for many years and amidst all the difficulties of life.

Ruth immediately began to attend Opus Dei formative activities and to receive personal spiritual direction from Fr. Sal, whom she considered "the holiest priest I had ever known." For his part, Fr. Sal was deeply impressed with Ruth, and particularly with her apostolic drive.

About a year later, in summer 1984, Ruth became a supernumerary member of Opus Dei. Michael had joined the Work a few months earlier. They began to live the members' plan of life, to attend circles and other means of spiritual formation, and to carry out a quiet apostolate based on friendship.

They also began to form friendships with other people connected with Opus Dei, particularly Jan and Tom Hardy. At the time, the Hardys had six children, which struck Michael as an unbelievably high number. "How could they manage?" he and Ruth asked themselves. "How was it possible to handle so many children and pay for the expenses?" But when they saw the Hardys' combination of Christian idealism, good sense, and ethic of hard work—and that they were no-nonsense critics of the "pro-choice" culture— they were impressed immediately and wanted to spend as much time with them as they could.

Pro-Life Activist

Ruth's involvement in pro-life activism was triggered by a debate she attended at Harvard. She was struck by the powerful arguments put forth by the pro-life spokesman and above all by the unwillingness of the pro-abortion spokesman to engage the argument that abortion involves killing an innocent human being. With Paul Swope, a graduate student at the Harvard School of Education, she founded a group called Harvard-Radcliffe Human Life Advocates.

After a while, so many Cambridge residents unconnected with the university became involved that Ruth decided to form a second group, called Cambridge Unborn Rights Advocates (CURA). Within a year, CURA had over three hundred active members and was sponsoring a variety of activities in Cambridge, including fundraising drives for the statewide right-to-life organization, Massachusetts Citizens for Life (MCFL); an annual dinner with a featured speaker; educational talks; sending buses to the annual March for Life in Washington, DC; door-to-door pamphleting; and collecting food, clothing, and baby supplies for expectant mothers. CURA viewed its own mission as primarily educational, but many CURA members also volunteered for crisis pregnancy centers and worked on the campaigns of pro-life politicians.

Board Member of Massachusetts Citizens for Life

A member of the Board of Massachusetts Citizens for Life reports that when she met Ruth her "first impression was that she was beautiful—physically beautiful—unbelievably articulate, and very intelligent. I thought, 'This is someone that we need to groom.' . . . We knew right away that Ruth was going to be a star."

In 1984, at the urging of MCFL officers who were impressed with the vitality of CURA, Ruth ran for and won a seat on the board of directors of the statewide organization. She soon found herself leading an effort to pass a state constitutional amendment to limit abortion rights to those explicitly recognized by the United States Supreme Court. The amendment failed by a small margin, but public debate on the issue gave many opportunities for broadcasting the pro-life view.

Political and Social Activity

Just before the 1984 presidential elections, Ruth wrote to a friend:

> I'm on the verge of becoming a registered Republican. The Democratic Party's
> wholehearted endorsement of abortion is what prompted my shift, but as I
> think through other issues, I find myself coming closer to the free enterprise,
> minimize-government mentality of the current administration. I have serious
> reservations regarding that approach in areas like pollution. I have serious res-
> ervations about arms buildup, but I know that abortion kills a member of the
> human race. That is not a religious belief; it is simply a biological fact.

A few months after the election, she told the same friend:

> I did vote for Reagan. I even urged others to do likewise and coordinated
> the distribution of roughly 3000 pamphlets aimed at persuading people to
> follow suit. My single reason for doing this (or, rather, the paramount reason
> for my doing this) is the abortion issue. It is to me quite obvious that abor-
> tion kills human beings. I used to ask myself, had I lived under Hitler, would
> I have spoken out in defense of the slaughter of innocent human beings? I
> still don't know what I would do if the price of speaking out were my own
> death, but it is inconceivable to me that I could sit idly by while our soci-
> ety condones the killing of innocent infants. I don't like leafleting. I don't
> like picketing, I don't like political activism; but I don't have the freedom to
> choose to remain silent.

Although primarily focused on abortion, Ruth was also concerned
about world poverty and hunger. Despite the family's very tight budget, the
Pakaluks continued to donate generously to organizations like Bread for the
World, Catholic Relief Services, and Oxfam. Ruth also made time to write
letters urging the United States to treat poor countries more fairly.

President of Massachusetts Citizens for Life

In 1987, Ruth was elected president of MCFL. Together with Paul Swope,
she worked to modernize the offices, increase fundraising capabilities, and
develop the group's capacity to issue press releases quickly in response to
developing news. Under Ruth's leadership, MCFL grew substantially. The

organization's ability to lobby expanded and it succeeded in turning back in committee some proposed state legislation in favor of abortion rights.

A few months after her election, she wrote to a friend:

> I am now president of our state pro-life organization. It's rather exciting. I have to hire staff, deal with the press frequently, make decisions about computer systems, do market research, etc. Thank heavens I don't have a 9 to 5 job, as most previous presidents have had. Towing three boys around with me is hard enough, but they're much more flexible than a boss.

Ruth's gift for public speaking about abortion and other "life issues" became apparent when, as president of MCFL, she was asked to appear on news shows or speak on campuses. She preferred debates to speeches. Even if the organizers of an event had not planned to make it a debate, she would try to persuade them to invite a pro-choice speaker. "If you hold a speech, a couple dozen people will show up, who are already convinced. But if you hold a debate, a few hundred will attend, many of whom really want to know."

Worcester, Massachusetts

In 1987, the Pakaluks moved to Worcester, Massachusetts, a city of about 150,000 inhabitants, forty miles west of Boston, where Michael had found a position at Clark University, a distinguished liberal arts institution. From an academic point of view, the appointment was attractive, but it paid poorly. Their search for a house revealed, in Mike's words, "the reality that the US economy was no longer designed for households supported by a single income. The reality was that even the least expensive starter house in the least attractive neighborhood of a relatively inexpensive city was not affordable for us, because now two incomes were usually chasing house prices." The best they could do was a small house in ill repair, in a neighborhood made up largely of illegal immigrants. When they moved in, they had no hot water, the carpets were forty years old, they had almost no real furniture, the stove and refrigerator clamored to be replaced, and their car was fifteen years old.

They worked hard to keep expenses to a minimum. On one occasion they were visiting a couple, both of whom were successful marketing professionals. They asked Ruth about her reasons for buying one product rather than another.

"It's easy," she said, "I calculate the cost per unit, and I buy the least expensive brand."

"You don't have any preferences for brands? You don't like Crest toothpaste over Colgate, for example?"

"Crest or Colgate!"

Ruth replied, "You've got to be kidding me. Those are much too expensive, even when they are on sale."

Despite their small income, the Pakaluks lived within their means and did not feel that they always needed more money. They continued to tithe. One year when they discovered that they were going to receive an unexpectedly sizable tax refund, they thought it was too much to spend on themselves, so they gave it to Catholic Relief Services for poor people who, they thought, needed the money more than they did.

Mike recalls that although financially stressed,

> Our house was cheerful and in its own way blessed with abundance. For example, every day when school was over, Ruth would have something freshly baked waiting for the children and their friends; or on a hot summers day she would pile everyone into the car, friends and all, and take them to Bell Pond or Rutland State Park to go swimming.

About a year after they moved to Worcester, Ruth was asked to join the professional choir of the cathedral. She was delighted and wrote to a friend:

> I'm singing in a choir again. Not just any old choir, but the Cathedral choir, a professional choir. Get this—I get paid to go out without the kids and sing beautiful music. . . . I just can't get over it. I'm not one of the best singers, but I'm working on it. It's been a very long time since last I concentrated on pitch and blend. Lucky for me I still sight-read reasonably well and I count better than most of them (why are singers generally such bad counters?).

Death of a Child

The Pakaluks' fifth child, Thomas, was born in September 1989. Seven weeks after his birth, he died of sudden infant death syndrome. The family was devastated, but Ruth and Michael embraced their suffering and saw in it, in Michael's words, "a 'severe mercy,' a sharing in the Cross of Christ which would bring many blessings and graces." Immediately after Thomas's funeral, Michael wanted to go home, be alone with the family, and maybe sleep. Ruth wanted to celebrate. Leaving Church after the funeral Mass, she clasped her hands together, smiled broadly, and said, "Okay, let's have a party!" She wanted to celebrate Thomas's having gained the joys of heaven.

Her desire to celebrate Thomas's being in heaven did not mean that she did not feel the loss of her infant son or that she failed to grieve his loss. When someone commented that because Thomas was in heaven, he had not really suffered any loss, Ruth responded that Thomas had lost "growing up as a boy and enjoying all of the beauties and joys of the world that God had created."

A few years later, a friend who had just lost an infant son asked Ruth whether it was true that the wound from that loss never goes away. Ruth replied:

> The spiritual or emotional wound, the grief, is a lot like a physical wound. And it heals imperceptibly. You can't function with your heart bleeding all over the floor. And your son knows that. Yet not a day goes by that I don't have recourse to Thomas for something. Find some devotion to your son and weave it into your daily prayer life. That way you don't have fear of either ripping the wound open or forgetting.

Ruth herself made it a practice to kiss her brown scapular each day when she put it back on after showering, saying,

> Let this kiss be a token of affection for Mary, my mother in heaven—asking her to pass along some expression of affection to my son, Thomas—asking him to pray for his mother, to pray for his father, to pray for his siblings, grandparents, and cousins, to pray for the Father's [the Prelate of Opus Dei] intentions, and to pray for the pro-life movement.

Her sense that Thomas was looking at her from heaven helped Ruth become more generous in her interior life. As she wrote to a friend:

> Thomas is already doing a good job of keeping me on the straight and narrow. It is not contemplating Our Lord's wounds or the Virgin at the foot of the cross that moves me to do my norms [the practices of piety

that make up the plan of life of members of Opus Dei]. It's the feeling of shame that my infant son is gazing at me and wondering why his mother is so silly that she thinks typing newsletters or folding laundry is more important than prayer.

Michael recalls: "Ruth prayed that her grief might be consoled by another child, and when Sarah Esther was conceived less than a month after Thomas died and was born less than a year after his death, in the manner of many women of the Bible, she regarded this blessing as a concrete answer to her prayer." As Ruth later confided to Sarah, "You brought so much happiness and emotional healing to me after the sadness and emptiness of losing little Thomas. You were a great gift and blessing from God for your mother."

Cancer at Age Thirty-Three

In July 1990, while pregnant with Sarah, Ruth discovered a lump in her breast, but her doctor assured her it was nothing to worry about. By the fall of 1991, the lump was visible and she again brought it to the doctor's attention. Although he again dismissed her concerns, Ruth insisted on a mammogram, which revealed a four-centimeter cancerous tumor. She underwent a radical mastectomy for stage 2-B cancer in October and began a five-month course of chemotherapy.

Ruth recovered quickly and easily from the surgery, but she wrote to a friend, "The chemo is just plain unpleasant. . . . [It] really only puts me back totally for two or three days, but I have to take it a little easy for a week or so." At Christmas, she confided to another friend, "I have total peace that God will bring good out of this experience, whatever the outcome. Still, I'd appreciate the spare prayer."

In a letter to a woman with cancer, she said:

> I did not live a totally normal life on chemo. I spent a lot of time thinking and praying and reading. I did try to force myself to keep some normal things, even though I felt overwhelmed. For instance, I continued to give pro-life presentations at high schools. It was difficult, but I was always glad after the fact. Dropping the baby off at the sitter and getting dressed up and getting out of the house early in the morning often

seemed impossible the night before, but I would just keep plugging away and found I was able to do it. Catholic spirituality emphasizes "offering up" our sufferings. That can sound a little pie in the sky, but I found it very helpful. Jesus came from heaven to share our life. He even wanted to share our experience of pain, fear, loneliness, suffering, etc. When we experience these unpleasant things, it is helpful to think about Jesus alone or in agony on the cross. We want to be like Him. We want to share His sufferings with Him, to keep Him company, not falling asleep like Peter, James, and John. He will accept our patient endurance of trials and turn them into glory, like his resurrection.

She told another woman with cancer that during the chemo she constantly felt vaguely nauseous.

But what was more difficult for me was the toll it took on my psyche. I have never been a worrier, never subject to much anxiety or depression. But while I was on chemo, I would experience dramatic panic attacks. I would be sitting comfortably on the sofa, and suddenly, my heart would start pounding, adrenaline would flow, and I would experience all the symptoms of total terror. I would try to dispel the symptoms by telling myself there was nothing to fear, but it wouldn't work. I'm confident that this was not suppressed fear of mortality. It was just a side effect of the chemo and it went away within weeks of the end of my treatment. That is the aspect of my experience I most want to convey to you: life after chemo is great. No matter how sick, tired, and depressed you feel during it, you will return to feeling like yourself when it is over. I think some people begin to think that the way they feel on chemo is a result of the cancer, but it isn't. Really it is just the chemo itself.

A few weeks after chemotherapy ended, Ruth reported to a friend,

I'm feeling like a normal human being again. It is so good to feel well—after feeling slightly and vaguely ill for so long, you forget how great it is to feel normal. These days, I'm constantly ecstatic just to be able to taste and smell normally, etc. I wish I could stay in this state and not take it for granted again, but that's human nature.

Ruth's surgeon advised waiting at least three years before trying to have another child. At that point, the risk of cancer recurring would be less.

Earlier, it might come back at any time, and if it did, pregnancy would pre-clude many forms of therapy. Furthermore, pregnancy might encourage the cancer to grow more rapidly. Ruth and Michael weighed the surgeon's advice carefully and asked God for light. Ultimately, however, they felt, as Ruth put it, that "it would be better to live life with the hope that my can-cer would not recur rather than cowering in fear. Even if my life were to be cut short by recurring cancer, we felt it would be a beautiful thing to give life to more children." Soon she was pregnant with Anna Sophia, who was born in April 1993.

Malpractice Lawsuit

Michael recalls that when Ruth learned she had cancer, her first reaction

> was a feeling of humiliation, of being made the fool or a chump, because she trusted her doctor's statement, "It's not cancer," and walked around for a full year with an easily detectable malignant cancer growing within her breast. . . . She had a brief period—very brief, only a matter of a day or two—when she was in great emotional turmoil, feeling first very angry at her doctor, then feeling emotions of pity for him and forgiveness.
>
> She resolved all of this very quickly—and I was amazed by this. She forgave her doctor personally, and, as far as I could see from everything she did or said, never nursed a grudge or held any continuing resentment toward him.

This did not, however, prevent her from filing a lawsuit. The settlement allowed the family to purchase a better house and pay tuition at Catholic schools and later at private colleges.

Further Pro-life Activities

After the initial chemotherapy ended, Ruth quickly recovered her strength and resumed her whirlwind activities. For about a year and a half, she enjoyed what seemed to be good health. Besides running the household and continu-ing with Opus Dei activities, such as giving a weekly class to cooperators of Opus Dei, she had a full schedule of pro-life speaking engagements at

Harvard Divinity School, Mount Holyoke College, MIT, Columbia, Fordham, Brandeis, Brown, and Amherst.

After the Supreme Court's 1992 *Casey* decision, Ruth felt it no longer made sense to focus on overturning *Roe*. In her pro-life activities, including many presentations to high school students, her goal was, as she said in an interview, to persuade her listeners

> that they don't want to have an abortion themselves, or that if they knew someone who was contemplating an abortion, they might actually dissuade her from doing it. Maybe I can persuade some to become active, as I am. So that's what I try to do, to persuade people that this is not a good thing, that there are better alternative solutions.

According to Michael, Ruth conceived the abortion controversy

> not as a difference of opinion as regards some philosophical thesis—"is the fetus a person?" as people often say—but rather as a difference between two cultures: given that (as everyone really knows) the thing in the woman's womb is a living human, do we act on the principle that all human beings are fundamentally equal, or do we proceed as if we believe that it is permissible to kill some human beings to solve our problems? The first is the Culture of Life, and the second the Culture of Death. These two cultures, she thought, were vying for the allegiance of the young people she was addressing, and her concern was to teach them what they should know in order that they might choose life.

Ruth did not believe in culture wars and their accompanying rhetoric. She constantly sought ways to build bridges and find common ground not only with those who were undecided but even with abortion advocates. One of her adversaries in the abortion controversy, a former president of Mass Choice, wrote to express her sympathy when she learned that Ruth's cancer had spread to her liver. Ruth responded with a cordial and surprisingly intimate letter:

> The one thing I most frequently regret about my current situation is not having another baby. . . . For a Catholic, it is truly a blessing to have almost certain knowledge regarding the imminence of death. I have

enjoyed, no—savored—these past years more than any others of my life. . . . I have almost eliminated committee meetings from my schedule and let only speaking engagements take me away from my family. I have made greater efforts to make our family life peaceful, joyful, fun, and loving. I think I have had some (modest) success. . . . I do not feel afraid of dying or of being dead. I have to admit that every now and again, I actually look forward to getting out of this fray. If you are given the gift of empathy, you can imagine how painful it must be for us pro-lifers to live in this country. Imagine how frustrating it must be for us to see women viewing their own offspring as adversaries to be destroyed, throwing away the priceless gift God has lavished upon them to love and by whom to be loved. As Mother Teresa says, the greatest evil of abortion is the death of love in those who participate in it.

Involvement in Politics

Ruth gradually became more involved in local politics, becoming a regular political commentator on a local cable news show. She wrote to a friend:

> Here's another piece of funny news. I've been asked to be a participant on a local Cable TV news talk show—the host wants to do a local version of the McLaughlin Group. He said I could be their Eleanor Clift [the progressive commentator]. Over my dead body, I felt like saying—more like Pat Buchanan [the right-wing commentator] in drag). I think this will be lots of fun. You know how I have always loved to argue. But who'd have thought back at Northern Valley that one day I'd be the orthodox Catholic right-wing Republican?

She also began to host her own monthly television show, which involved an interview with some interesting figure or leader in pro-life, Christian, or pro-family circles.

Even during chemotherapy, Ruth had worked with her friend Mary Mullaney to successfully oppose the implementation in Worcester of a sex education program designed by Planned Parenthood, which stressed "safe sex" and treated premarital sex as a perfectly valid personal choice. They formed a Committee for Responsible Sex Education. In a matter of weeks, it mobilized hundreds of Worcester citizens to express disapproval to the school committee. Not content with opposing the proposed program, they also crafted guidelines for an alternate program. Ruth would return from meetings completely exhausted, but she pressed on, and eventually the Planned Parenthood program was dropped in favor of a more acceptable, though still imperfect, one.

Perhaps encouraged by the success of this effort, Mary decided to run for the school board. Ruth, who had by then recovered from the chemotherapy, worked actively on her campaign. She coordinated an effort to distribute leaflets to every house in the city and to get women to stand on street corners with signs. Despite long odds, the efforts paid off. Ruth confided to a friend: "I love politics. It is a great competitive game with real stakes, but if you lose, there's always another election coming up so you can try again."

Ruth's participation in Mary's campaign, her pro-life activities, and her involvement in many other affairs sometimes caused tension at home. Michael recalls she would never commit herself to something like Mary's campaign without first consulting him and that he would enthusiastically encourage her. But when real sacrifices would later need to be made, he would sometimes gripe and complain about them. He recalls one occasion.

> Over dinner one evening during Mary's campaign with the five children sitting around the table with us, we were planning the activities of the coming week. There were a couple of events I really wanted both of us to go to—I can't recall now what they were—but as I mentioned them, one by one, Ruth said that she wasn't free, "I can't because I have this commitment with Mary's campaign." This was after weeks and weeks of Ruth's being tied up with the babysitting, leafleting, strategy sessions, and so on. I had had enough and lost my patience. In anger I stood up and said, "F--- Mary's campaign!" and then stormed out of the dining room. Just as I was leaving that room and entering the kitchen, I turned and looked at Ruth, who smiled, gave me the finger, and said firmly, "Well, f--- you!" The children, who witnessed all this, were horrified—because we almost never fought in front of them and absolutely never used obscenities. But the fight lasted only a few minutes, and naturally, I apologized to Ruth in front of the children.

Ruth also worked on the campaign of a candidate for the State House. She helped hone his message, but she also stuffed envelopes, went door-to-door, and stood at busy intersections with campaign signs.

Wife, Mother, and Friend

The most visible part of Ruth's apostolic activities involved directing pro-life organizations, debating, and appearing on television. But at the core of her apostolate were prayer, sacrifice, dedication to her family, one-on-one conversations based on friendship, and the power of her example. The core of her life lay in her role as wife and mother. A friend wrote:

> I like to dwell on how Ruth chose to be a wife and mother and to grow in holiness doing that. . . . Ruth truly is an example of growing in sanctity where you are, in the day-to-day, in the laundry, in driving from Point A to Point B. . . .
>
> I think she grew in sanctity in her duties as a wife and mother, and the way she offered that up. I think that's how she grew in sanctity, and in the moments she had to pray and offer up her works. And from that grace came the energy to use her talents to do the other things. I think the other things were just extra. And at the center of her life, I think, was being a wife and mother.

Ruth herself wrote:

> Housewives have lots of physical work and drudgery in the psychologically difficult task of listening to children fight, cry, and whine. But we have more free time to think our own thoughts and converse with our friends than most people ever do. I cannot picture a job that would be more appealing to me than this.

Ruth highly prized friendship and made a point of really getting to know the people she met. One of her friends recalls that "she was very quick to grab somebody, whoever showed up. She wouldn't let you slip away without really introducing herself and having a conversation." For example, Mary Mullaney, a Notre Dame-educated lawyer who met Ruth at a monthly meeting of a reading group, recalls:

Neither one of us being much for small talk, we got onto the subject of the infallibility of the church's teaching on birth control. Ruth said that it was infallible, but I wasn't sure about that. The next day Ruth arrived at my house—I remember seeing her trudge up the steps—with four big books in her arms. She sat on the couch and showed me all the citations in support of her position. I was awestruck. I couldn't believe that a casual conversation over coffee would prompt someone I had just met to go home, collect materials, organize her argument, and cross town again to convince me of the error of my position.

From that moment, Mary knew that Ruth was someone she wanted to have as a good friend. Reflecting on Ruth's impact on her life, she realized:

It wasn't so much any argument or anything that anyone said at the meeting [of the reading group] which affected me. It was just plain looking at Ruth. . . . When you're a young lady, you don't realize the joy that is part of motherhood. So that's what Ruth was an example of for me. It was a matter of: look at the joy that is there and then just get in line.

A friend talking with Michael after Ruth's death recalled:

I saw how much Ruth was able to do during a day. And also, your house on Shelby Street was not big. And yet Ruth entertained there. It felt very much like a home. We always had a good time. And, seeing that, I opened up our house more. I invited a lot more people over. I was much more willing to do things, after seeing how much Ruth did in a day.

Another woman, Grace Chaffers, recalled that when she first got to know Ruth she was impressed by how she was "so happy and so at peace. There was a sense of peace that she had. I didn't have that, and I wanted it." This eventually led Grace to rethink many aspects of her life, and concretely her decision not to have more children. She explained:

Before meeting Ruth, I had just offhandedly rejected the Church's teaching on contraception. I had never been challenged by anybody to rethink that. But it was not by any talk or lesson that Ruth challenged me on that, but just by being the mother of all those children. I gave her the kind of reaction that I always get now: "You have how many children?" (People kind of look at me in disbelief.) And she just very pleasantly explained that this was part of her faith. There was no doubt; there was no wavering. She was just cheerfully doing this.

After she discovered her own vocation to Opus Dei, Grace thanked Ruth for her prayers. Ruth, who didn't have a dishwasher, smiled, looked down at the floor, and said, "Well you've had my breakfast dishes for the last year." Grace didn't say much in response, but she thought, "Wow. This is Opus Dei."

Cancer Spreads to Her Bones

Just before Christmas 1993, Ruth discovered that cancer had spread to her bones. At the end of her Christmas letter, after talking about each of the children, she shared the news with relatives and friends:

> We ended 1993 with some difficult news. My cancer has returned to the right hip and backbone. Conventional medicine cannot cure metastasized breast cancer, so my years are numbered (in single digits). So far, Mike and I are (no doubt supernaturally) accepting of whatever God has in mind. We've gotten somewhat used to His ways not being our ways.

Ruth had formed a Rosary group whose members would meet once a week, bring their small children, and say the Rosary together, followed by coffee and conversation. At the January meeting, Ruth told her friends that her cancer had metastasized. "I'll tell you everything I know about my condition and the treatment, but after that, let's talk about something else." She explained that bone cancer could be controlled for two or three years, and in some cases even longer. So long as it stayed in the bones, she was going to be treated with a hormone, which wouldn't have such serious side effects as her original chemotherapy. Then she clapped her hands and exclaimed, "Right!—Now let's pray the Rosary for the intention that Michael finds a young wife to marry!"

The thought that Michael needed to remarry for the children's sake was not a passing one. She told her friends: "The worst suffering is the fear of dying while my children are still so young. What are the chances my husband could marry again with six children? . . . I hate the idea of my children growing up without a mother." Less than three months before she died, in a moment of particular intimacy, Ruth confided to Michael that she thought he should marry Catherine Hardy, the eldest daughter of their friends Tom and Jan Hardy.[1] She wrote to a friend, "I trust God to arrange things for the best, even if it doesn't appear that way to us. I have total peace that God will bring good out of this experience, whatever the outcome." To another friend, she wrote:

> It's funny that the prospect of dying does not bother me that much. I really do believe that whatever God wants is going to turn out best. If he wants me to die before getting out of my 30s, I trust that good will come of it. I pray that all my friends will come to have a strong faith, that my sister will be reconciled to the rest of the family, that my children will grow up in the faith—that sort of thing. I'll ask you again to say this particular prayer card [to the founder of Opus Dei]. This is the guy who ought to be looking out for me. He also has a reputation for blessing people who say this prayer card faithfully. I'd love to see that work for you.

The news that cancer had spread to Ruth's bones put an end to the uncertainty of the previous year of whether she had beaten cancer or not. Ruth wrote about this to a woman also diagnosed with breast cancer:

> This [doubt] was resolved for me . . . when I was diagnosed with metastatic disease. But that period of uncertainty was still a good time—it helped me become much more abandoned to God's will. Now, oddly enough, I am happier than I have ever been in my life. . . . I trust you will also find that this experience brings you closer to God, trusting His sometimes-inscrutable wisdom to bring blessings out of suffering.

Ruth's doctor suggested a well-known hormone treatment that had some benefits but offered no hope of a cure. Ruth was concerned that maybe she should press instead to receive Bone Marrow Transplant (BMT) therapy. This

---

1. At the time, this seemed highly improbable, among other things because Catherine Hardy was at least fifteen years younger than Michael, not much older than Ruth's oldest children, and about to begin graduate school at Harvard. In 1999, however, Michael and Catherine married.

painful and debilitating treatment was very risky because the immune system would be temporarily destroyed and because if the bone marrow transplant failed to "take," the patient would die quickly. It involved being hospitalized for weeks and debilitated for months. But it might offer some prospect of long-term survival. Ruth felt it would be a shame to ruin the little time she had left with debilitating treatment if it did not succeed. But she was concerned that, maybe even because of her faith in God and her growing desire to get to heaven, she was discounting the potential benefits of the treatment. She spent weeks reading medical literature and consulting with specialists about it. She decided against BMT, but remained open to the possibility if new information pointed that way.

Five Years with Bone Cancer

For five years, Ruth's cancer was contained to her bones and allowed her to lead a very active life. She carried on with the many things that had made up her life until then and even did new things. Shortly after her diagnosis, her friends the Swopes proposed that she go skiing for the first time in her life. Ruth enthusiastically accepted their invitation and along with the Swopes and her older sons spent a week skiing in New Hampshire. By the end of the week, she was making it down the mountain without falling.

Ruth had always been a "people person," but now she began to give even greater priority to spending time with family and friends. As she explained in a letter:

> Knowing that I have rather limited time left makes me a lot more willing to abandon the laundry and housecleaning in order to do things like attend the concerts of close friends. This is another very interesting question (like the interesting question of what is important to pass on to children as "family heritage"). When you know you have little time left to live, how should you conduct yourself? To a certain extent, I am glad that I have no burning desire to live any differently. I really enjoy the way my life has turned out. But I do feel it is important to spend more time with people I enjoy being with.

In January 1998, Ruth learned that cancer had spread to her liver and that she had less than a year to live. That same evening, she gave talks to children at a local school. The next day she attended a dinner for teachers in the Confraternity of Christian Doctrine program. The day after that she gave a talk at a high school. Two days afterward she began chemotherapy for liver cancer, and a few days later she gave a talk to more than one hundred high school students. Until it proved absolutely impossible, she continued to serve as parish Director of Religious Education, run the high school youth group, sing in the cathedral choir, host a monthly book discussion group, and teach classes for cooperators of Opus Dei. All of this in addition to taking care of her home and family.

At the end of June, Ruth co-taught a four-day course at the University of Notre Dame on the Basics of Catholicism with Professor Ralph McInerny. In August, during a family vacation in New Hampshire, despite having a steel rod in her leg to strengthen the bone which had been eaten away by cancer, she hiked down Mount Washington, the tallest mountain in New England, after having driven to the top.

Chemotherapy for liver cancer caused premature menopause and deeply affected Ruth's emotions. As she wrote to a friend at the end of March:

> I've been alternating between deep, painful unhappiness and a kind of serene joy. I try to remember that I should be glad of the opportunity to unite my sufferings with Christ. Then, when I actually feel miserable, this all goes right out the window. It's tedious. Another odd thing is that for many years it seemed to me as if I experienced very few emotions, all within a pretty reasonable range of intensity. There was the happiness caused by the children. There was exasperation when Michael was difficult and contentment when things with him were on an even keel, and that was about it. Now it seems to me my emotions utterly dominate my perception of reality. This must be menopause. It's interesting, occasionally pleasant, often horrible.

At about the same time, she wrote a long letter to a high school friend who was a nonbeliever:

> My cancer grinds inexorably on. It has spread to my lungs and liver. I am going to be on one form of chemotherapy or another for the rest of my life, which in all likelihood will not be that much longer. I don't complain, though. I have had a great life. I have known wonderful people. I have

done interesting things. I have had many gifts and talents that made life lots of fun (singing, acting, public speaking, etc.). My husband is great. My kids are great. And I really believe the Catholic faith. This life is short and it is merely the qualifying exam for the real thing. I regret that I have not written regularly to you. Your friendship has been a great source of happiness.

At the end of April 1998, Ruth wrote again to the same friend:

I am not afraid to die—not by a long shot. I go beyond just accepting what the Catholic Church teaches. Ever since I knew I had incurable cancer, I have thought long and hard about how I live my life and what I think death means. I have loved the life God gave me. There is no other life I would rather have lived. But I recognize God is the author of this life, as well as the author of the lives of all the people I love and the world, which is so beautiful and interesting. I want to see God; I want to see the One who thought all of this up. I cannot imagine that He will be less interesting and beautiful than all of the things He has made, and of course, I hope to see all the best people in heaven anyway, even you, to whom I (and so many others) owe so much. This life is short and eternity is—well, it's eternal.

Ruth did not finish that letter for another three weeks, when she added several more pages before sending it off:

Not wanting to seem maudlin, but this could be my farewell letter. I hope not, but just in case, let me thank you for your great friendship and for the world of literature and culture you encouraged me to know and love. Though I have been a very poor correspondent, you have been daily in my thoughts and prayers.

Naturally, I hope you will manage to return to the faith of your baptism. Really, what else could be true? There is no God at all? There is a God, but He hasn't bothered to communicate with us? There is a God, He has communicated with us, but we don't know whether it was through Buddha, Mohammed, Jesus, someone else, or all of the above? The last possibility seems much more likely than the first two. Then it is a matter of figuring out which of the great religions actually seems to be most likely to be the true communication of God to man. I have no doubt that if you were to turn your considerable intellectual powers to this question, it would only be a matter of time before you realized there is no explanation for the Catholic Church's existence except that, in fact, the guy named Jesus from Nazareth really did die and his corpse really did rise from the dead and he really did walk around talking to those rather uninspiring eleven who somehow, after this experience, transformed the course of human history. And for the better.

Well, thanks again and farewell. With love & gratitude.

Death

By early September, Ruth was bedridden and on oxygen. In the final days of her life, many people came to pray with and for her, or just to be with her. She died on the afternoon of September 23, 1998. That afternoon, dozens of people showed up spontaneously. This was before cell phones. No one sent out a message. They just "knew" somehow and showed up. As she lay dying, they kept vigil with her. As the rector of the cathedral, who was their pastor and a close friend, observed,

> The place was packed with people, all just sort of sitting around and pray-ing, praying with her. I'm sure that was a source of strength. . . . [It] would have been easier to just be quietly with the family; instead of having the front door open, just as on New Year's Eve. But [it was a wonderful thing] to let those people come in and see her in that weakness and those last hours, and the great dignity that was there.

Ruth died as she had lived, surrounded by people whom she loved and who loved her.

CHAPTER TWO

Tomás and Paquita Alvira:
Early Married Members of the Work

Tomás Alvira, the first married member of Opus Dei, was a soil scientist, a high school teacher, and a university professor of education. His wife, Paquita, a very early member of the women's branch, worked as an elementary school teacher and principal, but after the birth of their first child, she became a full-time homemaker. The Archdiocese of Madrid has opened causes of canonization for both of them. This chapter devotes more space to Tomás than to Paquita, not because his life illustrates more about the vocation to Opus Dei than hers does, but simply because his career as an educator led his colleagues to leave a record of many details of his life. Paquita's life taken as a whole is inspiring, but because it unfolded largely in their home we know far less about its details.

Getting Started

Tomás graduated from college with a degree in chemistry during the turbulent period just before the outbreak of the Spanish Civil War. He found a job teaching in a small public school in a rural town. Despite his youth and his reputation as a practicing Catholic, in 1935 his mostly anti-Catholic left-wing colleagues unanimously elected him director of the school.

In July 1936, Tomás went to Madrid to take national exams for a permanent position in the public high school system. A few days before he was scheduled to return home to Zaragoza, war broke out between right-wing, pro-Catholic Nationalists led by General Franco and left-wing, anti-Catholic Republicans.

Tomás found himself trapped in leftist Republican-controlled Madrid, where being a practicing Catholic could easily lead to being assassinated. One day on the street, he met the Republican mayor of the town where he taught. The man gave him his phone number in case Tomás found himself in trouble. Their professional relationship and the affection of the mayor's eleven-year-old daughter for her teacher trumped their political differences.

On another occasion, a Socialist colleague who had traveled to Madrid with Tomás for the exams and with whom he was sharing a room, decided to enlist in the Republican Army. At their last meeting, he asked Tomás to give him his watch. He explained his unusual request by saying, "I think that the watch is the thing I will look at most frequently and it will remind me of you. I want you to know that I will never shoot to kill someone on the opposing side. They are your people, and I don't want anything to separate us."

For more than a year, Tomás frequently went to study with a college classmate, José María Albareda. In Albareda's apartment, he met Isidoro Zorzano and Juan Jiménez Vargas, two of the first members of Opus Dei. On September 1, 1937, Albareda introduced him to the founder, Fr. Josemaría Escrivá. Tomás was impressed with "the forceful personality of that young priest, the supernatural vision that informed everything he said, his optimism despite the difficult situation, his admirable serenity, and his affectionate dealings." Tomás recalls that "from the day I first met him, I put my soul in his hands."

At the time, all the members of Opus Dei had embraced apostolic celibacy. They urged Tomás to join Opus Dei and do the same. Escrivá, however, understood that Tomás had a vocation to marriage. He told him that for the moment Opus Dei could only have celibate members, but that the time would come when he could join as a married man.

Early Years

In the fall of 1937, Tomás joined Escrivá and several other members of the Work in a perilous effort to cross the Pyrenees Mountains into France and, from there, enter the Nationalist zone of Spain. Several days into the grueling trek through the mountains, Tomás collapsed, exhausted. The group's guide wanted to leave him behind, but Escrivá objected vigorously. Turning to Tomás, he said, "You'll come with us, like everyone else, to the very end." With this encouragement, Tomás summoned up the energy to continue and successfully crossed into the Nationalist zone.

At the end of the civil war in 1939, Tomás won a position as a science teacher in the newly established Ramiro de Maeztu Institute in Madrid. The school had been created by the Spanish government to serve as a model for other Spanish state-run schools. In addition to teaching at Ramiro de Maeztu, Tomás was active in the Institute of Soil Sciences of the Higher Council of Scientific Research (CSIC), directed by his friend José María Albareda. Tomás also served as deputy director of the CSIC's Institute of Pedagogy.

In June 1939, he married Paquita Domínguez, whom he had met years earlier in Zaragoza. He was thirty-three and she was twenty-seven. She continued to teach in the Zaragoza area until the fall of 1941. The first of their nine children, José Maria, was born in 1940 but died of measles when he was four. Many years later, Paquita wrote to a great-niece who had just lost a young child:

> I understand your state of mind, asking the Lord how he could have done
> this to you. What I'm going to say may seem absurd, but the reason is that
> God had confidence in you. He knew that you would continue loving him

and having confidence in him and would realize that through this evil he would give you many good things. That is what he did with Tomás and me. When we were happy seeing our José Maria running around, when he was most beautiful, God took him from us to heaven in a few hours. It seemed to us that we would never again have anything to look forward to in life. The pain was enormous, but God is a Father and always provides for our good, even though we do not understand. Try to have the security that everything that has happened will fill you with blessings and good things. . . . You have in Heaven the best of your love, an angel who will watch out for all of you. Ask the most holy Virgin of the Pillar to give you the strength that you so much need now, and joy will soon become once again the characteristic feature of your life.

In 1947, the Holy See approved new statutes for Opus Dei. They made it possible for married people to belong to Opus Dei, with an ascetical bond to the Work, living its spirit and participating in its apostolate. Tomás joined Opus Dei on February 15, 1947, thereby becoming its first married member.

Director of a Boarding School for Orphans

Tomás's work at the Ramiro de Maeztu Institute, where he became deputy headmaster, and in the CSIC's Institute of Pedagogy, soon won him an outstanding reputation in Spanish educational circles. In 1950, the commander of Spain's Civil Guards, a militarized national police force similar to the French Gendarmerie Nationale or the Italian Carabinieri, asked Tomás to direct the Infanta María Teresa Institute, a boarding school in Madrid for five hundred orphans whose fathers had been civil guards.

At first, Tomás was inclined to reject the offer. He was deeply committed to the Ramiro de Maeztu Institute and very happy working there. The Infanta María Teresa Institute was a deeply troubled institution with a depressing atmosphere. The boys, who ranged from six to eighteen years of age, were housed in dormitories of one hundred beds each, with a number over each bed. All their heads were shaved, and they were subject to severe discipline with frequent corporal punishment. Gangs of older boys terrorized the younger students.

The conditions and traditions of the school were diametrically opposed to Tomás's ideas of education. He had always conceived of education as a joint effort of parents and teachers, but here all the students were orphans. He gave great importance to freedom, but discipline, not freedom, was the keynote in this military school in Franco's Spain. The teachers were dispirited, and the level of instruction was low.

Tomás did not immediately reject the offer, however, because he saw that if he could turn the school around, he would greatly improve the lives of five hundred boys. He talked it over with Paquita and thought and prayed about it a great deal. Eventually, with Paquita's support, he decided to accept the appointment with two conditions: complete freedom to act and the right to directly consult with the head of the Civil Guard, who had ultimate authority over the institution.

The Alviras moved to the director's house on the grounds of the school with their then-five children, ranging in age from nine to two. During the seven years they lived at the school, they would have three more children. The house was considerably larger than their previous apartment and had a garden, but at first, it had no heat and they had to wear their coats indoors. Living on the grounds permitted Tomás to get to know the students better and to be more aware of everything that happened at the school. Eventually, he would know a large percentage of the students by name. He congratulated them on the feast of the saint each child was named for (their "name days") and birthdays and often inquired about their families. On more than one occasion, he spent a large part of the night at the bedside of a sick student.

The first, and in many ways most difficult, task, was improving the attitude and working conditions of the faculty. Tomás's strategy was to set goals and objectives but give individual teachers wide latitude in achieving them. Remarkably, within a year he had transformed the faculty. A professional magazine published an article entitled "An Example for the Teaching Profession to Meditate On."

Tomás also set about improving the physical conditions of the school and the boys' living quarters. He began by taking down the numbers over their beds and working to clean up the school. Eventually, he replaced the one-hundred-bed dormitories with apartments for eight students each, comprised of two bedrooms, two bathrooms, a living room, and a small terrace.

He encouraged the students to decorate their rooms with personal objects that might remind them of their family and their hometown. Not content with transforming the physical environment, he also changed the structure of the school, opening it up to sons of active-duty civil guards so that not all the students would be orphans.

When Tomás took over, attendance at Mass and the Rosary were obligatory. He made them voluntary. At first, very few students attended. The students who did come to say the Rosary said it very quickly, rushing through the prayers and the closing litanies. One day Tomás came by when they were saying the litany and interrupted them, "My sons, don't you realize that you are paying compliments to your mother the Virgin, calling her Mystical Rose, Morning Star, Tower of Ivory, House of Gold. . . . Say those things with affection, as if you were talking with your mother." Years later, one of the boys said that this was "the most beautiful thing I have heard, and I carry his words in me. . . . When I pray the Rosary, I always remember him." Little by little, thanks in large part to the efforts of the chaplain, the number of boys attending Mass and the Rosary grew. Working with the chaplain, Tomás also made the celebration of major Church feast days more important in the life of the school.

After seven years, Tomás resigned as director of the Infanta María Teresa Institute and returned to Ramiro de Maeztu. He left behind him a completely transformed institution. Thirty-eight years later, at an assembly of school alumni, the thousand men present gave him a ten-minute standing ovation.

According to a long-term collaborator and close friend, the seven years in which Tomás served as head of the Infanta María Teresa Institute

seem to have been years in which Paquita and Tomás grew exceptionally in their closeness to one another. Work and family were intimately intertwined. Tomás came home from his experiences in the school with no intervening time at all—no time to switch gears or recuperate. He was a positive, optimistic person, but many of his days at the school, especially in the first months, were difficult. Coming home to Paquita restored him. She understood the situation, and fully accepted that he might leave the house at any hour of the day or night to look in on the school. She shared his concerns. As time went on, the students became aware of her affection for them, and she won their hearts.

Shortly after he returned to the Ramiro de Maeztu Institute in 1957, Tomás became assistant headmaster for education, a position he held until his retirement in 1976. After the headmaster permanently lost his voice, Tomás's role expanded to the point that many people thought of him as the de facto head of the school.

Founding Private Schools

In the early 1960s, St. Josemaría began encouraging Spanish members of Opus Dei who had school-aged children to start schools. The purpose was to give their children an excellent education while also transmitting the spirit of Opus Dei, particularly a love of freedom and a spirit of hard work. The first such school, Ahlzair, opened its doors in Córdoba in 1963. That same year, Tomás Alvira and another member, the well-known pedagogue Victor García de Hoz, started an institution to give guidance and support to these schools: *Fomento de Centros de Enseñanza* [Development of Educational Centers].

Following the principles developed by Alvira and García de Hoz, the schools strive for academic excellence through personalized education. They stress the central role of parents in their children's education and involve them in all aspects of school life. Religious and spiritual formation in *Fomento* schools is entrusted to Opus Dei, and participation in religious classes and activities is completely voluntary.

Thanks in large part to Alvira's dedication, optimism, and drive, *Fomento* grew rapidly. Today, it sponsors thirty-five schools with twenty-four thousand students spread throughout Spain. In 1975, *Fomento* reached the point that it felt the need for a teachers' college that would train new teachers, not only in basic pedagogy but also in character development and promoting an atmosphere of freedom. Although Tomás was almost seventy years old, he took on the task of founding and developing this new institution, which received government approval in 1978.

Teacher and Pedagogue

Tomás was a born teacher who took a deep personal interest in his students. In his view, the two key elements to successful teaching were, first, loving the students and, second, helping them experience the joy of learning. A teacher whom Tomás interviewed for his first job recalls that "he was not interested in whether I knew how to teach but rather in whether I liked to educate, whether I was in love with my profession." A seasoned teacher, giving a talk to young teachers, stressed the need to be understanding with students. After the talk, Tomás said to him, "Much more, Antonio, much more. We have to go way beyond understanding. We have to love them unconditionally. Otherwise, education doesn't sink in and becomes something small." When teachers complained about their students' shortcomings and about how difficult it was to win them over, Tomás would respond, "But, have we tried loving them?"

Tomás's love for his students was not merely a matter of words. One former student recalls: "He couldn't do enough for his students. How often he paid for textbooks or asked for used ones from students who had already graduated! He bought sandwiches for boys he realized were hungry but gave them in such a way that they didn't regard it as charity but as payment for some job or service done in the classroom." One of his high school students was certain he wanted to become a bullfighter. Rather than treating his aspiration as a childish dream, Tomás put him in contact with a friend of his who was a former bullfighter and arranged for the boy to work there so he could form an accurate idea of what a bullfighter's life is like.

In the classroom, he was guided by the principle that "we have to accustom students to feeling the joy of making an effort to achieve what they desire. Joy in study is one of the most important goals that an educator can aim at." Later in life when he was the head of *Fomento*'s school for teachers, Tomás formulated this as the characteristic feature of what he called the "Full-Life Class." A "Full-Life Class" is "one in which the teacher tries to awaken in the students the desire to know, a love of attaining knowledge, considered as a good in itself. We shouldn't try to get the students to study by presenting them with a possible reward or punishment; we must get them to want to know."

Tomás cared for not only the students and teachers but everyone who was connected with the school. During the many years in which he was deputy director of the Ramiro de Maeztu school, for example, he made an effort to get to know each of the janitors. He habitually spent time with them and took a sincere interest in their families and needs. At Christmas, he visited each of them at home to wish them a Merry Christmas and spend some time with their family. Often, he would take one of his children with him on those visits.

For many years, a poor old man used to sell candy and snacks just outside the school. When Tomás learned that one of his children had given the old man a hard time, he was deeply upset and spanked his son, something he never did. On another occasion, when the old man failed to show up for several days, Tomás made inquiries and learned that he lived alone, had no close relatives, and was in the hospital. Tomás took one of his sons to visit him in the hospital.

A Bright and Cheerful Christian Home

St. Josemaría often proposed the ideal of creating a "bright and cheerful Christian home." The Alviras worked hard, and successfully, to achieve this goal. Their home was characterized by a joy that a family friend characterized as "contagious, or better, radiant." Although both Paquita and Tomás preferred classical music, they cheerfully listened to the Beatles at high volume and even did a little rock and roll dancing with their children. The entire family celebrated both birthdays and name days, even of children who had grown up and were living in a foreign country.

They also celebrated the major religious feast days, including the Feast of Our Lady of the Pillar, the patroness of Zaragoza. Although the Alviras lived in Madrid for many years, on her feast day the family always awoke to music from Zaragoza; the house was decorated, and celebrations continued all day long. At Christmas time, Tomás transmitted to the children his enthusiasm for building a crèche. They all worked on it together. One of his daughters recalls:

> There was a wonderful atmosphere of joy and festivity in the whole house, with Christmas carols playing in the background. When we finished building the crèche something unforgettable happened. We put out the lights in the living room (where the crèche was) and left lit only the little lights that illuminated the crib scene. Then we sat on my father's knees, and amid our great expectation, he told us the story of the coming of the Son of God into the world.

The Alviras' style was to give the children a great deal of freedom, but also to demand that they take responsibility for their decisions. One daughter testifies that she does not remember her parents ever forbidding her—or any of her brothers and sisters—anything.

> We always felt free, but responsibility was a very important factor. It was something they had explained to us, but that you really learned by living. In cases of doubt about doing something, you knew that you could do it, but you weighed the pros and the cons. At times they gave you some facts to consider in deciding if it was worthwhile.

Another daughter recalls a time when her father refused to allow her to attend a particular camp. Without giving reasons he simply said, serenely but clearly, "You should not go there." She remembers because she was quite disconcerted by his refusal without giving any explanations, since he habitually explained his decisions. Yet another daughter sums up her home environment saying, "I never felt afraid of my parents. I told them very openly where I went. . . . My parents knew everything I did, and I always felt that they trusted me."

When someone got out of line and had to be corrected, Tomás and Paquita rarely lost their tempers or raised their voices. When one of his daughters came home with a miniskirt, Tomás asked her with a smile, "My daughter, why did you buy a skirt a couple of sizes too small for you? Here's some money. Go with your sister and buy a skirt that fits you and give that one to one of your little sisters." On the rare occasions when he did lose his temper, Tomás would apologize publicly to the entire family.

Trust and mutual confidence were essential in the Alvira family. On one occasion one of the children borrowed some of his father's markers without telling him. Soon, Tomás needed the markers and spent quite a bit of time looking for them. When Paquita saw that the child had them, she told him to bring them to his father. When the boy returned the markers to his father, Tomás did not raise his voice or show irritation over the time he had wasted looking for them. He simply said, "My son, if you need something ask me for it." His son recalls that he added, "alluding to what he had deepest in his heart and what he knew most mattered to each of us, 'Could it be that you don't feel comfortable with me?'"

Tomás's usual style was dialogue. When the children asked questions, particularly about topics of morals or religion that were being discussed in society and at school, he didn't simply answer their questions. Rather, he made them think. One of his daughters says that he "never wanted us to accept blindly his principles or ideas. In our home, there was an extraordinary climate of freedom, precisely because there was so much love and trust. I can't remember anything ever being forced on me or any of my siblings." Nonetheless, she also says that when he did speak, usually at the end of a dialogue, "What he told us had such authority and certainty that the things he said were engraved in our heads, giving us security."

For many years, even after car ownership became quite widespread in Spain, the family did not own a car. One of his daughters recalls what happened when she asked her father why they didn't have a car.

> He looked at me closely and, with the air of someone who had thought about it well, he said: "My daughter, don't forget what I'm going to say to you. There is one thing fundamental in this life: knowing how to be in your place." I don't recall his adding anything else. I understood that I had to go beyond the question of a car to understand my parents' attitude. If they had wanted to, we would have had a car. But it was not the right moment nor was it indispensable. For that reason, it would have been out of place for us at that moment. There were other priorities. I understood that my parents didn't let themselves be carried away by the desire of doing what everybody else was doing.

The Alviras had nine children. All eight of those who survived childhood went to college, so money was always short. Paquita handled the family's finances. For about four years when things were particularly tight, Tomás worked as the human resource manager for a bank in addition to his work as an educator. Often the younger children wore hand-me-downs from their older siblings, but Paquita would spruce them up, so they didn't look old or worn.

A good part of the peace and joy that characterized the Alvira home came from Paquita's and Tomás's deep love for each other. One of the children recalls Tomás saying, "I have always tried to surprise your mother and to love her more each day." When they went to a movie, Tomás would choose one he thought Paquita would like, even if he wasn't especially interested. He often spoke to the children about their mother's gifts, especially her artistic talent, and about how she had put those talents aside to dedicate herself fully to raising them.

At eighty years old, Tomás wrote on the back of a photo he gave Paquita, "How much happiness God has given us." A young woman who met Tomás toward the end of his life observed:

> When I met him, the main idea I came away with was that he was a man deeply in love with his wife. This was obvious in his old age, which really made an impression on me. The refinement, the tenderness, the exquisite tact that he employed when he looked at her, spoke to her, or just referred to her, reflected an intense love for her that did not seem to have lost any of its vigor in an entire lifetime. At that moment I understood clearly that his vocation to matrimony consisted in falling more in love with his wife each day. . . . He is a yardstick for measuring the affection and self-giving that can be lived in marriage.

Paquita and Tomás transmitted their love of God and piety primarily by their example.

One of their children recalls:

> From when I was very little, I considered visiting the Blessed Sacrament something natural, a custom that formed part of being a Christian, because my parents always did it. If we went out with them to go shopping or for any other motive, before returning home we entered a church. In summer, we used to all go together to the church of the [small town where the family spent the summer] to make a visit.

Another childhood memory involved weekday Mass:

> When I turned fourteen, I began to realize that my father went to Mass very early every morning, always at the same time. From when I was little, I recall him seated in a chair reading. Now I understood that early in the morning he was spending some time in prayer. When I realized all this, I asked him to wake me up so I could go with him. I think this was his ordinary way of teaching: to do things and let his coherent life sink into us. Everything that he said was backed up before by what he did.

Looking back years later, a daughter said about her parents:

> With their example and their words, they helped us to discover the secret of the incomparable joy of an authentic Christian life: the intimate, constant,

and loving presence of God in our existence, the loving vital encounter with Jesus Christ. Seeing my parents, I have understood that Christianity is not a theory, but a joyful life with Christ. It is possible. It is not an unattainable ideal. It is the path of the fullness of happiness.

Both Paquita and Tomás hoped that their children would receive from God a vocation to Opus Dei. When they told St. Josemaría about their desire early in their marriage, he urged them to pray a lot for their children and "to leave them in peace." They took this advice very much to heart, and never so much as suggested that any of their children attend activities at an Opus Dei center. When one of their daughters told Tomás that she had joined Opus Dei, he limited himself to asking with great affection, "My daughter, do you understand well what you have done? Did you do it freely? Are you content?" When she replied "Yes," he kissed her and that was that.

Eventually, all the Alvira children joined Opus Dei. When the last child became a member, Tomás asked one of the older children to "help me give thanks to God. What have I done to deserve such a wonderful thing? My time to live is too short for thanking God enough."

Tomás's Old Age and Death

In 1981, at age seventy-five, Tomás underwent surgery for prostate cancer. He said to one of his children, "I entered the operating room holding the hand of the Blessed Virgin and our Father [St. Josemaría]. You can't be safer than that." The surgery was successful, but afterward, his family and colleagues urged him to slow down or retire. When one of his colleagues raised the issue, he answered, "Doesn't the Constitution say that every Spaniard has a right to work? You must have noticed that it doesn't say anything about age. Therefore, I intend to exercise my right up to the end." When one of his children broached the same subject, he cited a different authority: "I have read in the Bible that God made man to work, but I haven't found any passage that indicates that man should work until he is seventy." Only at age eighty-two did Tomás officially retire.

A few years after his retirement, Tomás began to suffer debilitating effects of the prostate cancer that had spread to his bones, but he continued writing. He also continued going to daily Mass, despite the effort it cost him.

If anyone suggested that he didn't need to go to Mass, Tomás responded that his sacrifice was very small compared to the great sacrifice of the Mass.

When he could no longer go, a priest brought him Communion each day. "It's something magnificent, truly magnificent," he said, "to have the Lord in my house."

As the end approached, he commented to one of his daughters, "They tell me no, but it looks to me like the end is near. Whatever God wants will be what happens, and that's what I want. But I'm not downcast. I offer everything for the Father [the Prelate of Opus Dei], but I ask the Lord to take me." Tomás died on May 7, 1992. At his wake, a very close friend and collaborator found himself thinking, *Thanks, Tomás. How well you did everything! Thank you, Lord. What marvelous things you do among men.*

Paquita: Mother and Homemaker

Paquita's father died when she was only two, and her mother faced severe economic challenges in raising five children. At that time in Spain, Paquita's education would normally have ended with grade school, but a teacher convinced her mother that it would be a shame for such a talented girl not to go to high school. Her mother asked the other children if they would be willing to make the sacrifices necessary for Paquita to continue her education, and they agreed.

When she finished high school, Paquita obtained the highest score of the one hundred students who took the entrance exam for teachers' college. This won her a scholarship that made it possible to obtain her teaching degree. In exams for a position in the national corps of teachers after graduation, she again finished in first place. In 1934, at the age of twenty-two, she began to work in a three-teacher school in Sástago, a small village about fifty miles from Zaragoza.

Paquita and Tomás were married just after the end of the civil war in June 1939, but they could not make ends meet without Paquita's salary so, for the next two years, she remained in Sástago and he in Madrid. Finally in fall 1941, she resigned her position and joined Tomás in Madrid. It would have been possible for her to find a teaching position in Madrid, but their first child had been born in 1940 and they were hoping to have a large family, so she decided to become a full-time mother and homemaker.

Paquita was fully aware that she was extraordinarily talented and better educated than most women of her generation in Spain. She could have had a successful career in education or some other field. She did not, however, consider that turning her attention primarily to taking care of her family meant wasting her time or talents. Paquita was convinced, as she wrote, that "work in the home can be just as professional as any job a woman can hold outside the house." In addition, she saw, as she wrote in a magazine article, that "taking care of the house and the children with a spirit of sacrifice, taking care of the details and trying to live in the presence of God provide an occasion for living all the Christian virtues."

Paquita found housework fulfilling because she did not do it out of a sense of duty. Each one of the things she did was done for someone concrete. One of her daughters recalls:

> My recollection is of work well done and done with joy. Some women don't like to take care of the house because they've heard their mothers complain about having to do so. Mama transmitted to us a very high concept of the value of work in the home, putting one's head into it and filling it with affection.

A cousin observed:

> I have seen her give herself totally to her family, forgetting about herself, without complaints or laments, without ever referring to the tiredness that raising such a large family must have brought with it. Rather her smile and her welcoming expression seemed to manifest her own happiness and that of her family.

Paquita took advantage of the time when the children were in school to do housework, go shopping, and visit friends. She also played an important role in starting and running many apostolic activities connected to Opus Dei. One of her daughters wrote: "She was never a woman shut up in the house. . . . She always had very open horizons." She tried to keep up with current events and to be well-informed so she could talk with her older children about everything. But, as one of her biographers says:

> When it came time for the troop of children to arrive home, the door would burst open with cries of "where's mama?" And she was always to be found just a few steps ahead with nothing else to do but listen to them. She

understood each one of her children and continually accompanied them as they grew from infants into little soccer players or teenage girls wearing their first high heels.

A niece who spent several summers with the Alvira family recalls that their house "was always filled with joy. It was a home where one could feel the presence of God. Without spending much, they celebrated everything: some pickles and a few chips were enough to make for a good time."

Precisely because it was a happy home where a spirit of freedom reigned, the children's friends liked to come to the Alvira apartment to study and have an afternoon snack. Even though the house was crowded with the eight Alvira children, Paquita always welcomed them.

A Woman of Virtue

One of Paquita's outstanding characteristics was her cheerfulness. A friend commented, "I recall her as always being happy. I used to think to myself, *she must have concerns, but it's evident that she resolves them with God. Otherwise, it wouldn't be possible to always be like that.*" Another friend said, "I enjoyed being with her. When I was with her, time went by quickly. She was like a magnet for me." One of her daughters expresses a similar experience: "She was always happy. Hers was a quiet, not a noisy happiness. Her smile was permanent. She knew how to laugh openly, and her smile was contagious."

Late in life, Paquita wrote to a niece telling her about how much she had enjoyed the fact that all the children had been able to come home for their parents' fiftieth anniversary. The niece responded:

> How well you know how to appreciate and thank the Lord for the happy moments! I admire you! You don't say anything about the suffering you must have experienced when they left or how empty the house felt. Your strength is extraordinary and undoubtedly the Lord is with you. I tell you sincerely that you are an example.

Paquita had a big, welcoming heart, and people who spent any time with her soon noticed her warm affection. One friend found that "getting to know her was like finding a second mother. I felt very much at home with her and she with me. She had very special affection for me. When I was with her, I was happy. Her life was always an example for me, and when she died, I thought that the best person I had ever known had died."

Another friend said that Paquita

> transmitted peace and joy with her words, with her gestures, and with her smile. When I visited her, I poured out my heart talking about what was worrying me at the moment. If I told her about someone who was making me suffer, she downplayed the matter and helped me to forgive them. She always talked about others with affection and a positive sense.

One of the women who got together with her in her home to make vestments for Opus Dei oratories in the Third World says: "I was won over by the environment I found. She created it, orienting the conversations and making you notice that she loved you, that you were not indifferent to her. . . . Her self-giving to others was obvious. She was always looking after everyone. In her house, you were really at home."

For many years, Paquita's sister-in-law lived with the Alviras. Paquita treated her so affectionately that some people who saw them together thought they were sisters.

One of her daughters who spent the nights with her during the final weeks of her life testified: "Being so loved gave me incomparable joy. Her affection was profound and disinterested. Her expression of thankfulness and joy when I arrived in the evening and the joy I felt in seeing myself loved that way made me think many times about what the love of God in heaven would be like."

A Woman of Prayer

When Paquita first came into contact with Opus Dei, she found it hard to imagine how the mother of a large family could find time for the practices of piety that make up the plan of life of a member of Opus Dei. Gradually, however, she learned how to find the time. In a letter to a young mother who had raised the same objection, she shared her secret:

> You can do the prayer or read a spiritual book, while you rock your baby in the cradle. You can pray the Rosary when you go to the park with your children. You can find time to go to Mass when your domestic helper or

your husband is at home. And during the whole day, you can be in the presence of God, offering your work and your tiredness with joy.

Paquita was not content with simply finding time for getting to Mass or praying the Rosary. She actively sought ways of praying better and cultivating a deeper sense of God's presence. She confided to one of her daughters that, after the children's baptisms, "I placed each of you next to my heart, and there adored the Blessed Trinity in you, thinking, *Now it really is a fact that the Holy Spirit is inside this daughter or son of mine.*" On one occasion, when she sensed a special need to thank God, she felt that she didn't know how to do so well. So, she said, "I looked for a trick that I think must please the Lord. I asked his mother that she be the one who thanked him in my name because naturally, everything tastes better if it is your mother who tells you about it."

She had great devotion to the Blessed Virgin Mary, especially to Our Lady of the Pillar, who is venerated in Zaragoza. On many occasions, she was heard to say, "What would we do without her?" In May, during the last year of her life, she arranged with a florist to deliver a fresh rose every day for the image of Our Lady in the Opus Dei center where she attended formational activities.

For a number of years, Paquita suffered from severe insomnia, but she filled the time praying the Rosary. She would sometimes comment, "Last night I tried to unite myself to all those who suffer." When the breakup of Yugoslavia led to war in Bosnia in the early 1990s, Paquita spent the night thinking of all that the women in Bosnia were suffering and sending them what she could—the help of her prayer. One day she said to her daughter Pilar, "Today I have been a Bosnian woman, all day. I thought it would be the most powerful way for me to pray to Our Lady for those women."

Paquita suffered a serious stroke on April 20, 1994, that left her in a deep coma. She died on August 29, 1994, two years after Tomás. Her cause of beatification, along with that of her husband, was opened by the archbishop of Madrid in 2009.

CHAPTER THREE

Carlos Martinez:
Fish Seller

Carlos Martinez's father was a shoemaker and his mother sold fruit at an open-air stand in Oviedo, the provincial capital of Asturias, in northeastern Spain. Often the family didn't have enough money to buy even bread, and their meals would consist entirely of spoiled or damaged fruit that his mother had not been able to sell.

Early Life

Poverty forced Carlos to leave school at age nine and begin working at a fish store. At about the same time, he started to steal parts from the railroad and sell them to a scrap iron dealer. He joined the youth group of the Communist Party, and after work he sold the Communist newspaper in bars.

His father died in 1934, when Carlos was fourteen, and was buried in a common grave. That same year, Carlos enthusiastically greeted the revolutionary movement that swept through his hometown and the surrounding area. When the government crushed it with brutal force, he felt like "a loser." *Once more*, he thought, *we poor people continue to be crushed under the boot of oppression.*

At the outbreak of the Spanish Civil War in July 1936, army units that supported General Franco's revolt against the government occupied Carlos's hometown of Oviedo. They called themselves "Nationalists," but Carlos considered them fascists. For four months, left-wing Republican militia groups mostly made up of miners besieged the city in an effort to expel Franco's forces. Food and other supplies were very scarce, and aerial and artillery bombardments were frequent. Finally, in October Franco's troops defeated the Republican forces.

A few months later, Carlos and his older brother fled from Oviedo to the nearby city of Gijon, which was still controlled by Republican forces. Because he was only sixteen, Carlos failed in his attempts to enlist in the Republican Army, but his older brother succeeded. Their younger brother, who had stayed home with his mother, was shot by Franco's forces for refusing to reveal where his two older brothers were. In the fall of 1937, Carlos returned home after the collapse of the Republican forces in Gijon and the rest of the surrounding region. Although he was only seventeen years of age, he was arrested and sentenced to eighteen years in prison.

After the war ended in 1939, Carlos was offered the possibility of reducing his sentence by two days for each day he would work, but he refused to cooperate with his captors. In prison, he read, took classes, and developed an interest in literature. He was, in his own words,

> a fairly quiet young man who walked back and forth in the prison patio wrapped up in my own concerns. I couldn't find answers to the many questions my life raised. I saw the events that ended up with me in prison as if they did not affect me. My conclusion was always the same: the poor are left wing and the rich right wing. They are in charge for the moment. I need to keep quiet.

At this stage of his life, Carlos rejected religion, which he saw "as something for rich people, who were now the victors."

As part of an amnesty that covered many people, Carlos was set free in August 1941. Once back home in Oviedo, he recalls:

> I thought a lot about my brother who had been executed because he refused to betray us. Things were made worse by the fact that I didn't know where his body had ended up. In some strange way, my heart pardoned. I don't know why. Perhaps it was a grace from the God whom I barely knew, but the fact is that hatred didn't find a place in my heart.

Carlos found work in a fish store. After hours, he began to write short stories. The father of a friend was impressed by them and urged him to go to Madrid and try to begin a literary career. In Madrid, Carlos supported himself by working in a fish store. Although he was able to meet some major literary figures, he could not gain a foothold in the literary world and decided to return home to Oviedo. There his left-wing past and prison sentence caused him many problems. He had to report every week to a political commissar of the Franco regime. People often confused him with another Carlos Martinez who had spoken at Marxist meetings in 1929. In vain, Carlos protested that he was only nine years old at the time.

One day in 1945, Carlos came across a recruiter for the Spanish Foreign Legion. The Legion asked no questions about the political or criminal past of recruits, and serving in the Foreign Legion would erase the past. Once you were discharged, you were no longer who you had been before enlisting, but simply a veteran of the Legion. Carlos enlisted without hesitation. Despite the harshness of the discipline, Carlos identified with the spirit of the Legion, which seemed to him "a poem of toughness and manly spirit." He was moved by its warlike maxims such as, "A legionary will never say he is tired till he drops exhausted."

Back in Oviedo

Carlos was discharged from the Legion at twenty-eight and returned to Oviedo. Once again, he found work in a fish store and began to dedicate much of his spare time to writing. In 1951, he began dating a seventeen-year-old girl named Ester. She was the daughter of the owner of the fish store where he had worked immediately following his release from prison. After a while, Ester's father asked him to stop seeing her because she was still very young. This posed a great conflict for Carlos because he was in love with Ester but had great respect and affection for her father, to whom he felt deeply indebted. He stopped seeing Ester for a time but was so disturbed he had to spend several days in bed.

Ester's father had brought Carlos to a meeting of HOAC, the working-class branch of Catholic Action. He liked what he saw, returned several times, and finally joined the organization. Carlos was deeply concerned about the poor, prisoners, and the sick. In the early 1950s, he visited them frequently. He was especially diligent in visiting political prisoners despite the difficulties this caused him. Carlos recalls his visits:

I tried to take care of them as I would have liked someone to do for me during my years of solitude and isolation in prison. I tried to accompany them, share their concerns, and encourage them to take advantage of the time they had to read or study. I also tried to cheer them up, encouraging them to be concerned about others and giving them hope of getting out soon.

They waited for me anxiously, perhaps thinking about the time we would spend talking and about the small gifts that I used to bring them: cigarettes, books, and a little bit of money to buy coffee. My visits and the company I was able to give them improved their spirits and behavior. This led the guards to treat them better and to be well-disposed toward me.

When, for whatever reason, I was unable to visit them, I sent them cigarettes and money through someone who was quite well known in Oviedo, a former prison inmate who worked as a shoeshine boy and whom people called "the bullfighter" or "the legionary," because of how long he had spent serving in the Legion, where we had met. He was already old and lived alone because he had no family. I tried to help him, paying his rent, and giving him some fish when the store was closing Saturday afternoons.

At this time, many people from the impoverished southern parts of Spain were emigrating to the better-off northern areas, including the area around Oviedo. Shantytowns of improvised shacks without running water, electricity, or sanitation sprung up. One day, Carlos stumbled across an unusually poor shantytown occupied by Romani (or Gypsies, as many people called them at the time). They were almost all illiterate and lived on the margins of society. The Spanish police contributed to their marginalization by controlling their movements and denying them access to many areas. Carlos, moved by their desperate poverty, began to take an interest in helping them. He recalls: "I began to do things, and I gradually acquired what I could for them: food, clothing, medicines, etc. Little by little, they began to accept me. I spoke with a businessman from the area and asked him to give me some space in a warehouse where I could organize classes for the Gypsy children. Surprisingly, he accepted."

A Dramatic Change in Life

A major turning point in Carlos's life came in June 1954. He was trying to decide whether to propose to Ester despite her father's opposition or to break off their relationship altogether in deference to her father. He entered a church late one afternoon and looked at a statue of Our Lady.

I began to pray and think about my life, and what I should do with it. I was moved. Suddenly, I found myself crying. I only recall two other occasions on which I cried. In both, I did it in the same way, without sobbing. It's the same effect as when a few drops fall into a glass that is already full of water: All the pain flows in silent tears.

I spoke with great emotion to the Virgin. I told her about my problems. I had written them out in two letters which I had in my pocket. They were both written to the same person, Ester Moyano. I continued to be in love with her and I couldn't bring myself to accept her father's opposition. At the same time, I could not see going against his wishes, especially since I owed him so much gratitude. That's why I had written two letters. In one I proposed marriage. In the other, I cut completely with her.

During this period of prayer, I felt consolation and deep peace. The problems continued to be there, but now I saw them with a vision full of hope, and I felt a relief that occupied the place of my anguish. I understood that the Most Holy Virgin was carrying me toward her Son. And I said to him, "How many years, Lord, without recognizing you. It is because I didn't see, Jesus."

Immediately, almost without time for my tears of pain and hope to dry, I begged our Lord to put me on a path of reparation, love, and self-giving. I didn't say it to him in those words, because at that time I didn't really know what they meant. But the Lord read my heart. How quickly he answered my prayer. When I left the church, outside in the street, I took the two letters out of my pocket and gave them their definitive destination. I put in the mail the letter breaking off relations, and I tore up the other. Ester understood my attitude.

From that day on I went daily to that church to see Our Lady. . . . I sat quietly in front of her, looking at her, without saying anything. I had written a letter to Heaven, and I was waiting for a response. God wanted something from me, but I did not know exactly what it was. I needed my life to have a clear sense, and I was sure that Our Lady would make me know what it was.

I don't know how many days I went to see her, to talk with her. One of those days, the idea of going to Confession came to me. I had become accustomed to being receptive to the things that occurred to me because I saw that they were things from God. So, I decided to go to Confession. I went to the church and knelt down in a confessional.

"Father, I have not been to confession since my first Communion." I told him that I had been in jail, had been a Communist, and continued to be one. That priest must have been perplexed because he refused to give me absolution. Sometime later, I learned that communism meant denying faith in the church and was incompatible with Christian life. But at that time, I didn't know anything about all that.

I recalled that in the HOAC I had met a priest, Fr. Rosendo, and I went to him. He knew me well and had no problem in granting me absolution.

Later, Carlos wrote a more intimate and penetrating recollection of some of these events:

How long were you there? You don't know. But when you finally left you felt your cheeks tight and your eyes burning. From that day on, every day you visited that image of Our Lady, staying there a long time, seated in the semi-darkness, in front of her.

You were comfortable there and you felt an almost physical sensation that something oppressive and painful was leaving you. You were finding yourself. . . . Your breast awoke to a miracle of tenderness. A few days earlier, you felt old, tired, and without hope. But that day, do you remember? Something began to tell you that living was worthwhile. You told the Mother of God your story once and again. Repeating past things under her affectionate gaze, you came to discover, in what was a true revelation, something that today seems very simple: the influence of God in everything that was happening. Yes, of that God that you forgot shortly after your first Communion, almost certainly by nine years of age when you began to work.

Joining Opus Dei

This interior conversion did not lead to any dramatic external change in Carlos's life. He continued working in the fish shop, reading, writing, and helping the Romani. It was precisely while he was trying to teach an older Romani how to read that a young man, who had also been trying to help the Romani, came up and said that he would like to talk with him. The young man told him that he belonged to Opus Dei. He explained that

Opus Dei was made up of men and women, both married and single, who search for holiness in ordinary life, in their work, each one in his place. He said that it had been born in Spain in 1928 but that its calling was universal, and that it had already spread to several countries in Europe and America.

I listened to him attentively. Everything he was saying seemed to me new and marvelous. He told me that the members of Opus Dei continued to be what they had been before: teachers, doctors, miners . . . or fishermen. He said that each one lived in the place and circumstances in which God had put him.

When he finished, I was assailed by the recollection of my prayer in the church, and of the letter that I had written to Heaven. This was the response that I was waiting for. I saw the hand of God behind very ordinary events, that for others may have been simple coincidences, but not for me.

Those thoughts of mine, while I listened to that young man whom I had just met, completely demolished all my plans for the future. . . . With this encounter, Lord, you answered in a tangible way my petition of wanting to love you above all things!

That was my first conversation with José García Monge, who was a couple of years younger than me. That day he entered my life and became a friend forever. With the fire that an ideal gives when one embraces it without limitation, he talked to me about an adventure that I could take part in and which from the beginning was very attractive. I think this was my first real encounter with Jesus Christ.

Carlos visited the Opus Dei center in Oviedo and talked with both the chaplain and the director of the center. On his first visit, Carlos came to understand "that Opus Dei is a family. A family of supernatural bonds, but a real family. They treated me with an affection which I have been short of all my life." The director was impressed with Carlos. He noticed in him the effects of a hard life as a fish seller, a prisoner, and a legionnaire. But above all, he saw that he was a good man. He was impressed by Carlos's ability to share the pain and suffering of others. He saw, he says, that Carlos had a "great soul." Carlos began to receive spiritual direction as well as religious instruction.

"'Let it be done,'" Carlos recalls, "was my response and, leaving everything behind, I asked to be admitted as an associate member of Opus Dei." At first, everything about life as a member of the Work was easy, almost effortless. Years later, Carlos asked himself:

> How could I describe those first times of following up on my conversion and giving myself to Opus Dei? They all seem so far away! There were no shadows, no hesitations, no difficulties to darken, detain, or obstruct me as I walked down this new path. In the words of the Founder of Opus Dei, "the divine paths of the earth had been opened up." How good our Lord is! In those days I was like a little child in the interior life. I would not have persevered if trials for my generosity or occasions to demonstrate that my love was above any attack of the enemy had come in the form of temptations or trials.

Of course, things were not always easy, and later Carlos had his struggles:

> How often nonetheless, this security was troubled, even broken, by the old man! How often you forgot what God did for you and the ardent promises of eternal fidelity that you made to Him! Do you remember how often, in a groan whose source you yourself did not know, you said to Him: "No, I cannot. I cannot. I want to live my own life."
>
> You came back to reality and, asking pardon from the Lord, you returned with more intensity to your plan of spiritual life, put more effort into your apostolate, and had greater joy in encountering setbacks.
>
> Time went by and a vague idea settled into my soul that Jesus loved me less, and that the goal of sanctity was each day further away. In reality, that was not true. In the moments in which the Lord made me see this, my heart was filled with thankfulness and a lacerating desire to be faithful.

His Own Fish Store

With the encouragement of the director of the Opus Dei center in Oviedo and other friends, Carlos decided to start a fish shop of his own in the best part of the city's market, even though there were already other fish shops there. Not surprisingly, when he went to get the necessary permits from the city, he ran into opposition from the owners of the existing shops. At about this time, however, the city threatened to shut down one of the shops for failure to meet sanitary standards. Carlos quietly worked behind the scenes so that the city would give his future competitor an extension of time in which to correct the conditions. When the man learned what Carlos had done, he withdrew his opposition and begged Carlos's pardon. The two became friends, and the competitor returned to religious practice.

Eventually, Carlos got the necessary permits and scraped together the money needed to rent a store. The previous occupant had been a sewing goods store that had gone out of business, and Carlos's lease required him to purchase the remaining stock of that store. So, for some months, in addition to fish, Carlos found himself selling thread and buttons.

Carlos understood well that "Opus Dei does not take you out of your place. Quite the contrary, it helps you to see how to take better natural and supernatural advantage of the place in which the Lord has placed you." When he speaks about taking "supernatural advantage," he means trying to sanctify his work and to sanctify himself in his work by doing it carefully for the love of God, thereby turning it into prayer. "I was a fishmonger, and this profession was the hinge of my vocation and the material I had to sanctify, so I worked at it more carefully." Gradually, Carlos learned to be aware of God's presence throughout the day and to offer up his work and its demands.

> You have to get up very early and walk several kilometers to go look for fish at the wholesale market. There are frequent changes in temperature, in the old days with ice and later going in and out of the refrigerators. You have to lift heavy weights and remove the scales and cut and clean the fish with sharp instruments that require a great deal of attention and can easily cut you. You have to spend many hours standing. These are things that I have had to do my whole life long, but since God gave me a vocation to Opus Dei, I learned to offer them as reparation for my sins and those of the whole world.

Taking supernatural advantage of work also meant finding ways to bring other people closer to God through his work. In the store, Carlos had a nativity scene which he kept up year-round. In addition to the traditional figures, it had members of the Spanish Foreign Legion and the Civil Guard. Carlos also had some shelves with spiritual reading pamphlets and books which he sold to customers. In a fish shop, Carlos said, "you talk a lot with the clients about the fish and the best way to prepare it. I told them everything I knew." But his conversation was not limited to fish and how to prepare it. "I talked about my life and my way of thinking while I cut up and cleaned the fish."

The people he saw most frequently and interacted with most intensely were, of course, his employees. He was a demanding employer but showed concern for his employees' material and spiritual needs. Over the course of the years, a number of them and some of their family members received the grace of a vocation to Opus Dei. This was largely thanks to Carlos's conversations with them and his prayers for them.

Working with Romani

Helped by several other members of Opus Dei, Carlos continued his efforts to aid the Romani encamped outside of Oviedo. At one point, the civil guards ordered them to move on, probably because of pressure from neighbors. Carlos intervened on their behalf with the commander who had issued the order. After a long conversation, Carlos not only convinced him to allow them to remain but got the commander's son to help look for work for the Romani in local factories. The civil guard sergeant, who had ordered the Romani to move on, accompanied Carlos later that same day to give them the news that they could stay. When the sergeant saw that the room where Carlos gave them classes had no benches or desks, he offered to arrange for a carpenter he knew to make them.

Carlos organized a Romani soccer team and managed to get it admitted to a league, an important step in integrating the Romani into the larger community. With the help of some Opus Dei members as well as other friends, he formed a nonprofit organization called ACUDEL, Cultural and Athletic Association of Lugones, to help the Romani. He convinced some factory owners and other businessmen to hire them. This not only provided them with a steady income but allowed them to obtain the identification papers they lacked.

Gradually, modest houses were built, and eventually, the shacks in which they had been living completely disappeared. Nevertheless, some of the neighbors were unhappy with what Carlos and his friends were doing. There were demonstrations, and on more than one occasion Carlos had to flee from angry neighbors and the Civil Guard.

With the discovery of his vocation to Opus Dei, Carlos's efforts in favor of the Romani took on a new and specifically Christian meaning. One day, one of the Romani asked him to prepare his four children for baptism. Carlos had to teach them the most elementary truths of the faith as well as how to read. Little by little he managed to involve other members of the family and became good friends with them. Soon afterward, another Romani approached him on the street and said he would like to get married and baptize his children. Carlos filed all the necessary paperwork and arranged for the local parish to take care of the ceremonies. This was the beginning, Carlos says, "of many baptisms, marriages, confessions, communions, and last sacraments. Thanks be to God, hundreds of people received the light of the faith and discovered that they too were children of God."

Carlos liked to go with the Romani to the most prominent shrine of the Blessed Virgin in the area, Covadonga.

> Entire families went to spend three or four days of prayer, formation, and rest close to our patron. Bringing them closer to the Virgin was fundamental in assuring their Christian life. It was also fundamental to be very open with them and to let them see that they were really loved. This is the only way—for them and for anyone—to recognize the sense of friendship and understand the Christian spirit that we wanted to transmit to them. To go to pray to Our Lady of Covadonga did a great deal of good to them, and to me. As we say in my part of the world, she is so pretty.

Reaching Out to Coal Miners

Oviedo lies just north of Spain's most important coal mining region, where much of the work was still done by hand. Few mines had adequate safety equipment. Ventilation and measures to control dust were poor, and many miners contracted silicosis at an early age. Almost all were ill-educated. Although baptized, few practiced the faith.

By the late 1950s, the situation of the Romani had greatly improved, and Carlos had created a stable organization to help meet their ongoing needs. He and other members of Opus Dei increasingly turned their attention to the miners, asking themselves what they could do to help improve their social and religious situation. Carlos began making occasional trips to the area, especially ten miles south to the town of Mieres, where he tried to get to know people. He was soon joined by his young nephew, also an associate member of Opus Dei, who worked for Carlos in the fish store.

At first, they traveled by bus, but as their trips became more frequent, the slowness of bus travel became a problem. Carlos purchased a motor scooter, but the cobblestone roads, often slick with rain, proved dangerous. Neither Carlos nor his nephew suffered any serious injuries, but they took so many falls that Carlos eventually decided to buy a small truck that he could also use for his business.

Among the people Carlos got to know in Mieres was a young man who, in addition to working in the mines, was studying for certification as a mine engineering assistant. He soon became an associate of Opus Dei. After a while, Carlos and other members of the Work rented a small apartment in Mieres. At first, it was difficult to attract miners to the apartment and its activities. As Carlos observed, they were "very tough men with many human virtues," but they faced a bleak future with the prospect of early illness and death, and little chance to improve their situation. Most were more interested in drinking than in attending talks on cultural and spiritual topics. After a while, however, the first miners began to come, as well as clerks, other workers, and students from the public high school and the School of Mine Engineering Assistants. In addition to talks on cultural and spiritual topics, they also organized a club that sponsored excursions to mountains nearby.

The miners had little in common with the students, clerks, and delivery boys who also came to the apartment. They were significantly older and came from a completely different social milieu. But by 1963, the number of miners coming to activities had grown to the point that Carlos and the other members of Opus Dei decided to rent a separate apartment for activities with them. Two years later they rented a three-story house with a small soccer field. It was big enough to accommodate activities with miners and other groups without interference.

The Peñavera center offered classes for apprentices and delivery boys so that they could get a certificate of grade school graduation. This allowed them to work legally and be insured by their employers. It also began to offer courses in accounting and a high school course via radio.

In collaboration with a mining company, Peñavera organized courses of professional training for miners. It was difficult to recruit students for the first course. Looking back, Carlos says, "If we managed to put together the first forty students, it was not thanks to our advertising but to the work of friends and acquaintances."

Although the vast majority of the classes were technical, there were also some classes on basic education and religion. It was not easy to attract the miners to those subjects. In the first such session, when the speaker said that human beings have a soul, a young man said, "I don't believe I have a soul." In a session on criminal law, the speaker asked one of the students at the end of class to sum up what they had learned. "Don't bother asking me. I know the criminal code backward and forward, by experience." Despite his youth, he had already been arrested four times.

According to Carlos, "The first days of the course were hard, but then personal contact, the professional quality of the course, friendship, and affection won the confidence of those tough men. They had little education but big hearts and were generous and good companions." The student who was convinced he did not have a soul eventually had a heart-to-heart talk with Carlos and told him that he wanted to learn, become a believer, and understand the significance of the Mass.

An important part of the professional program for miners—and of all the programs in Peñavera—was individual mentoring. The mentors were often able to win the confidence of the miners and talk in-depth about their personal situations and attitudes. Thanks to the efforts of the mentors, as well as to activities like weekend workshops and retreats, many of the miners began to frequent the sacraments and some of them became members of Opus Dei. The organizers of the workshops and retreats often invited Carlos to give one of the presentations and tell the participants something about his life. Carlos was convinced that, "In some way, this helped them understand the mercy and the grandeur of God. They also laughed hearing about some of my adventures."

In the small towns where most of the miners lived, the sight of men receiving the sacraments caused something of a stir. Carlos remembers one case in particular. "When Andres decided to go to Communion after ten years without setting foot in the church, his neighbors in the town imagined the strangest motives to explain his new attitude. But it didn't take them long to realize that this was something serious. Many people changed and decided to live their religion intensely."

Not content with the burgeoning activities in Mieres, Carlos traveled regularly to other towns, where he met with people wherever he could: a drug store run by a friend, a café, or a bar. He was always ready to go anywhere to talk with anyone he thought he could bring closer to God. On one occasion, a relative of a very bright high school student who lived in Pola de Lena asked Carlos to see the boy. Little by little, the young man began to pray and come closer to God. Quite soon he discovered that God was calling him to give himself completely. Today he is a priest of Opus Dei.

In 1973, Carlos decided to make a fifty-mile pilgrimage on foot to the shrine of the Blessed Virgin in Covadonga. He convinced twenty-three people to accompany him. The group set out under light rain after work on Saturday and reached the shrine at noon on Sunday.

Retirement and Death

In 1985, Carlos reached Spain's mandatory retirement age of sixty-five. He was still in very good health and ran every day, usually with someone else. He also swam frequently in the ocean regardless of the weather. Carlos continued volunteering in Peñavera in the afternoons and evenings, but now he also had the mornings free.

Even before his retirement, Carlos had frequently visited patients in the hospital. Now he began to do so on a systematic basis and as an official volunteer. Three hours a day, six days a week, he visited patients, especially those the staff told him didn't have visitors. He had a great ability to strike up a conversation with anyone and bring the conversation around to spiritual topics. In a short time, if the person wasn't opposed, Carlos spoke to him about the possibility of being reconciled with God. At times the results were so extraordinary that he was especially aware of the hand of God being present.

Toward the end of his own life, Carlos was hospitalized in a room with two other men. He noticed that the older of the two didn't look very pleased when a priest came to visit. One time, when the man was out of the room, Carlos asked the man's daughter if she would object to him talking to her father about meeting with the priest. She responded that in her sixty years of life, she had never seen her father pray or enter a church. Carlos was not discouraged, and when the man came back to the room, he proposed that the man talk with the priest the next time he came. The man said that he had been separated from the Church for seventy years, but that he didn't mind talking with the priest because he seemed to be a pleasant man, and he had noticed that when he left Carlos seemed to be especially happy.

After the priest and the old man talked at length, he went to confession and asked to receive Communion. The following day, while the priest was going to the chapel to bring him Communion, the man died suddenly. When Carlos asked his younger roommate if he would like to go to confession, he responded that he would, but not if he would die suddenly as the older man had.

Carlos died in May 2000 at eighty years of age.

CHAPTER FOUR

Dora del Hoyo:
First Numerary Assistant

Dora del Hoyo spent her life as a homemaker, not as a mother creating a home for a husband and children, but as a numerary assistant in Opus Dei, creating a home for her sisters and brothers in the Work. Although known as Dora del Hoyo, her full name was Salvadora Honorata del Hoyo Alonso.

Early Life

Most of the two hundred inhabitants of the village of Boca de Huérgano in northern Spain where Dora was born in 1914 barely managed to scratch out a living from the arid soil. Dora's family was no exception. In the evening, Dora and her siblings wove cloth to make clothes for the family while their father knitted socks. She soon learned to work in the fields, butcher cows, and make sausage. One year she defeated all the village boys in a contest for reaping with a scythe.

The school where Dora learned to read, write, and do simple arithmetic had only one book, Cervantes's *Quixote*. After a few years, she left school and began to work for the village doctor's family. She did the laundry by hand in a pool of a nearby stream, even when she had to break through a skim of ice.

Around 1934, Dora and her sister decided to look for better opportunities in Astorga, a larger town about ninety miles (140 km) away. She found a position as a maid in the home of a small factory owner. Soon, however, the growing level of violence during the period leading up to the Spanish Civil War made her employer worry about what might happen to the young women on his household staff, and he dismissed them all. Dora had to return to Boca del Huérgano, where she spent the three years of the Spanish Civil War (1936–39).

The hunger the civil war brought to Madrid and other large cities did not affect Huérgano, but it was a period of great tension for the family because one of Dora's brothers was serving as a soldier in the Nationalist Army and fought in the battle of Teruel, one of the bloodiest of the war. Communications were so poor that for long periods the family knew nothing about his situation.

During the war, a young man with whom Dora had been close friends was killed. Although she began to go out with another young man, she concluded he would not make a good husband and broke up with him.

In Madrid and Bilbao

At the end of the war, Dora was twenty-five years old. According to a biographer, she was "a good-looking young woman, well-mannered, intelligent, with a great capacity for manual work and quick to serve others. She was a woman of few words, rather dry and unemotional, but with a big heart." From her parents, she had acquired solid Christian piety and a strong work ethic. She decided to look for work in Madrid.

There, the Congregation of the Daughters of Mary Immaculate for Domestic Service helped Dora find a position in the home of a noble-woman. Subsequently, she worked in several other houses in Madrid, Santander, and Bilbao. In 1943 she was working for the Duke and Duchess of Nájera in Madrid. The position was well-paid and the working conditions good, but Dora wanted to see more of the world and learn other languages, so she eagerly accepted the opportunity to join the staff of a Spanish diplomat who was about to move to Berlin. Although the tide of World War II had already begun to turn against Germany, she was not concerned about the risks of going to Berlin. Her father, however, thought differently and dissuaded her from going, so she returned to working for the duchess.

At this time, three young women members of the Work had taken responsibility for the cooking, cleaning, and laundry at Opus Dei's recently opened Moncloa residence for one hundred male university students.[1] All three came from middle-class families and knew little about housekeeping and nothing at all about running an operation of this size. The situation was further complicated by shortages of food in Spain, and by the fact that construction was still underway in the residence.

When St. Josemaría realized that the three women were completely overwhelmed, he turned for help to the Congregation of the Daughters of Mary Immaculate for Domestic Service. The mother superior knew that Dora was free and asked her to lend a hand. Dora was not at all interested in working in a student residence. Not only did she find work in a student residence unattractive, she and her sister had started making plans to open a guest house in Madrid. But she agreed to lend a hand for a week to help get things organized.

---

1. These tasks and the people who carry them out are referred to in Opus Dei as the Administration.

At the end of the first week, Dora agreed to stay one more week. Week after week, she promised herself she would leave after one more week, but she stayed on; at first primarily out of respect for the mother superior of the Daughters of Mary Immaculate; and then out of affection for the young women of the Work and for St. Josemaría, whom she was getting to know. Looking back years later, Dora recalled thinking, *I can't leave. I have to help the Father*, or *I'll stay. I don't want to make the Father unhappy*. After a month, she decided to stay till the end of the academic year. And when the end of the academic year came, Dora agreed to stay another year.

Work in the residence was arduous. Money was short and it was difficult to find qualified people, so the staff was too small. As Dora put it, "Too much work and too few hands." Food was rationed and hard to find. The equipment was primitive. Clothes, for instance, were pressed with heavy irons with burning charcoal inside, and it was even difficult to find good-quality charcoal. At times, Dora and the others stayed up all night ironing clothes.

She could easily have found a better position, but Dora had a growing conviction that Opus Dei and the apostolic activities of the residence were God's undertaking and that she was needed there. In addition, she was inspired by the generosity of the members of the Work and their dedication.

St. Josemaría visited the Moncloa Administration regularly. After meeting with the members of the Work, he often stopped to talk with Dora and the other employees. He spoke to them about the importance of their work and how necessary it was—as important, he said, as the job of a doctor or an architect. He made them feel proud to be home workers, carrying out their work in a professional manner and loving their uniforms as much as soldiers loved theirs. He often told them, "You have to be very happy—very, very happy—because you are daughters of God. All of us have to be overflowing with joy. All of us, because I too am a son of God."

Dora was a godsend for the Administration of the residence. One of its directors recalls:

She had a heart of gold, and the way she worked was a wonder to behold. She was an expert at ironing, dry-cleaning, and sewing. She cleaned the house with incredible thoroughness, served at table without making the smallest mistake, and was a first-rate cook. . . . She was able to teach the other girls with authority but with kindness and consideration. She did have a temper, but she strove to master herself.

In 1945, Opus Dei decided to open a university residence for men in Bilbao. Women of Opus Dei would oversee the cooking, cleaning, and laundry there. The director of the Administration of the Moncloa residence asked Dora to join the initial team. At first, she refused. She disliked the idea of living in Bilbao. Several years earlier she had taken a fall while working in a home there, and her employer had asked only whether the glass she was carrying had broken, showing no interest in whether she had been hurt. Eventually, however, she agreed to go. Another housekeeper from the Moncloa, Concha Andrés, also agreed to join the team. As had been the case at the Moncloa, things were very difficult at first. Construction had not been completed, and neither the kitchen nor the laundry was working properly.

Joining Opus Dei

Despite everything, Dora was happy in Bilbao and growing rapidly in her spiritual life. At Christmas, one of the members of the Work gave her a copy of *The Way,* a book of short spiritual considerations written by Escrivá. She stayed up all night, reading it in a single go. Gradually, she began to feel that God was asking for her whole heart. She explained to her parents that she was thinking of dedicating herself to God in celibacy, seeking sanctity in her life as a domestic worker and living in a center of the Work with other members. Her father responded that at thirty-one she was old enough to decide on her own.

At this point, some background is called for. From the time of Opus Dei's foundation in 1928, St. Josemaría had seen it as a family with himself and his successors as the father of that family. Although Opus Dei's family spirit does not depend on living under the same roof, it does require that the centers in which some members live and the apostolic activities are held should be Christian homes with all the warmth of a close-knit family. In the first center, the DYA Academy-Residence in Madrid, the people hired to take care of the cooking, cleaning, and laundry were all men. The residents, including the first members of the Work, were quite happy with how things were, but Escrivá was not. Although the house was clean and the meals well-prepared and served, something was missing: the warmth of a family home.

After considerable thought and prayer, St. Josemaría concluded at the end of the Spanish Civil War that only women could supply the missing element. Creating a family environment in the centers of the Work while taking care of cleaning, cooking, and laundry, he decided, would be an important apostolic activity of the women's branch. Women of Opus Dei, just like its men, would work in all professions. There would be doctors, hairdressers, schoolteachers, factory workers, professors, store clerks, stay-at-home mothers, and a whole host of other professions. Some would dedicate themselves professionally to taking care of the housekeeping in Opus Dei's centers. Their work would make such an essential contribution to all the other apostolates of Opus Dei that Escrivá often described it as "the apostolate of the apostolates."

There were very few women members at the start, and they lacked experience. At first, therefore, Escrivá asked his mother and his sister to take responsibility for the household services in the Work's centers. In the years following the civil war, they hired other women to help them, but they also did much of the work themselves. Their work and sacrifice helped create a family atmosphere in Opus Dei's centers. During those early years, Escrivá's mother and sister also trained the first numerary members of the women's branch who would become administrators of centers. Their primary responsibility would be to hire, train, and supervise housekeepers, laundresses, and cooks. They would, however, also do those tasks themselves whenever necessary.

Escrivá also foresaw that some of the women who would primarily do the physical work of taking care of the house would be called by God to dedicate themselves to him in apostolic celibacy as members of Opus Dei. They would not be considered or think of themselves as hired help but would take care of the centers as their family home. They would not be content with just making sure that the food was well-cooked and the house clean. Rather, they would focus on creating a home for the members of the Work. At first, they were referred to as numerary servants. Later, as society changed and the term "servant" began to take on negative connotations, they would be called numerary assistants. For the sake of simplicity, we will use that term throughout this chapter.

On March 14, 1946, Dora wrote to St. Josemaría asking to be admitted as a numerary assistant. She was the first in Opus Dei. She had already begun to turn to God frequently as she worked, to offer her work to him, and to do it as well as she could precisely because it was what she had to offer him. Now she intensified those efforts, because she came to see her work as the same as the Blessed Virgin's and because she came to appreciate more deeply the importance of work in the home. She incorporated into her daily schedule the norms of piety that make up the plan of life of a member of the Work, seeing them as a way of becoming a contemplative soul in the midst of her daily work. She also began to pray for more vocations to Opus Dei, especially among the young women working in the Administration at the residences in Bilbao and Madrid.

Beginnings of Opus Dei in Rome

In 1946, Escrivá asked Dora, two other numerary assistants, and two numeraries if they would be willing to move to Rome as part of Opus Dei's efforts to set up its headquarters there while working toward approval from the Holy See. He did not hide that the beginnings would be difficult. Opus Dei had very little money, and Italy was still reeling from the effects of World War II. In a December letter, he said: "Those who come to Rome are going to know what real poverty is; what real cold is (damp and with no heating); what it is to live in someone else's house until we 'coerce' the Heart of Jesus. They need to be ready to take up these delightful little crosses with their habitual cheerfulness and enthusiasm."

Dora and the other women who would begin Opus Dei in Rome flew there on December 27, 1946. They stuffed their suitcases with things for the center, wearing most of the clothes they were taking in multiple layers.

Dora carried an extra coat in her arms and tied its sleeves with string to form little bags where she carried an assortment of items including a few forks and spoons. St. Josemaría and Fr. Del Portillo met the travelers at the airport and accompanied them to the apartment near St. Peter's that was Opus Dei's only center in Rome.

The three numerary assistants shared a bedroom that had only one bed, which they gave to the eldest, Julia Bustillo. Dora and Rosalía López Martínez slept on the floor, as did most of the men of the Work, who lived in a separate area of that first center in Rome. Food was scarce, and some days neither the women of the Work nor Escrivá and his companions had anything at all to eat. Rosalía recounts: "We were happy being so poor. Dora made me realize that we were living as our Founder lived, and we would become saints by *loving* that." Rosalía observes that in later life, Dora "never complained about things we did not have. She learned this during those early years. Then there was no choice about being poor—as poor as beggars—but she was happy to be so. Her example helped me a lot. We were so happy in the Work that I honestly believe we did not miss anything." Rosalía adds:

> I learned so much from her! . . . I saw how she battled very happily, despite her quick temper, to fall in love with Christ and to find him in every little household task; to accept all that poverty freely; to work hero-ically, trying to give all the glory to God. If I was tired or complained about some inconvenience, Dora would encourage me by saying something like this: "Don't you see, we're living like the Father [the founder of Opus Dei]?" And then she murmured, as though to herself, "And how much he loves us!" That was all it took to restore my peace of mind.

At Villa Tevere

In 1947, Opus Dei acquired a villa in Rome that would become its inter-national headquarters. They called it Villa Tevere. Dora and the other four women who had taken care of the apartment moved there. Escrivá arranged for them to have a private audience with Pope Pius XII in Castel Gandolfo. Protocol required that they wear black dresses. The only black dress Dora had was the uniform she wore for waitressing, but she solved the problem by adding a simple but elegant collar.

By January 1953, some fifty people were living in Villa Tevere. Dora was in charge of the kitchen, and at times cooked for the whole house single-handedly. A few years later, the number of people had grown to more than two hundred, mostly students studying ecclesiastical subjects in Rome in preparation for priestly ordination. There was no money for sending clothes out to be cleaned, so Dora switched from cooking to dry cleaning. Because the benzene she used was toxic, she worked outdoors in a courtyard. It was a very unpleasant job, especially in the cold days of winter, but Dora did it cheerfully. Eventually, they acquired dry-cleaning and steam-pressing machines, which greatly reduced the work. Dora became an expert not only in using the machines but also in maintaining them. Many years later when a technician was overhauling them, he was amazed to see how well they had been maintained.

As the number of students living in Villa Tevere increased, so did the number of women working in the Administration. Their time there was a key period in their formation as members of the Work. Many recall the lessons they learned from Dora. She had made very much her own the idea that God cannot be offered shoddy work. If something was poorly finished, she said so clearly, even firmly, but also lovingly. An English woman recalls:

> "Dora taught me patience with little things in my work by working alongside me and teaching me how to care for little fiddly things which made the finished product much better. I appreciated the fact that she worked with me rather than just telling me how to do things and was willing to teach me her little tricks to work better."

During the first years at Villa Tevere, money was so short that food and other supplies had to be purchased day by day. Finally, in the late fifties, the situation eased enough to permit buying wholesale at Rome's General Market. Periodically, Dora and another member of the Work set out early in the morning via public transportation to shop. At that hour the buses and trams were packed with workmen, many of whom wore badges showing their membership in the Italian Communist Party. The situation was not dangerous, but being surrounded by men who openly declared themselves

Communists brought back bitter memories of the Spanish Civil War to Dora. She and her companion made the trip in silence. Once they reached the market, however, they relaxed and laughed at the tense moments they had just experienced.

In the market, Dora prayed to the guardian angels of the people she met and occasionally spoke to some of them about God. She displayed a keen eye for finding fresh, good-quality produce at a reasonable price. At first, she followed the usual practice of carrying her purchases on her head to a rented van, but after they acquired a small car, she also bought a cart for moving things around the market. Soon many other women also began to use carts.

In the spring of 1957, Escrivá's sister Carmen, who had moved to Rome to help get the Administration started there, was diagnosed with terminal cancer and given only a few months to live. During those months, Dora moved to her apartment and helped take care of her. Carmen was greatly relieved to have someone who could foresee her needs, pray with her, and help her bear her sufferings cheerfully. Carmen died peacefully on June 20, 1957.

Summers with St. Josemaría

Many summers, Escrivá and his two principal assistants, Alvaro del Portillo and Javier Echevarría, spent a month or two in a small, rented house working outside of Rome and its suffocating heat. In order not to put more strain on the members of the women's branch in the locale, they asked some of the women from the Administration of Villa Tevere to rent accommodations nearby and take care of the Administration of the house. In 1958, they rented a house in London and the director of the Administration of Villa Tevere asked Dora if she would like to go. Dora did not understand that she was talking about a month or two and assumed she was being asked to move to England. Although she did not speak English, she responded she would be delighted to go. Asked whether she wasn't worried about the challenges of working in an English-speaking country, she responded, "No—we go wherever we're needed, so I'm delighted to move to London." When the director clarified that she would be returning to Rome, she answered, "Well then, I'm even more delighted."

Although Dora was usually not very expressive, she spoke admiringly about the cleanliness of London, its orderliness, and the way things worked there. She appreciated the beauty of the English countryside, the buildings, the prosperity of the country, and the art in the museums and gardens they visited. She also discovered domestic appliances in London that were still virtually unknown in Italy and Spain. St. Josemaría liked to hear her explanations of what she had learned about them and suggested that she visit the sales representatives to get more detailed information. One of the other members of the Work who was with her that summer says that she expressed her admiration for what she discovered "with such enthusiasm that it helped us to value more the good things we had around us and left us with a very positive outlook."

The Founder wanted his daughters who had taken care of the Administration that summer to have a souvenir of their stay in London. He suggested that they each buy something they would especially like. Dora purchased some earrings, which she wore on special days. Although they were very dear to her, she was not possessive about them. Another member of the Work who was with her in the late 1960s recalls:

> "She did not mind sharing; in fact, she spontaneously offered to lend me those earrings when my parents came to Rome in 1967. She wanted my parents to find me looking pretty. She offered them to me quite simply. It was only many years later that I learned they were a gift to her from the Father."

During the periods in which Dora helped take care of the houses where the Founder, Del Portillo, and Echevarría worked during the summer, her close contact with St. Josemaría helped her to grow in her spiritual life. She spoke from time to time about one occasion in northern Italy in July 1970. As she was setting the table in the dining room for lunch, she saw St. Josemaría praying with four hydrangea flowers in his hand. He went into the room that served as his office, planted himself in front of a picture of the Blessed Virgin, and offered her the bouquet as a child might. That loving gesture moved Dora to pray more intensely and to urge others to pray for the Father. During those summers, Escrivá suggested verses from Scripture to the women working in the Administration, as well as aspirations they could incorporate into their personal prayer. In August 1971, he confided to them that whenever he entered the dining room and turned on the light, he tried to see Jesus, Mary, Joseph, St. Joachim, and St. Ann in the house of Nazareth. This made a deep impression on Dora.

Albarosa

During the twenty-five years Dora worked in Villa Tevere, it served not only as the Work's international headquarters but also as the provisional home of the Roman College of the Holy Cross. There, members of the men's branch studied philosophy and theology in preparation for the priesthood or for serving on Opus Dei's regional and local governing bodies. Finally, in 1974, the Roman College was able to move into a new residential campus on the outskirts of Rome called Cavabianca. The new facilities could accommodate 150 men.[2]

Cavabianca would need a large Administration to take care of so many people. The women who worked there would contribute to the students' formation by creating a warm, welcoming environment in which Opus Dei's spirit of working well for the love of God would be visible. The center for the new Administration would be called Albarosa. Women from all over the world would come there to support the formation being given in the Roman College of the Holy Cross and to deepen their own formation in the spirit of Opus Dei while learning to carry out the task of administering a large center of the Work with greater professionalism.

In the final stages of construction, St. Josemaría asked Dora to inspect the workspaces and domestic appliances and give her professional opinion about them. Dora reported that the dining room seemed too small from the point of view of the waitresses who would be working there, but because of regulatory limitations, nothing could be done about that. She also suggested covering the kitchen and laundry machine that had already been installed to prevent their being damaged during the ongoing construction.

2. The women in Opus Dei also have their own Roman College, where they too come from around the world to pursue graduate studies in theology and philosophy, and they usually return to their respective regions and teach in a variety of Opus Dei formative activities.

For Albarosa to fulfill its role as a center of formation for the women's branch while contributing to the formation of the men studying in the Roman College of the Holy Cross, the initial staff needed exceptional women. Getting things off the ground would not be easy, and at first the physical conditions would leave much to be desired. Dora was already sixty, approaching the age at which most women working in physically demanding positions were thinking about retirement. Escrivá thought, however, that Dora's human and supernatural gifts, her common sense, and her fortitude would help get Albarosa going. She unhesitatingly accepted the invitation to form part of the original team. There she would be called upon to help set up a large center that was still under construction and teach young people how to work, leading from the front with her experience and good example.

When Dora arrived on March 7, 1974, the heating was still not working. A woman who had arrived a day earlier put a hot water bottle in her bed. Dora laughed to see herself treated, as she said, like an old lady, and used the hot water to wash some handkerchiefs. She immediately threw herself into the work of setting up the newly constructed buildings, making up excuses for taking on the most demanding tasks while leaving easier ones for others. She also helped create a garden with flowers, fruit trees, and fragrant shrubs like thyme, rosemary, and jasmine. Dora's special interest was pumpkins, because she loved to make a Spanish pumpkin-based jam called *Cabello de angel*. In later years, she would prepare enough to send jars to all the numerous Opus Dei centers in Rome.

An Important Person Despite Herself

Because she was the first numerary assistant, members of the Work wanted to see Dora and talk with her. She never took her status as a point of pride but as an incentive to be faithful and generous in living her vocation. Dora made St. Josemaría's motto her own: "To hide and disappear so that only Jesus may shine." One year, some girls who had come to Rome for a congress organized by people of the Work were anxious to meet her. When they passed her in a hall without knowing who she was, one of them asked her name. Dora answered "Salvadora" and moved on.

In Albarosa, she tried not to stand out. Even when she was in her eighties and could easily have justified getting up later, going to bed earlier, or taking a nap, Dora followed the house schedule without looking for excuses. A young woman who worked with her at the reception desk recalls: "I considered her an elderly person and felt I ought to help her with everything. Great was my surprise when she told me, kindly, 'Look, you shouldn't think that you're here to serve me. We are all here to serve, and the more the better.'"

Dora did not hesitate to point out things that were badly done. An Italian woman recalls: "I can honestly say that I never saw her get annoyed about anything personal. What really upset her was work badly done, dirt, and, above all, seeing people doing something halfheartedly." Another person confirms: "Sometimes she did get annoyed and scolded us. It usually happened when we had been careless or left something badly done in our work." Her annoyance, however, was short-lived and people did not feel hurt, in part because they "never saw her feel offended or resentful toward anyone."

When Dora corrected people, she inspired confidence and even gratitude. As a woman from the Philippines said, "She noticed every detail and corrected us, not in a bossy way, but trying to teach us to love our work, out of love for God." A Mexican woman who lived and worked with her for thirty years says, "It was a pleasure to work with her, because I felt she trusted me, and she smiled easily." Another woman who worked with her at Albarosa recalls that "she made me feel tremendously confident. [On one occasion, when I felt overwhelmed by how much there was to do] she said to me: 'It doesn't matter whether you get a lot done or very little; but what you do, do it well, and do whatever you can manage.' She made me feel so confident." Yet another person recalls an occasion when Dora came across her in the kitchen, obviously in a bad mood.

"'What are you doing, Marjoy?' 'Peeling apples!' I replied in a bothered manner. She drew up a stool and began to help me. . . . After a little, I asked her how she kept calm when things annoyed her, and she said: 'I just ask God what virtue He wants from me in the situation and then I give it to Him.' I was struck because I realized that this was her sanctity, that God asked and she always and simply said, 'Yes.'"

From the time she joined the Work, Dora struggled to overcome her tendency to overreact and gradually learned to be gentler. By the end of her life, she had made great progress. One day, a year or two before Dora's death, Rosalía López, who had come with her to Rome and spent more than fifty years with her, commented: "Dora, nobody who saw you then would believe it if they could see you now. You're like a different person."

Although she was far from outgoing by temperament, she made a point of trying to make newcomers in Albarosa feel at home. An English-woman recalls:

> She would take them under her wing as any mother of a family would. Many people commented to me that they felt as if Dora had a special soft spot for them, especially when they first arrived. Only later they would find out that she was like that with everyone; that her motherly affection for you radiated in her details of making you feel at home and also in work-ing alongside you.

Another person who knew her only in her later years was impressed by the fact that "she knew each person and knew how to make us feel at ease with her."

Even in old age, Dora remained open to new ways of working, different tastes, and other ways of thinking. A young Italian woman, commenting on Dora's openness to new things, says that she once told her, "'Dora, some people think the clothes I bought were too dashing.' She answered: 'But if you don't wear it now when you're young, when will you? I couldn't wear it, but on you, it looks splendid!'"

She had great affection for St. Josemaría and his successors, Blessed Álvaro del Portillo and Javier Echevarría. The title by which the head of Opus Dei is known in the Work, "the Father," reflected the reality of Dora's relationship with Escrivá, Del Portillo, and Echevarría. She was deeply concerned about their well-being, prayed for them a great deal, and tried to support them with her work. When St. Josemaría died, Dora began to feel filial affection for his successor, Álvaro del Portillo, as she had for the Founder. The same thing hap-pened when Javier Echevarría succeeded Del Portillo. Someone who was with her during the elective Congress after Del Portillo's death recalls:

You could see that she was deeply recollected, undoubtedly praying for the next Father. When she was told that we once again had a Father, her face brightened with gratitude. I can never forget how moved she was when she saw Don Javier for the first time after his election. From the beginning, she called him "Father," and she couldn't help telling us afterward: "To think I knew him when he was so young!"

Dora felt completely at home with Escrivá and his successors as head of the Work. During the summer of 1983, for instance, Del Portillo was evidently exhausted after several long pastoral journeys to various countries in Europe and the Americas. He looked so tired that Dora was angry. She told Rosalía, who served his meals in the dining room, that she wanted to speak to Don Javier Echevarría, who was Del Portillo's closest collaborator. When Rosalía said that Dora was annoyed and wanted to speak with Don Javier, Del Portillo asked why, but Rosalía simply insisted that Dora wanted to speak directly with Don Javier. A few days later, Del Portillo said, "Dora, my daughter, I've brought Don Javier. I believe you want to tell him something." Dora then told Echevarría he should not let the Father get so tired. He protested that the trips had given many people an opportunity to see the Father and that there had been many conversions. But Dora insisted that he should not allow the Father to become so exhausted.

Until the late 1980s, Dora worked steadily without significant health problems. In 1987, at age seventy-three, she suffered a serious heart attack, followed in quick succession by two more. The cardiologist gave her only a five percent chance of survival, but she recovered and lived another seventeen years.

On January 11, 1994, Dora turned eighty. At Albarosa, her birthday was celebrated as a big feast day. At Mass, all the women in the center wore their best clothes. She received birthday cards from people all over the world, many of whom had never met her. A good number said they had learned to love homemaking from things they had heard about her and her dedication to God through housework. In the evening, the Prelate of Opus Dei, Don Álvaro, attended the celebration organized for her in Albarosa with songs, humorous poems, and skits. He gave her a chain with a commemorative medal of the Founder's beatification.

A few weeks later when she passed through Madrid, the directors of the Work organized a get-together so younger members could get to know her and ask her questions. She was miffed. She said she wasn't the Father and questioned why people should want to meet her. Nonetheless, she cheerfully answered questions and talked above all about sincerity and allowing themselves to be formed.

Another anniversary came in 1996, fifty years since Dora and Rosalía had arrived in Rome. Once again, she was annoyed at being the center of attention and protested: "I've celebrated the twentieth, the thirtieth, the fortieth, plus whenever Rosalía wants." Nonetheless, on December 27, the Administration transformed the ironing room at Villa Tevere into a Roman restaurant, and the whole house gathered around Dora and Rosalía.

Final Years

When her two sisters had to enter a nursing home, Dora made a point of calling and writing them more often. When arthritis made her handwriting illegible, she asked another member of the Work to write the letters for her, saying whatever she would say to her own sisters. Although Dora said she didn't need to review the letters before they were sent, she did, of course, make suggestions, sometimes rather pointed ones. For example, after seeing photos of a niece who had put on weight, she said it didn't suit her and suggested she try to reduce.

Arthritis finally forced Dora to use a cane, but she rejected offers to help her make her bed or wash her clothes. She even continued to clean her closet every month. As a young woman, she had dyed her hair to experiment with different colors. When the first grey hairs appeared in early middle age, she began to dye it to cover them up. Even in the 1950s when Opus Dei was so short on money in Rome that there was not enough to eat, Escrivá had encouraged her to buy dye. In her final years, she found bending over the sink to dye her hair increasingly difficult, but as long as she could, she rejected offers of help. In 2002, when she was eighty-eight years old, she remarked to a young woman who had helped her do her hair, "How difficult it is to be a saint. I really didn't want to get up this morning, but I can't become lazy."

That same year she broke several toes, and her foot was put in a cast. The accident made it impossible for her to attend St. Josemaría's canonization, but she accepted that disappointment as God's will. One of the people who was living in the center with her at the time remarks:

A person of eighty-eight with her leg in a cast ought to be someone to pity, but not Dora! She took it with the sporting spirit of a young girl. Immobility did not suit her at all. The doctor had advised her to keep her foot off the ground most of the time. But she walked on it so much so that she wore out the synthetic material that kept the wooden sole in place, and we had to fix it back on with adhesive tape, which needed to be replaced almost every day because she wore it out. To prevent her from walking so much, we took her in a wheelchair for longer distances. If she got half a chance, she set off without the wheelchair, but, whenever she was told she had to use it, she did so without protest.

When she was going down a corridor in the wheelchair, she liked to catch someone unaware and give her a light tap with her cane to clear the way. When the person turned around to see what had hit her, she found Dora with a wide, mischievous smile on her face.

Dora insisted that she did not want to celebrate her ninetieth birthday, stressing that she celebrated her name day rather than her birthday. She spoke about her death in a joking tone, peacefully and without fear. "If you take such good care of me, I'm never going to die." On one occasion she said, "We are all going to die, sooner or later, but I am praying that our Lord will take me before I become helpless or lose my mind."

On the first day of the last course of formation which Dora attended, the director announced that, because of their age, Dora and Rosalía would not be helping with cleaning. Dora answered, "No; please don't leave us without any cleaning to do. Rosalía needs to walk, and it's the only time I can move around and do something. So please let me do some cleaning, even if it's only the benches in the garden." The director gave in and assigned Dora to an area of the garden as part of a two-person team. One of the people who attended that course says that even at her advanced age, "She arrived first for the cleaning. . . . Whenever she saw something that wasn't as it should be, she would put it right herself if she could."

During the last months of her life, Dora's arthritic pain became constant and intense. One time when she complained, she corrected herself immediately saying, "I'm sure our Lord is expecting great things from this." One of the people who cared for her during the last weeks of her life was impressed that "Dora was so detached from her health and so happy, that she infected everyone with peace and joy. We could see that her faculties were diminishing by the day, but that did not dim her joy and good humor—nor ours, thanks to her."

During her final illness, the Prelate of Opus Dei, Bishop Echevarría, visited her several times, talking to her about the importance of the work of Albarosa for the formation of the priests of Opus Dei, and thanking her for everything she had done. He reminded her that in those moments of sickness, she was an even better support for souls than when she had been working with all the energy of youth.

At the very end of 2003, Rosalía López went to say goodbye. She recalls:

> I began reminding her about those lovely times we had spent with the Father and Don Alvaro, and how much we had prayed for many vocations for the Work and the fidelity of them all. I said to her that even though we are now old and have lived years of great poverty and suffering, we had been so lucky to belong to Opus Dei and as numerary assistants at that. "Dora," I said, "that's something that nobody can ever take away from us." Then she opened her eyes, looked at me in joyful agreement, and closed them again. It was our farewell.

Dora died around four in the morning on January 10, 2004, the eve of her ninetieth birthday. Bishop Echevarría arrived at Albarosa at 6:30 in the morning and offered Mass for her in the main oratory. At her funeral Mass the next day, he said:

> The Lord turned her into one of His most faithful daughters in Opus Dei. How well he has done it! Through her availability in total joy, she became the driving force behind many works of apostolate that were just dreams when she joined Opus Dei in 1946. She has opened up the road, by being the first numerary assistant. And I am sure that now, from Heaven, with the same naturalness as she had here on earth, she is telling us, "Don't

think that I have been anything special. You have the same job I had. You are a splendid piece in the mosaic. You too have to constantly give light, showing God's greatness through the path of Opus Dei."

Eight years after her death, Dora's cause for canonization was introduced in Rome.

CHAPTER FIVE

Eduardo Ortiz de Landázuri:
Professor of Medicine

duardo Ortiz de Landázuri, a nationally known Spanish physician and professor of internal medicine, was born in 1910. He applied to the naval academy but was not admitted. Faced with the need to choose some other career, he put slips of paper with the names of things he could study in a bag and pulled out "medicine." Despite this haphazard reason to become a doctor, Eduardo ended up deeply in love with medicine and completely dedicated himself to it.

Eduardo entered medical school in 1927 and became a disciple of Carlos Jiménez Díaz, the best-known Spanish professor of medicine in the first half of the twentieth century. He joined the Socialist Party and served as vice president of the Professional Association of Medical Students, a left-wing group. He was very pleased to see Spain reject the monarchy and become a republic in 1931.

He graduated from medical school in 1934 and began working in an infectious disease hospital in Madrid. At a time when there were no antibiotics, the hospital was a grim place, but there Eduardo met his future wife, Laura Busca. She had finished a degree in pharmacy and was doing research for her doctorate. As a condition for going on their first date, she insisted on splitting the bill.

In 1936, at the beginning of the Spanish Civil War, Eduardo's father, a professional artillery officer, was condemned to death by Republican authorities. Eduardo had some connections with important Republican politicians and managed to get the death sentence reversed, but on condition that his father serve in the Republican Army. That he refused to do. Eduardo, together with his mother and his sister Guadalupe, accompanied their father in his prison cell during his final hours.

His father's execution was a turning point for Eduardo, both spiritually and politically. He had been religiously indifferent as a student and during his first years of medical practice, but now began to take his faith seriously. Politically, he decided that he could no longer be a member of the Socialist Party and even secretly joined the Falange, a party that took much of its inspiration from Italian fascism and supported Franco. During the war, he harbored in hospital wards several dozen people who were in danger of being arrested because of their political views and activities, or simply because they were known as practicing Catholics. He also sheltered in his home people who were in danger, including two nuns. During the civil war, he was mobilized by the Republican Army as a medical officer but was not sent to the front. Throughout the war, he continued to work in a Madrid hospital.

When the civil war came to an end in 1939 with Franco's victory, Eduardo was tried by a military court because of his membership in the Socialist Party and because he had served as a medical lieutenant in the Republican Army. Because he sheltered people during the war and belonged, albeit secretly, to the Falange, Eduardo was found innocent of political wrongdoing and declared eligible for employment. He got a position supervising medical care in prisons and opened a small private office. In 1944, he defended his doctoral thesis on malnutrition.

A Decade in Granada

In 1948, Eduardo won a chair as Professor of Medicine in Granada, a medium-sized city 250 miles (425 kilometers) south of Madrid in the foothills of the Sierra Nevada that was renowned for its outstanding Moorish architectural monuments. The next ten years went very well for Eduardo and his family. At the medical school, he combined research, teaching, and clinical care of patients in innovative ways that made him stand out among his contemporaries. He became Dean of the Medical School and built a team of some forty doctors and scientists associated with the Department of Internal Medicine. He frequently attended medical conferences in Germany and England and was making a name for himself in the world of international academic medicine. In 1958, he was named Vice-Rector of the University and was well-positioned to become its next rector. His private practice also flourished, and he gradually became the leading internist in Granada and the surrounding area.

Eduardo and his family were very content in Granada and looked forward to a fulfilling and happy future there. The family had many friends in the university and in the city, and Eduardo's private practice supplemented his salary handsomely, which permitted the family to have a chauffeur and a beautiful home on the outskirts of the city. It also allowed him to personally pay for medicines like penicillin for poor patients he treated in the University Hospital.

Move to Pamplona

In 1952, after making a retreat at Molinoviejo, the first Opus Dei conference center, Eduardo became a supernumerary member of the Work. That same year, a handful of Opus Dei members started an institution of higher learning in Pamplona called, at the time, the Studium Generale of Navarra. It began with a law school and added a school of medicine in 1954. Its founders hoped it would become a full-fledged university. Given the Spanish government's tight control over higher education, it was not clear, however, how it would ever achieve government recognition as an independent institution.

In Spain, students enter medical school directly from high school. The first few years of medical school are limited to classroom instruction with no clinical component. This made it possible for the medical school of the Studium Generale to make do in the first few years with classroom space in an old building on the grounds of the Provincial Hospital of Navarra.[1]

In the fall of 1958, Navarra's Medical School had the original leased building and a recently built four-story building on the grounds of the Provincial Hospital at the outskirts of Pamplona. The new facility had classrooms, a cafeteria, a library, some rudimentary laboratories, and an outpatient clinic, but no beds and no space for clinical instruction. A university hospital with beds and operating theaters would be needed, but it was not clear where the money would come from.

---

1. At the time, Spanish hospitals were government-run institutions to care for the poor. Patients with any money were seen in a doctor's private office. If they needed in-patient care, they went to private clinics.

At this juncture, the dean of the fledgling medical school approached Eduardo about joining the faculty. On its surface, the offer was unattractive, even crazy. The move would require abandoning a large number of friends and uprooting his family. Pamplona was a small market town that provided services to the surrounding agricultural communities. In contrast with Granada, it was architecturally undistinguished and had little to offer in the way of culture or social life. The skies were often overcast and most of the year it rained at least ten days a month.

Professionally, Eduardo would be giving up a secure position in a stimulating environment to join a recently established school with no official recognition, inadequate facilities, a tiny faculty, and a very uncertain future. On the other hand, there was something exciting about becoming part of a university project which, if it succeeded, might break out of the ossified molds of the official government-run universities. He would be able to shape the medical school in the light of the vision he had received from his mentor, Dr. Jiménez Díaz, by combining research, teaching, and clinical practice. Most importantly, he knew that the Founder of Opus Dei was deeply interested in the project.

Eduardo consulted his wife, Laurita, who said she would be happy to do whatever he thought best. He also sought the advice of Dr. Jiménez Díaz, perhaps with the thought that he would dissuade him from doing something so crazy. On the contrary, Jiménez Díaz encouraged him to accept. "In my opinion, the offer is very attractive, and knowing you as I do, I think it is very interesting." Later in a letter, he wrote, "Come on, Eduardo. The three kings went further, and they were only following a star." Naturally, his friends and colleagues in Granada attempted to dissuade him.

Eduardo also informed his friend Dr. Gregorio Marañón about his decision. Professor of endocrinology at the University of Madrid and a prolific author who published extensively in many fields, including history, Marañón was one of the best-known and most respected physicians in Spain. Eduardo was very encouraged when he received his response:

> "As soon as I heard about your decision, I felt strongly that it was the right one. . . . The School in Navarra can have a beneficial and perhaps definitive influence on the transformation of the spiritual life and the efficacy of Spanish universities. . . . Although I don't think it will happen, if you should ever have a moment of doubt, know that you have in me a friend who will fortify you and your conviction."

Eduardo and his family moved to Pamplona in September 1958, just in time for the beginning of 1958–1959 academic year. He immediately began teaching and established a program of research suitable to his new conditions. He also made an effort to meet people in Pamplona, including members of the provincial government who would be crucial to the school's development.

It was common at the time for Spanish medical school professors to see private patients in an office outside the medical school. In Granada, Eduardo had followed the normal practice except that, at the suggestion of his mentor, he had set his fees five to ten times higher than what other doctors charged. He did so not to get rich, but because in that way, he would be able to earn enough for his family without taking too much time away from the medical school. The strategy had worked well. People felt that if he charged so much, he must be very good, and they soon discovered that he was. He became the doctor of choice for the well-to-do in Granada and the surrounding area and made a lot of money without taking much time away from teaching and research. He also saw many patients for free or for very low fees in the medical school clinic, so he was never the doctor for only the rich.

The dean of the medical school in Pamplona assumed that Eduardo would open a private office somewhere in the heart of the city. He was surprised when Eduardo said he would see private patients at the medical school. The location was inconvenient, and some potential patients would consider it beneath them to see a doctor on the grounds of the hospital where the poor went for treatment. Eduardo, however, thought that in this way he could better carry out his mission in the medical school and contribute to its prestige, although he would undoubtedly earn less money. This generous decision contributed greatly to the establishment and development of the Clinic and later the Hospital of the University of Navarra, which today is accredited by the Joint Commission International and widely considered one of the best hospitals in Spain.

Shortly after arriving in Pamplona, Eduardo established Saturday morning teaching conferences modeled on those at the Massachusetts General Hospital. They consisted of a literature review followed by a discussion of a case. The teaching conferences, attended by many doctors from Pamplona and nearby towns, helped raise the level of medical practice in the area and contributed to the reputation of the fledgling medical school.

Eduardo was a prodigious worker. During his long career, he saw something like 500,000 patients. He published more than 200 articles and spoke at more than 100 conferences. He taught innumerable classes and directed 36 doctoral dissertations. In addition, he did a great deal of administrative work for the medical school and the university.

He also made time for his many friends. In a letter to a former colleague, he said, "If there is something in this world that reflects in the highest degree the gifts that God distributes to men, it is friendship. Everything great, like self-giving and with it love, begins with friendship." One of his colleagues observed: "He was very disorderly in his work precisely because he was governed by criteria of a higher order, that of charity. If he saw that somebody needed him, he went to help wherever that person was." On one occasion, Eduardo traveled from Pamplona to Madrid simply to tell a friend in person, rather than by phone, that his brother had cancer.

To do so much, he cut back on sleep. Eduardo went to the clinic to see his patients on Sundays and holidays. At times, he spent the entire night at the bedside of a critically ill patient. He often visited his patients late at night. In part, this was to make sure they were receiving proper medical attention. He once said, "At three in the morning, you can save a life. At nine, all you can do is sign a death certificate." But he also simply wanted to visit them and reassure them.

Often, he invited graduate students to join him at home to review the literature and discuss cases. These sessions began at around 11:00 PM, after Eduardo's late Spanish supper, and went on well into the night. At times he would nod off but then wake up and continue as if nothing had happened.

A Master Clinician with a Great Heart

Eduardo once told a friend, "There are two languages: the language of logic and the language of affection. Logic has limits. Therefore, when you reach the limit of logic, and there is no way of reaching an agreement, the only way is affection. Everything I have done in my life, in all areas of life, I have always done on the basis of affection." This was especially evident in his care of patients.

Eduardo's approach to medicine, formed in the school of Jiménez Díaz, relied heavily on compiling a detailed clinical history for each patient. It was governed by the principle that "the patient is always right." This meant that hidden in the patient's narrative of his illness lay the clues that would lead to a diagnosis. If the doctor listens closely, he believed, the patient will guide him to a proper diagnosis. As the years went by, Eduardo incorporated into his practice the laboratory tests and other modern diagnostic tests that were becoming available. Still, he continued to rely on clinical history as a key element in diagnosis.

In his view, even more important than the doctor's diagnostic skills is his "ability to penetrate the personality of the patient. Only in this way," he believed, "do doctor-patient relations, which are the crucial point in the practice of medicine, acquire their greatest authenticity."

During Eduardo's years in Pamplona, the structure of the medical profession was changing rapidly. Jiménez Díaz had viewed medicine as a unified whole, a pyramid with internal medicine at the top and specialties as subordinate parts of internal medicine. As the years went by, and as more and more complex diagnostic tools became available, the specialties became increasingly independent. Eduardo had a hard time accepting this, because he viewed it as a loss of the patient-centered unity of medicine. He suffered as areas of the University Clinic that had been parts of the Department of Internal Medicine broke off and became departments in their own right. Although he recognized that this had some advantages, he feared it involved losing sight of the patient as a human being.

The principle that the patient is always right also meant to Eduardo that it was very important to give weight to the patient's view of his illness, to his subjective perception of his situation, and his needs. He believed there were

> two possible states of mind both for the doctor and for the patient. As regards the doctor, he can consider the patient as a clinical case, subject to the scientific rules of diagnostics, treatment, and prognosis. Or, without omitting the former, the doctor can consider him as someone who suffers from physical and mental pain. The patient can simply accept the doctor as a professional functionary who fulfills his duty. . . . Or he can value him in his human aspect, as a friend in whom he confides.

Eduardo was firmly convinced that "the patients need attention. The mission of the doctor," he said, "is not only to cure them. He has to give them affection, confidence, and a desire to live, which some of them lack."

According to his daughter, he was "totally dedicated to his patients. He loved them as if they were members of the family."

The key to Eduardo's practice and his teaching, according to one of his colleagues, was the individual patient.

> When Eduardo spoke about patients in the classroom or in scientific gatherings, he did it with rigor and with rational and scientific analysis. Nonetheless, when he was in the hospital or at the bedside of a patient, even though he was talking with other doctors or medical students, he never spoke about clinical cases. They were his "little patients" [*enfermitos* as he used to call them in Spanish]. He took care of each person with special affection. He pampered them. He was concerned about the individual patient and his overall situation even more than about the illness. Of course, he was concerned about diagnosis and treatment, but he concentrated above all on how the person was dealing with illness. His greatest desire was to help each patient see that their sufferings had positive value and that they were an opportunity to improve as a person.

> When he made rounds in the Clinic, he often sat on the edge of the patients' beds and held their hands or gently stroked their heads. No matter how busy, when with a patient he always seemed to have all the time in the world. He knew how to incorporate into his conversation a gesture of affection, of true love for the sick person. Sometimes it was a question of holding their hand in his, others a light touch on the cheek, and always, an affable word.

A nurse who worked with him for many years recalls:

> I admired his cordial dealings with the patients. He never gave me the sensation of being in a hurry or under pressure. His dialogue with his "little patients," as he often called them, was cordial. He listened . . . He always listened and took notes of what the patient said, even though it seemed trivial. He rarely interrupted. He took notes. The patient was the only protagonist.

One patient wrote to him:

> With just the right words, you encouraged me, gave me consolation, and the resignation I needed to bear up under my ills. You are like a good fairy come to watch over the sleep of children, because a patient, when all is said

and done, is not something different from a child. You cannot imagine how both I and my family appreciate all your kindness. What our mutual friend Dr. Lana says with his sharp intuition is true, "Dr. Landázuri has cured more patients with his affection and amiability than with his medical treatments, although the treatments have cured innumerable people."

In 1966, Eduardo became St. Josemaría's physician. This allowed him to get to know the founder of Opus Dei personally. He said that he emerged from his visits to Escrivá "feeling free and flying like a bird." They gave him "the sensation of wanting to begin once again in my professional life."

Dedicated to the University

In Pamplona, Eduardo dedicated himself to developing the School of Medicine and the rest of the university. He radically cut back his efforts to make a name for himself in the world of international academic medicine and centered his attention on the needs of the institution. In addition to teaching, research, and patient care, he focused on negotiating with local and provincial government authorities, getting to know people in the city, fundraising, and developing the University Clinic as a place where private patients would want to go for medical treatment.

He also took great interest in the School of Nursing and in the work of the nurses. He saw them as crucial in the struggle to transmit a Christian sense of life. "Considering the whole range of professions for which the University prepares its students, it is hard to find any other which is so important in the struggle against materialism. The nurse, who lives at the side of the patient and his family in decisive moments, should irradiate the light of the truth." He urged nurses to see themselves as collaborators of the doctors, not just assistants. He urged them to leave behind their personal problems when they entered the clinic. When on duty, he told them, the patients should be the only thing that matters. He encouraged them to aspire to make the patients feel more comfortable and at home than they do in their own homes.

He constantly gave nurses, as well as other doctors, a clear example of this kind of dedication to the patients. A doctor who worked closely with him recalls a particularly dramatic incident. Eduardo was at his mother's side when she died in the University Clinic. He stayed a few minutes longer praying but then went to complete his rounds. On his way back to his office he met a patient's husband. The conversation dragged on, and the doctor who was with Eduardo wanted to cut it off by telling the man that Eduardo had just lost his mother. Eduardo stopped him by discreetly tugging at his white coat. When his colleague later commented that the husband could have been briefer, Eduardo responded, "We have to dedicate time to the patients and explain their situation to family members."

Teacher and Dean

Eduardo was an outstanding teacher who enjoyed an easy, natural relationship with the students. One day a student came up to him in the hall and commented, "Professor, how little doctors know." "Yes," Eduardo responded, "but you have to know that 'little' to pass the exam." He was willing to take the time to help students who were experiencing difficulties and treated them with great affection. For instance, he wrote to a first-year student that he would like to give him

> much peace and much strength, so that simply and with a smile on your lips, you can accept the difficulties which will arise, the mistakes of the people who surround you (which they will commit because they are human) and the other little hardships of someone studying first-year medicine, which is a difficult year.

Referring to an outdoor shrine of the Blessed Virgin near the entrance to the campus, he added, "As you will recall, on the Campus you will find Our Lady of Fair Love."

He did occasionally lose his temper with a student, but reacted quickly and made amends. One day, a student representative criticized a young faculty member at a meeting in ways Eduardo thought inappropriate. He dressed him down severely and ended up saying, "You are no longer a student in the School of Medicine." That same afternoon he looked for him and gave him a hug that practically lifted him off the floor. Nothing further was said about the matter.

Eduardo was Dean of the Medical School from 1962 to 1978, with a break from 1966 to 1969 when he served as Vice-Rector of the University.

It is possible to get an idea of his schedule and way of life as dean from a letter he wrote to a friend who had recently been named the dean of another medical school. He insisted on the need to continue to do research, see patients, and teach. Time spent on administrative duties, he urged, should be kept to a minimum. He suggested the following allocation of time: two hours a day of classes; one hour seeing students; two hours seeing Social Security patients; two hours seeing private patients; two hours doing research; one hour of work on the deanship; and two hours to pray. In the evening, one hour to study. Without the two hours of prayer, this was an eleven-hour workday.

When he relinquished the deanship in 1978, he became the president of the Association of Friends of the University. He would have preferred to leave fundraising and cultivation of supporters to others and to dedicate his time to teaching, research, and the care of patients, but he gave priority to the university's needs. His work in the Association of Friends taught him, he said, "to be patient and persevering, above all looking for the friends the university needs so badly and doing apostolate with them."

Father of a Large Family

According to his son Carlos, Eduardo's family was more important to him than his profession. One of his colleagues corroborates that "despite his extraordinary activity and the way he put himself entirely into everything he did, whether research, teaching, or care of patients, his principal, constant concern was for his family. He was not able to dedicate to the family as much time as he would have liked, but the time he was able to dedicate was very well employed, and he made it yield."

One of Eduardo's daughters recalls that he was very concerned about us, his children. Despite the intensity and amount of his professional activity, "he was always concerned about our things, especially about things that concerned my mother. The two of them, my father and my mother, were very close to each other and understood each other. He kept a close eye on our things, even though they were unimportant, and he put his heart into them. He loved each of us in a different way. . . . He was affectionate, enthusiastic, enterprising, understanding and demanding, and very cheerful."

In Granada, though he had a chauffeur, he normally drove the children to school to spend more time with them. Throughout his life, he made a great effort to join his wife and seven children for the main meal at midday. He also had supper at home, though he was often late. His wife Laurita waited for him to arrive and, after supper, they said the Rosary together no matter how late the hour.

Eduardo did not preach to the family, but his example had a strong influence on them. One of his daughters recalls: "Although he never told us that we should get up early or go to Mass, the way he lived moved us. That is why I began to go to Mass before classes."

His wife recalls,

> At first in Pamplona, it seemed that he was going to have more time for the family. We went for excursions in the surrounding areas; we all went together to the movies; if he had to stop to see a patient, we waited for him. But soon he was completely absorbed. The twenty-four hours of the day were insufficient. He studied until late at night.

She sometimes objected that he worked too much, but his son Carlos notes:

> She had made her choice with full knowledge of what she was getting into, knowing perfectly the deepest motivations that move my father in each case and fully sharing them. She used to comment that my father had not changed in this aspect since she first met him. She said that she had fallen in love with him knowing perfectly well what he was like and that she liked him to be the way he was.

Eduardo himself seems to have understood that he spent too much time at work. In a 1977 letter, he said:

> Laurita is very happy, putting up with her health problems with simplicity and seeing with peace how little I accompany her. This university attracts me in such a way that in the end, people are going to say, "he did everything badly." It's a sort of half-humorous phrase we use when working very hard, perhaps we go too far.

Eduardo's concern for his family was especially evident in his care for his eldest son, who had a brain lesion and suffered epileptic attacks and outbursts of anger. His daughter recalls that her father had a special affection for "Eduardito," as he called him. He never shouted at him, no matter what he did. He saw him as "God's treasure, which we have to care for." Living with and caring for their sick brother, the other children learned how to live with understanding and charity in practical ways. Perhaps that is why Eduardo considered Eduardito "the salvation of the family."

By the time Eduardito was twenty years old, his fits of anger had become dangerous, especially to Laurita, who had suffered for years from a bad back. Finally, he had to be committed to a psychiatric hospital. For the rest of his life, Eduardo visited him at least once a week, usually on Sundays, late in the morning.

Life of Piety

Eduardo's day-to-day life was profoundly affected by what he learned in Opus Dei. When he met the future Saint Josemaría Escrivá for the first time in 1960, he commented, "Father, you asked me to come to Pamplona to help create a university, and we have done it." Escrivá responded, "I did not ask you to come to Pamplona to create a university, but to become a saint creating a university."

Eduardo said he learned three virtues from the Founder: "Affection for my neighbor, with his limitations and defects, so as in this way to love everyone; supernatural sense in the little activities of each day, which makes the way always a happy adventure; and enduring love for this university." On another occasion, he summarized what he had learned in Opus Dei as follows: "First, that the cross carried gracefully is the only way to draw near to Christ and that with Him, everything is peace and joy; second that ordinary work can be the conduit for the sanctity that should project itself on the family and on all the people who surround us."

Eduardo strove to live the Opus Dei member's plan of life well. He had an especially marked devotion to the Blessed Virgin. Despite his numerous professional obligations, he stopped at noon every day to say the Angelus. He said the Rosary with Laurita after supper in the evening, no matter how late or how tired he was. On Saturdays, the family sang the *Salve Regina* to honor Our Lady, and Eduardo often kissed a statue of Our Lady in their home. On the campus of the University of Navarra, there is an outdoor shrine with a life-sized statue of Our Lady of Fair Love given to the university by Saint

Josemaría. From the time it was completed in 1966, Eduardo made a point of visiting Our Lady there every day, no matter what the weather or how bad conditions were underfoot. He was committed to receiving the sacrament of penance every week. Toward the end of his life, he was having a hard time getting around even in good weather. On one occasion, the streets were treacherous with snow and ice on the day he usually went to confession. The director of the Opus Dei center was astounded to see him appear at the door. "Eduardo, what are you doing here on a day like this?" he asked. "I've come to go to Confession," Eduardo replied.

Eduardo was very anxious to help other people come closer to God. Toward the end of his life, for instance, he invited several people to accompany him on a retreat. Three did: a medical student, the owner of the store where his wife did her shopping, and a local businessman who was his friend. He often talked with terminally ill patients about going to confession and receiving the sacraments.

Illness and Death

Throughout his life, Eduardo enjoyed remarkably good health. He had some falls and minor accidents, but never felt sick enough to stay in bed. One day he said to one of his colleagues, "Do you know why I'm never sick? Because I never go to the doctor."

In 1980, however, he began to lose weight and suffer some other symptoms. He realized he should get a checkup but put it off. Over the next few years, he continued to lose weight and experienced weakness in his feet and legs. Although he had officially retired, he continued working very hard as president of the Association of Friends of the University of Navarra. The previous president of the association, who was in his eighties when he retired, told him one day the principles that guided his life: "First, to live as if I were going to die today; second, to work as if I were going to live forever; and third, to try to do at least as much today as I did yesterday." Eduardo fully accepted those principles, but as the months went by, he found it harder and harder to put the third into practice.

During the summer of 1983, he finally went to see a doctor, who diagnosed metastasized colon cancer. After surgery, he began to suffer nerve pain, which forced him to abandon both teaching and patient care, though he continued to work in the Association of Friends of the University. Unable to attend the annual meeting of the association in October 1983, he recorded a brief message in which he said, among other things, "Don't think that I am sad. In fact, I am very serene. I think that the Lord always prepares the best for us. He will not leave Laurita or any of us abandoned. If we are faithful, he will bring us to his side where we will meet the Father [St. Josemaría], the founder of this university which we love so much."

When the news of his illness got out, the local newspaper interviewed him and published a two-page article entitled "Message to the Dying." At one point during the interview, Eduardo said:

> There's only one thing that I'm really concerned about. I want to go to heaven. Yes, I believe in heaven, the place where I will enjoy the presence of God. How? My mind is too limited to understand it or explain it. But I want to go there.
>
> People say that God gives conformity to his will and that is true. Now I have come to realize that I'm going to leave the world, and I'm not going to say that I'm not frightened. . . . Nor am I going to deny that I would prefer to die without pain. I accept, nonetheless, whatever God wants to give me. I have faith in him and what I most ask for is that this faith that has always accompanied me may not abandon me now, in my final hour, when I need it most.

Many people contacted Eduardo after the article came out. One of his colleagues, Dr. Soto, wrote to him: "I owe you a great deal. Much more than what your humility will let you believe. You radiate fortitude, serenity, and especially a firm Faith united to Hope and Charity."

The reaction that most moved Eduardo was a letter from a man whom he had seen in the clinic twenty years earlier. The man wrote:

> I was a municipal employee in a small city. Now I am nothing: someone forced by cancer to retire. Like you, I await death, but in my case with fear.
>
> There are many differences between us. You are "religious and apolitical." I am "political and areligious." You talk about death without sadness; I with fear. You say that you have tried to go through life doing the good that

you could. I have tried to go through life forgetting that one can do good. You believe in heaven. Now I would like to believe. Before I thought that it was something that didn't affect me. . . .

After reading the interview and thinking about your cancer and mine (that's something we have in common), I began to feel a great desire to also go to heaven, a heaven in which I do not believe.

I went to confession for the first time in twenty years. The previous time was after visiting you in the clinic. Among the medicines you prescribed was that I go to confession. As someone who was sick and frightened, I did it; but I recovered and I forgot all about it. . . .

You are seventy-three years old. I am thirty-seven. Our age is not important. Neither of us has much time left before we go to the other world. You were told this "with clarity and charity." I was told it "in a confused way and without charity."

I'm writing you this letter because it seems to me that with it for the first time in my life, I do good to a friend. If I were to receive this letter it would make me happy to know that I have "done good to someone," undoubtedly because unlike you I am vain.

Doctor, if heaven exists and you go to heaven, don't allow me not to go even though I may still not believe.

Doctor, thank you for your message.

For as long as possible, Eduardo continued to work for the Association of Friends of the University of Navarra. To the doctor who was taking care of him, he seemed "like a runner who was reaching the limits of heroism, who did the final sprint until he arrived exhausted at the goal. He was heroic in many aspects."

During the years in which he served as St. Josemaría's physician, Eduardo was impressed by how the Father put himself completely into his hands, without asking questions or making suggestions. He decided to imitate that, leaving decisions about his healthcare to the physicians who were taking care of him. After the initial diagnosis, he was initially inclined to reject chemotherapy, but thinking and praying about how St. Josemaría followed his suggestions unquestioningly, he decided to leave the decision to the doctors who were taking care of him.

On one occasion, toward the end of his life, Eduardo's doctors were debating between an aggressive surgical attempt to solve a problem and simply allowing it to run its course. When they told Eduardo that they thought it better not to intervene, he exclaimed, "Blessed be God! I was praying for that." But he had not attempted to influence their decision.

When a group of doctors came to see him during the final hours of his life, one of them looked very distressed. Eduardo told him, "Andrés, let's see a happy face. This life belongs to those who are happy."

Eduardo did experience some periods of fear. He also felt there were things still left to be done and commented to one visitor, "How I would like to live another six or seven years." Nonetheless, he found peace in prayer. From his bed in the clinic, he wrote to a friend: "I am content and happy. After all, we need to offer something to our Lord." He commented to his son Carlos, "Now I see that my entire life has meaning, even the most humdrum things." Following the example of St. Josemaría, he prayed insistently, "Lord, increase my faith, increase my hope, increase my love, so that my heart may be like yours." This is the aspiration he was praying when he died peacefully on May 20, 1985.

Eduardo's cause for canonization was opened in 1998.

CHAPTER SIX

Fr. Joseph Múzquiz:
Engineer and Priest

Father Joseph Múzquiz[1] was a civil engineer who joined the Work in 1940, shortly after the end of the Spanish Civil War. He was one of the first three priests of Opus Dei and played a major role in bringing the apostolic activities of Opus Dei to the United States, Canada, and Japan.

Youth

José Luis Múzquiz was born in 1912 in southern Spain. He entered the School of Civil Engineering in 1930, after attaining the second-highest score among nine hundred applicants on the national entrance exam. Although the idea of living celibacy in the world struck him as "something odd and strange that could not succeed," José Luis accepted a friend's invitation to meet Opus Dei's founder in late 1934 or early 1935. He was very impressed when, in their first conversation, Escrivá said, "There is no greater love than Love," and he decided to attend the weekly classes on practical Christian life which Escrivá called "Circles."

While waiting for a job to open up after graduation, José Luis traveled to Germany to improve his German language and visit civil engineering projects. He was there when the Spanish Civil War broke out in July 1936, but he immediately returned to Spain and joined the Nationalist Army. He was convinced that Escrivá must have been killed by the violently anti-Catholic mobs that dominated Madrid during the early months of the civil war. When he learned that Escrivá had not only survived but had escaped from Madrid

---

1. Before coming to the United States, he was called José Luis. Later he was usually called Fr. Joseph. This article reflects that change.

and crossed into the Nationalist zone, he concluded that Opus Dei must be something "supernatural and desired by God."

José Luis joined Opus Dei in January 1940. From then on, his life was shaped by the conviction that he and the other members of the fledgling Work were, as Escrivá had written, "not just men who have joined other men to do a good thing. That is much, but it is little. [They were] fulfilling an imperative command of Christ." His overriding goal was to incorporate Opus Dei's spirit into his own life and contribute to spreading it as the specific way in which God wanted him to serve the Church. Escrivá's prediction was fulfilled in him: "The conviction of the supernatural character of the Work will make you happy sacrificing yourself for its accomplishment."

Almost immediately, Escrivá asked him to take over one of the classes of practical spiritual formation he had been giving to college students. Múzquiz's professional competence, calm, poise, good humor, and piety were an inspiration both to other young members of Opus Dei and to students who were discerning their possible call to Opus Dei. Laureano López Rodó, a law student who would become the Commissioner of Economic Development and Minister of Foreign Affairs, was struck by Múzquiz's smiling good humor when they met in Barcelona in 1940. During a conversation with Escrivá in Madrid a short time later, López Rodó began to think about dedicating himself fully to God in the world as a member of Opus Dei. At first, he was enthusiastic, but as the hours wore on, he began to think that such a vocation was "marvelous but impossible." But seeing Múzquiz "so serene and smiling," he recalls, "I immediately concluded: the life of total dedication is possible since José Luis Múzquiz lives it."

A Priest of Opus Dei

In late 1941 or early 1942, Escrivá asked Múzquiz if he would be willing to be ordained a priest. Although he was aware that Escrivá still had not found any way in which Opus Dei could have priests ordained, he had complete faith that a way would be found. He began studying for the priesthood as if there were no obstacles. Preparing for ordination involved a formidable amount of work. In addition to the philosophical and theological studies the Church required of all priests, Escrivá wanted the priests of Opus Dei to have a civil doctorate. At the time, no university in Spain offered a doctorate in engineering, so Múzquiz earned a doctorate in history. Escrivá founded in 1943 the Priestly Society of the Holy Cross. This made it possible for Múzquiz and two other members of Opus Dei to be ordained in June 1944. José Luis immediately began to travel extensively to offer pastoral care for Opus Dei's incipient activities in southern Spain and Portugal.

Starting Opus Dei in the United States

In 1948, Escrivá asked Múzquiz to lead an effort to bring Opus Dei to the United States. On February 17, 1949, he arrived in New York with another member of the Work, Sal Ferigle, a young physicist. From the plane, he wrote to Escrivá:

> We have been flying for five hours over a small part of America. A few minutes ago, we passed over Boston. We picked out Harvard University . . . and prayed to the guardian angel of the university and the guardian angels of each of the inhabitants. I think we will keep them busy. They must be sort of unemployed. The country is very big . . . and very small. And all of it has to be filled with tabernacles. . . . We are very happy and have great desires to work. From the plane, you see immense horizons. What a great harvest! [2]

From New York, Múzquiz, Ferigle, and José María González Barredo, who had been working professionally in the US for some time, traveled to Chicago, where they would open Opus Dei's first American center. They were soon joined by two other lay members of the Work. During their early months in Chicago, they faced formidable challenges. They had no money, had few friends, spoke little English, and were unfamiliar with the way of doing things in the United States.

Faced with these challenges, Múzquiz's first recourse was to prayer. He wrote to Escrivá at the end of March: "Every day I see more clearly what you have told us so often about the need for personal sanctity. I feel small and unworthy, but I see that our Lord loves me a great deal, and I want to love him a great deal."

---

2. Because Jesus present in the Eucharist is the heart of every Opus Dei center, Escrivá often spoke about a new tabernacle rather than a new center. Múzquiz's phrase about filling the United States with tabernacles expressed his hope that Opus Dei would have many centers in the country.

For Opus Dei to carry out its mission of serving the Church in the United States, it was essential to find young men and women who would dedicate their lives to God in Opus Dei, try to put its spirit into practice, and spread it to others. For that, a vital first step was to get to know young people whom God might be calling to this path of service to the Church. One place to do that was Calvert House, the Catholic Club at the University of Chicago. Múzquiz also contacted some Catholic high schools, and in many cases found the priests and brothers who taught there anxious to help him meet students who might be interested in Opus Dei's message.

The First Opus Dei Center in the US

In Spain and other countries, Opus Dei had opened student residences near major universities. They offered a homelike environment, an atmosphere of serious study, and an opportunity to receive the sacraments and Christian formation. They had greatly facilitated Opus Dei's apostolate with students. From the beginning, Múzquiz and the other members of the Work planned to open a similar student residence in Chicago.

The only suitable building for sale near the University of Chicago was a fifteen-room brick house just a few blocks from the campus. When the real estate agent asked Fr. Joseph if he could make a down payment of $25,000, Múzquiz thought he was asking if they could pay a total price of $25,000. Although they only had $2,000 at the time, he said yes. Later he clarified that the most they could put down would be $10,000. Sometime later he dropped that to $7,000, and eventually he confessed that they could only come up with $5,000 as a down payment. The agent was so impressed with Fr. Joseph's sincerity, innocence, and acceptance of God's will, that he offered to donate his entire commission to help them put together the down payment. The seller, convinced that the credit of a Catholic priest was good, offered to give them a first mortgage for two-thirds of the price. In August 1949, they took possession of the house they would call Woodlawn Residence. As Múzquiz wrote, they were essentially "broke," and there was no money to buy furniture. Nonetheless, they moved in immediately.

They were pleased to find inside a few old beds, a large dining room table, and a smaller table that Fr. Joseph used as a portable altar to celebrate Mass.

There were also a few wooden boxes they used to supplement the one chair they found in the house, which was immediately dubbed "The Chair." Little by little, various people they met gave them used furniture. Coming from a country where skilled labor was cheap, they were shocked at the cost of hiring painters, electricians, and other workers. Because doing it yourself was virtually unknown in Spain, they had no experience in remodeling, but they made up for their lack of knowledge with enthusiasm and goodwill. They recruited some boys they had met to help with painting, and a little more than three weeks after moving in, a temporary oratory was finished. On September 15, 1949, the Feast of Our Lady of Sorrows, Fr. Joseph celebrated Mass in the oratory and, for the first time, left the Blessed Sacrament reserved in the tabernacle of an Opus Dei center in the United States.

Múzquiz was delighted to have Christ present in the tabernacle. He wrote to Escrivá: "We are very happy to have our Lord at home with us. We don't know how to thank Him for having wanted to stay among us. Here, far away, one notices even more the need to unburden oneself with Him and to thank him for everything he has given us and is going to give us."

First Steps in the Apostolate

From their base at Woodlawn Residence, Fr. Joseph and the others worked steadily at putting together a group of young men whom they could help to develop a solid interior life of prayer and sacrifice, with the hope that some of them might receive from God a call to Opus Dei. By the end of October, they had a large enough group to be able to have Exposition and Benediction of the Blessed Sacrament on Saturday evenings and began organizing classes of spiritual formation patterned on the ones Múzquiz had attended himself in the 1930s. Fr. Joseph told the Founder, "The spiritual life is something new for them. It is a joy, however, to sow the seed, and when it begins to develop the harvest will be enormous. We are happy and we are beginning to see palpable fruits in some of the boys."

At the end of their first year in the United States, Múzquiz reflected on the experience thus far. He and the other members of the Work had explained the vocation to Opus Dei in some depth to more than forty young men they thought might be called to the Work. Writing to Escrivá, he commented:

The young men continue not to respond. I don't know if it is because they have a different mentality, that they have received poor formation, or if we still don't know how to deal with them. We are filled with peace by your saying that our work is very pleasing to our Lord and that the fruits will come soon. I think at times that perhaps things don't work out because our Lord is not pleased with us, but I try to reject that thought as a temptation. When I see the enthusiasm and the effort of some of my brothers, I feel sure that our Lord will soon do great things in Chicago.

First Vocations

The first American to join Opus Dei was Richard Rieman, a former naval aviator. At the time, he was working as the technical director of the mounted units at "Frontiers of Freedom," a summer show with a cast of 150, presented on the lakefront at the Chicago Fair. He joined Opus Dei in July 1950. In late 1950 and the first half of 1951, there was a flurry of new members, but only Rieman would persevere. Looking back on those events, Múzquiz saw a parallel with what had happened to Escrivá in the early days of Opus Dei when almost none of the very first members pressed on.

Three women of Opus Dei, led by Nisa González Guzman, arrived in Chicago in May 1950. Soon they were joined by two more Spanish members. Pat Lind, Rieman's cousin, became the first American member of the women's branch in June 1951. Soon thereafter, the women acquired a mansion a few blocks from Woodlawn.

By the end of 1951, only two years after the first members of Opus Dei arrived in the United States with no money and a rudimentary command of English, both the men's and the women's branches had substantial centers and were in touch with a growing number of people. Opus Dei was still a tiny reality in the United States, but thanks in large part to Fr. Joseph's prayer, sacrifice, and effort, it had begun to put down roots and to reach out to all types of people, men and women, single and married, laymen and priests.

The major apostolic activities at Woodlawn for several years were three-day retreats for groups of ten to twelve high school boys. They were a way of getting to know more students and teaching them the rudiments of the spirit of Opus Dei, especially the sanctification of their studies and the rest of their daily life.

Fr. Joseph's schedule was grueling. At times, especially during Lent, he would preach several retreats a week. Often, he finished one retreat in the morning and began another the same afternoon. In each retreat, in addition to offering Mass, preaching five or six half-hour meditations a day, and hearing confessions, he tried to have at least one personal conversation with each participant.

Those conversations were the heart of the retreat for many of the boys. They were effective because Fr. Joseph was so thoroughly a man of God. One person observed, "He had not the slightest hint of pretension about him, and neither did he show any particular interest in talking as an 'educated man' or as one able to discuss current issues and cultural topics. . . . He didn't talk about himself at all." Another person completes the picture: "His cheerfulness, his smile, his words, everything about him, inspired confidence. He was the sort of person whom you would tell, with great naturalness, the most intimate aspects of your life."

In 1948, Opus Dei opened the Roman College of the Holy Cross, an international center of formation for men. There, members would study philosophy and theology and learn the spirit of Opus Dei directly from the Founder. Some would be ordained priests of Opus Dei, and all of them would become much better equipped to live their calling and spread Opus Dei's spirit to others. In 1952, Escrivá suggested that Múzquiz consider which Americans might go to Rome. Fr. Joseph immediately began making plans to send people.

In the fall of 1954, Múzquiz sent Dick Rieman and one other American to Rome. The following year he was able to send a larger group. By Christmas 1955, a total of seven men from the United States were studying at the Roman College. That same year, the first two American women members went to Opus Dei's international center of formation for women, the Roman College of Holy Mary. The pace quickened during the following years. In the fall of 1956, nine Americans arrived at the Roman College of the Holy Cross. They were followed in 1957 by another six. Heading to Rome for several years when they were just beginning their professional careers or still studying at the university might have seemed imprudent or even crazy. Nevertheless, Fr. Joseph trusted in God's providence.

Sending a high proportion of the American members of the Work to Rome for formation involved serious sacrifices for Múzquiz as well as for the young men who pulled up stakes to go. It deprived Múzquiz of people who could help Opus Dei spread in the United States. With few exceptions, the centers were staffed almost exclusively by people who had joined Opus Dei only a short while before.

Despite the obvious drawbacks, Múzquiz was convinced of the value of sending many people to Rome. There they could live with the Founder and learn the spirit of Opus Dei from him. They could spend time with members of the Work from many different countries and acquire a personal sense of the universality of the Church and the Work. They could study philosophy and theology in depth, and some could train for the priesthood. When they returned to the United States in a few years as priests or as well-formed laymen, the benefits for the apostolate would be enormous.

Even in the short run, God blessed Múzquiz's generosity in sending people to Rome. In July 1955, he observed that "the apostolate is going much better than in other years. In fact, since the first Americans left for the Roman College, we have experienced a big push. In the year since they left, there have been quite a few more vocations than in the previous five years." Msgr. Cormac Burke, an Irish priest of Opus Dei who arrived in the United States in 1955, confirms this observation:

> When I first arrived in the States, I began to realize something of his concern to send those who had joined the Work to Rome to receive formation directly from St. Josemaría, as he had. His policy—which would not be normal in other times, but then showed an extraordinary depth of faith—was to send everyone he could to Rome, leaving the centers almost deprived of native members. Nevertheless (or more probably as a result of this exercise of faith) vocations continued to come in abundance in all those following years.

Years later, St. Josemaría observed that Fr. Joseph had been outstanding in grasping the importance of sending as many people as possible to Rome for formation.

Working in Rome

In 1961, Escrivá called Múzquiz to Rome to serve as a member of Opus Dei's international governing body, the General Council. When he left the United States, centers existed in Boston, Washington, DC, St. Louis, Milwaukee,

Madison, Wisconsin, and South Bend, Indiana. From the handful of people who accompanied Múzquiz in the early days in Chicago, Opus Dei had grown to several hundred members in the United States. Half a dozen young American professional men had been ordained as priests of Opus Dei, and a sizable number were studying philosophy and theology in Rome. Many of them would be ordained and others would return to help direct and expand Opus Dei's activities in the United States. Some would go to other countries to spread Opus Dei there. In addition, Opus Dei was getting started in both Canada and Japan, thanks in large part to Fr. Joseph's efforts.

At the end of September 1961, Múzquiz took up his new position as Central Priest Secretary. His duties involved working with Escrivá and the women responsible for directing Opus Dei's apostolic activities with women throughout the world. Serving on the General Council, like serving on any of the regional or local governing bodies of Opus Dei, was a collaborative, collegial affair. Most of the work was done in writing. Meetings were few and brief. Múzquiz had long been accustomed to this way of working, but previously it had occupied a fraction of his time, which was otherwise taken up with preaching, hearing confessions, giving spiritual direction, and traveling to cities where Opus Dei had centers.

Fr. Joseph had greatly enjoyed transmitting the spirit of Opus Dei to people through direct personal contact and loved traveling. In Rome, days and even weeks could go by in which he hardly ventured out of the buildings where he lived and worked, rarely seeing anyone except other members of Opus Dei. His days were taken up with paperwork. Escrivá reminded him and the other members of the General Council that they needed to see souls behind the papers and realize that their work made a direct contribution to bringing people closer to God. Convinced that this was true, Fr. Joseph offered his work for the people who would be directly affected by the projects he was working on, for friends and acquaintances, and for people in contact with Opus Dei's apostolates whom he had heard about but had not met. He cannot, however, have found this as immediately gratifying as interacting personally with people and seeing them grow in the love of God.

Even in a setting where hard work for the love of God was the norm, Fr. Joseph's seemingly endless capacity for work stood out. He worked very quickly, and his coworkers found his style and work habits distinctly

"American." Escrivá and the people who lived with him had to take pains to get him to rest and to take care of his health, since he didn't complain even when suffering from migraine headaches. One person who worked closely with him says that he would not even have known that he had migraines unless someone else had told him.

Leading Opus Dei in Switzerland

Opus Dei's activities in Switzerland had begun in 1956, but in 1963 they were still struggling. The women of Opus Dei had not begun working in the country, and the men had a single center, Fluntern, a small student residence in Zurich. Escrivá hoped Múzquiz's vibrant faith, drive, and enthusiasm might produce a breakthrough. He was aware, however, of the contrast between the highly structured character of Swiss society and Múzquiz's restless, freewheeling personality and rapid-fire style. Wanting him to see the virtues of the country before asking him to direct Opus Dei's apostolate there, Escrivá sent him in late 1963 to visit and report back. As Múzquiz was leaving, Escrivá spoke with him enthusiastically about Switzerland's importance as an international crossroads and about the "colossal" work that could be done there to contribute to Opus Dei's activities in many countries.

In July 1964 Múzquiz left Rome to head Opus Dei's activities in Switzerland. Immediately upon arrival, he threw himself into adapting to the country. During his years in Rome, Fr. Joseph had picked up some Italian, but his French and German were very limited. Nonetheless, he quickly began to hear confessions and preach in all three languages. German was especially challenging, but with careful preparation, he soon began to preach half-hour meditations in simple, but correct, German.

Hans Freitag, at the time a member of the governing body of Opus Dei in Switzerland, recalls that Múzquiz immediately set a "new, accelerated, pace in all our work. He was an example of hard work and good use of time." Building on his experiences in the United States, he suggested offering courses for high school students on study methods and introductions to various professions. The courses proved popular and brought many students into contact with Opus Dei. He had the building that housed the student residence remodeled, creating three separate zones. The student residence occupied the ground floor and the upper floors. Offices and living quarters for the Regional Commission were in a semi-basement. In what had been a dirt-floored cellar, they created a large activities area with a study room. To the surprise of many, Fr. Joseph rapidly raised the necessary funds for the project from local businesses.

Múzquiz quickly set his sights on Geneva as a target for Opus Dei's expansion, but the focus shifted to Fribourg when Pope Paul VI told Escrivá in a private audience that he hoped Opus Dei would soon begin apostolic activities in that city because an important Catholic university was located there. Soon they purchased a house in Fribourg for a student residence.

Shortly after Múzquiz's arrival, an avant-garde of two women of Opus Dei came to start the Work's activities with women in Switzerland. Although at first there were only the two of them, Múzquiz came to their house every day to say Mass on an improvised altar. In frequent meditations preached to these women, he insisted repeatedly on the same themes: love of God and confidence in him, doing things as the Father wanted them done, apostolate. Although both he and they were native Spanish speakers and it was slow work for him to prepare meditations in German, he began to preach to them in German almost immediately to help them learn the language.

The women had no sooner gotten started in Zurich than Múzquiz began urging them to make trips to Geneva. When they had been in the country a year and had held one German summer course for foreign students, he suggested they look for a house in Fribourg so that the next summer they could have a German course in Zurich and a French course in Fribourg. Money was tight, and one of the women observes that they managed only "thanks to his encouragement. Humanly it didn't make sense, but it worked."

Escrivá had pointed out to Múzquiz the importance of Switzerland as a world crossroads, and he quickly began to seek out foreigners who might understand Opus Dei. By hearing confessions in French, German, Italian, and English in a nearby parish, he met people from other countries. Some began to attend Opus Dei activities and a few eventually joined the Work.

Back to Spain

In the spring of 1966, Múzquiz was only fifty-four, but he had been working extremely hard for many years and was aging rapidly. Escrivá decided it would be good for him to return to Spain and take a less stressful position. At first, he was assigned as chaplain of an Opus Dei center in the southern city of Cádiz. As he did throughout his life, Múzquiz cheerfully accepted this new assignment. After about a year, he was reassigned as chaplain of Pozoalbero, a large conference center located in the countryside near Cádiz.

Múzquiz adapted quickly and apparently effortlessly to his new situation. Despite having spent most of his adult life in positions of authority in Opus Dei, he demanded no special attention, passing unnoticed as just one more priest. In this regard, Múzquiz was a magnificent example of the aspect of Opus Dei's spirit and practice that Escrivá described in a 1974 letter:

> Young persons and those not so young have gone from one place to another with the greatest naturalness or have persevered faithfully in the same spot without growing tired. When needed they have completely changed their work, leaving behind what they were doing and undertaking a different task of greater apostolic interest. . . . They have joyfully accepted hiding and disappearing, letting others move past them: going up and coming down.

Pozoalbero had facilities for retreats, workshops, and other activities for adults, along with an area for young people. In a separate part of the compound, there was a center for the Administration, women who formed the permanent staff of the conference center and were responsible for running it and taking care of meal service and housekeeping. Fr. Joseph's principal duties were to provide spiritual care to these women and to support their personal apostolate with women who lived in the area by giving mediations and classes, and by hearing confessions. The task of preaching the retreats held at Pozoalbero and ministering to the people who came there for workshops and other activities normally fell to the priest who accompanied each group, although Fr. Joseph often volunteered to help with confessions and give personal spiritual direction.

His assigned duties were minimal, compatible with a quiet semiretirement in the country, but his ten years in Pozoalbero were a whirlwind of activity. He threw himself with extraordinary generosity into the pastoral care of the women who worked in the Administration and the support of their apostolate with local people. In addition, he heard confessions and gave spiritual direction in nearby parishes and Opus Dei centers. He frequently visited the one hundred parish priests scattered around towns and villages in the area, organized retreats and days of recollection, and carried on a vigorous personal apostolate with many other people—including Americans stationed at the nearby naval base at Rota.

The physical labor of running a large conference center at a time when modern appliances were still unknown in southern Spain was often overwhelming. The women who worked in the Administration understandably felt they had little time for recreation or apostolic activities beyond what they were already doing: running a small catechism class and supplementary education program for girls from the immediate area and giving formation to members of Opus Dei in the area. On days when the conference center was unoccupied, they often took advantage of the break to clean more thoroughly, but Múzquiz would tell them that the house was already clean and would urge them to take the opportunity to get out and enjoy themselves.

He was especially interested in helping them extend their apostolate to more people. That seemed impossible for lack of time, but he helped them devise a work plan that gave each of them at least two free afternoons a week—time to visit friends or run apostolic activities. He urged them to keep a master list of all the women and girls they had met or even heard about, ranging from the wives of owners of vast rural estates to Romani girls living in shacks. Frequently he helped them review the list and make plans for working with each person on it. No matter how tired or concerned with the problems of running the center they were, he managed to rekindle their enthusiasm for the apostolate.

Not content with simply urging the members of Opus Dei who worked in the Administration to reach out to more people, Fr. Joseph generously supported their projects. Each week he spent hours in the confessional ministering to local girls who could hardly read. He treated them with fatherly patience, even when several would crowd into the confessional simultaneously.

Múzquiz frequently visited the nearby American naval and air base at Rota where he made friends with a wide range of people. The attendance at an annual open house that he organized at Pozoalbero for Americans was so large the police had to control the flow of traffic. On several occasions, Protestant chaplains came with their wives.

Fr. Joseph organized and preached days of recollection and even an occasional retreat in English. Among those attending were the commander of US nuclear submarines in the Mediterranean, an Anglican chaplain, the head Catholic chaplain at Rota, and a Catholic chaplain from an American base in Morocco. A number of the Americans whom Múzquiz met at Rota became members of Opus Dei when they returned to the States.

A primary focus of Múzquiz's apostolic activities was the diocesan priests in the surrounding area. All priests need support, encouragement, and guidance in their spiritual life. Priests who, like most of those in the area around Pozoalbero, live in isolated small towns and villages need help to avoid falling prey to loneliness and discouragement. Supporting their brother priests is a specific apostolate of the priests of Opus Dei, and Escrivá encouraged Múzquiz to dedicate himself especially to it by "loving them, dealing with them with affection, teaching them to serve the Church with refinement."

Whenever Fr. Joseph passed through a town or village in his travels, he stopped briefly to visit the parish priest. If he found him in, he would chat with him for a few minutes. If the priest was out, he wrote a short note and went on. Not content with visiting those whose parishes were on his way, he would systematically visit all the towns and villages of the area, no matter how small and out of the way and no matter how bad the roads were. Many were grateful for his visits. "They want to talk and many times to open their hearts," Múzquiz told Escrivá. "One told me, 'I didn't sleep all night I had so many worries. Fortunately, you came by, so I had someone to talk with about them.'"

During the years Múzquiz lived in Pozoalbero, priests needed special help to assimilate the teaching of the Second Vatican Council and to distinguish between what the Council taught and the aberrations some justified as the "spirit of the Council." Múzquiz tried to befriend all the priests he met, even those whom some other priests dismissed as "revolutionaries." In most cases, he realized, it would be counterproductive to engage in theological debates, but "at least I can reach out to them with concern and affection."

Múzquiz organized frequent talks, classes, days of recollection, and other means of spiritual and intellectual formation for priests. When Pozoalbero's schedule permitted, he held one- or two-day workshops that included talks about a topic in the news. Because the facilities at Pozoalbero were often not available and because it was hard for many priests to get there, Múzquiz also organized activities in roadside restaurants or homes. In his eyes, the content of the talks and classes he organized was not more important than the opportunity for the priests to spend a few hours or days together, becoming better acquainted and establishing bonds of friendship, fraternity, and mutual support.

All this required driving over bad roads to reach remote villages in a Seat 600, the cheapest car on the market, which was tinny, rough-riding, and so small that it was hard to get in or out. With a twenty-one-horsepower engine, it was badly underpowered. It had no air conditioning, although midday temperatures during the summer often hit 105 degrees Farenheit (40 degrees Celsius). Múzquiz frequently returned to Pozoalbero exhausted after a long day of driving in the heat, but he entered the house smiling no matter how tired he was.

Thanks to Fr. Joseph's spirit of sacrifice, a large number of priests began to attend workshops, days of recollection, retreats, and informal lunches and dinners. Over a few weeks at the end of 1970, he talked to more than a hundred diocesan priests. Some of them eventually joined the Priestly Society of the Holy Cross, part of Opus Dei that provides diocesan priests guidance and support. It helps them seek sanctity by carrying out their priestly ministry generously and being closely united with their bishop.

In his apostolate with both priests and laymen, a large part of Fr. Joseph's time was spent hearing confessions and giving spiritual direction. He was effective as a confessor and spiritual director because he combined deep faith, supernatural outlook, and love of God with humility and simplicity. What moved people was not what he said, but who he was. As one person observed, "In a way that is hard to define, he had an extraordinary capacity to communicate a sense of God, and even of God's presence, to everyone he met."

A priest to whom he gave spiritual direction recalls that when he first met Fr. Joseph he was "confused and in conflict" due to difficulties in carrying out the tasks assigned to him by his bishop.

> From the first time we met, he could see that I needed somebody to give me support. So, he singled me out. He would invite me, "Let's take a walk." As we walked, we talked. He would let me unload a lot of my frustrations and angry feelings, and then give me direction so that by the time we came

back, I was already feeling a lot more supported and at peace with things. The direction he gave me was very positive.

Thanks to Múzquiz's encouragement, support, and personal dedication, the apostolic activities conducted at Pozoalbero expanded greatly during his decade there. Many people of all social classes came closer to God, and a number discovered that God was calling them to Opus Dei.

Return to the US

By 1976, Múzquiz's health had improved considerably, and he had recovered his old energy. The head of Opus Dei asked him to return to the United States to head up activities there for a few years while Fr. Rafael Caamaño prepared to take over. Fr. Joseph gladly accepted the interim appointment. He returned to the US with just one small suitcase.

During the time Múzquiz spent at the helm of Opus Dei in the United States during this second stay, he managed to infuse a new sense of dynamism and energy into the apostolate. Nonetheless, he was fully aware of how much remained to be done. As the thirtieth anniversary of his first arrival in the United States approached, he wrote:

> It is a motive for thanksgiving to God, and at the same time to examine our consciences and see that things are going slowly—they have gone slowly, and they still are going slowly. We are just a few drops of water in the ocean that is this great country. I try, Father, to see things with serenity and a supernatural outlook and to encourage my brothers and sisters as much as I can.

Múzquiz's strong interior life was the foundation of his optimism and hope. A person who knew him well was impressed that he "never saw Father Joseph show signs of discouragement. He never lamented without hope the sad conditions of modern culture. He was keenly aware of individual and social sin against God and His Church, but he was so prayerful that they didn't cause him anxiety or despair."

As the time approached for Múzquiz's designated successor as the leader of Opus Dei in the US to take over, Del Portillo, Escrivá's successor as head of Opus Dei, asked where he would like to go when he stepped down. Múzquiz replied:

> You know that I have never expressed a preference for going to one country or another and that I would be happy in Spain, in the Ivory Coast which I visited in 1976, or wherever I'm needed. But since Rafa [Caamaño] said you wanted me to write you, I have thought about it in prayer, asking our Father's aid. I think the best thing would be to remain in the United States. This is not only because of the affection I have for this country, and especially for the members of the Work. The principal reason is that—although the people are good—I think they need to go deeper into the spirit and traditions of our family. I think that without the responsibilities of governing, I could continue to help as an older brother to transmit the marvelous family spirit that we have received from our Father.

Final Years

Múzquiz moved to Boston. There he served as chaplain of one center of the men's branch and three centers of the women's branch. He was happy to make himself available for whatever was needed and took great interest in the apostolic activities of the people he worked with. Since the centers where he exercised his priestly ministry were widely separated, he had to spend much time getting from one to the other, especially in the final years of his life when he could no longer drive and relied on public transportation. His ability to serve these centers, one person observed, "can only be explained by his extraordinary dedication and spirit of service, his sense of order, and above all his zeal for souls." Nor did he merely fulfill his duties. Each group he served "felt Father Joseph was 'their' priest. He communicated a real interest and involvement in all places."

On June 20, 1983, Múzquiz was in Arnold Hall Conference Center, south of Boston, serving as chaplain and teaching classes at a course for women members of Opus Dei. While teaching, he suffered a severe heart attack, dying later that night in the local hospital.

Fr. Joseph's cause of beatification was introduced in the Archdiocese of Boston in 2011.

CHAPTER SEVEN

Ana Gonzalo:
Eurocrat

na Gonzalo was a career administrator at the European Union who lived with cancer for most of her career.

Youth

Ana grew up in Madrid and joined Opus Dei as a numerary in 1973 when she was eighteen. At the time, she was studying geography and history at the University of Madrid. In her senior year, she won a scholarship to pursue a PhD at the University of Louvain. She moved to Belgium immediately after her graduation in 1977 and lived there for the rest of her life. She earned a master's degree in economic geography in 1980 and another master's degree in applied sciences in 1981. In 1987, she received a doctorate in urban affairs.

She began her professional career working in the Spanish embassy in Brussels as director of cultural events and press relations. Spain's 1986 entrance into the European Economic Community (which changed its name to the European Union in 1993) opened the possibility for Spaniards to be employed there. In 1987, Ana won a competition for a position in the General Direction of Agriculture. She spent the rest of her career working for the European Union.

Lebanon

Ana transferred to the General Directorate of Foreign Affairs in 1992. Her first assignment there involved planning and overseeing programs in Lebanon and Israel. Between 1992 and 1995, she made thirteen trips to Lebanon and one to Israel in connection with the European Union's programs there.

When Ana first visited Lebanon in 1992, the country was just emerging from fifteen years of civil and international war, including invasions by Syria and Israel. It was no longer at war, but was not at peace either. In a country of only three million inhabitants, the prolonged conflict had cost 150,000 lives, injured 300,000, led to the emigration of almost a million people, and brought the state to near collapse. Beirut was in ruins, and there was a large Syrian presence.

On Ana's first trip to Lebanon, she was met at the airport by an embassy car with two driver-bodyguards, one Christian and the other Muslim. At the numerous checkpoints, many manned by Syrians, matters were taken care of by one or the other depending on whether they were in a Christian or Muslim neighborhood.

The majority of the EU projects which Ana supervised in Lebanon involved the reconstruction of roads, electrical systems, water supplies, sewers, and other infrastructure. She was especially interested, however, in a small project which involved reestablishing agriculture in an area with a mixed Druse and Christian population. As a way of trying to overcome divisions between the two communities, the EU insisted that they share the agricultural equipment it furnished, even though they had been at each other's throats only a short time before.

Ana also took a particular interest in the construction of infrastructure in the Palestinian refugee camps. The Lebanese government had no interest in spending money on the camps, so the refugees lacked even the most basic facilities like sewers. When Ana visited, she was moved by the desire of the children to take a picture of themselves with the European lady who had come to visit them. When they offered her fish and fruit, she forced herself to eat some although the fish had been caught in polluted waters and the fruit was shriveled.

During her visits to Lebanon, the numerous invitations she received to visit and eat with families and individuals allowed her to encounter in-depth the reality of life in Lebanon, even though they forced her to cut back severely on sleep. Very quickly, Ana became known not only as a representative of the European Community but also as a "fervent Catholic." This led to invitations to visit several sanctuaries, including the monastery of St. Charbel Makhlouf, where the superior gave her a relic of the recently canonized saint. On several occasions, she visited a monastery of Carmelite nuns. On one visit, one of the nuns, whose information about Opus Dei came mainly from her contact with Ana, said she thought the charism of Opus Dei was smiling. When Ana explained that it was the sanctification of work, the nun replied, "Yes, but with a smile."

Israel

Given the high per capita income in Israel, the European Community did not carry out aid projects there. It limited itself to financing some projects of industrial cooperation to promote relations between private businesses. For that reason, Ana went to Israel only once.

Her busy work schedule did not permit her to visit many holy sites, but on her way to the Golan Heights she was able to stop at the Mount of the Beatitudes and Lake Tiberias, which she had imagined much larger than it is. Similarly, she found that her image of the Way of the Cross was mistaken.

> For me, the Way of the Cross should have been a place where one prayed the Stations of the Cross because that is where the way of the Cross really happened. Everything should move people to adoration. It should be an enormous sacred and silent place. Nothing could be further from the truth. Narrow little streets with fruit stands, potatoes, onions, Arab sweets, candies, rags, balloons, peanuts. . . . The streets are full of people: tourists, local people, shopkeepers, shoppers, merchants shouting out their wares. It wasn't easy to move. You couldn't stop to pray, but I prayed intensely. I realized that this is what the Lord's way of the cross must have been like. The Gospel and tradition speak many times of the crowds pushing their way through to go and console the Lord. Although I would have liked it to be a sacred place, I understood that it was a sacred place in its own way, the real way. At first, it surprises you. Later it helps you to pray.

In Israel, Ana was struck by the sharp divide between the Jewish and the Palestinian populations. It seemed to her that the two societies were

> watertight compartments. What does the future hold for these worlds? I would dearly like to see the superposition converted into living together. The watertight compartments become permeable. The differences become

diversity with rich fruits. I would like men to understand that we are all children of God and that this God is the same for everyone. I would like them to grasp that differences in civilizations, even ones as big as you find here, cannot hide the fact that we all have the same human nature. All men are the same, and fraternity is possible because our nature is identical, and we share being sons of God.

Something tells me that this is a hope, a desire, and almost a prayer. But no matter how hard I try to convince myself that it is not a dream, that it could happen, I don't entirely achieve it. Will we want to reconcile these two worlds?

In the plane on the way back to Belgium, she shared her impressions with a Jewish seatmate. He responded, "You have to realize, ma'am, that God did not create the world in a single act. He took his time, one week. He did it little by little. Much more than God, we need time." Ana recorded her reaction in her travel diary: "I find that quite convincing, and with my whole heart, I pray that as time goes by, people's will and desires may change. They are the actors and the makers of their history, although God is its author."

Ana did not find it easy to get to daily Mass in Israel, but she was determined to do so. She experienced, for the first time, something that would happen often during her career. Trying to find a Mass permitted her "to get to know the streets and the people, to escape from the featureless international hotels where you don't know where you are because . . . everything is the same everywhere. The monotonous offices in which our work meetings take place, which are also always similar."

Although she was often required to travel in official limousines, Ana liked whenever possible to take public transportation. She believed that "you don't begin to know a country until you take its public transportation, whatever an ordinary citizen, who doesn't go around in official cars as I normally do, would take."

First Appearance of Cancer

In late 1992, shortly after beginning to work in Foreign Affairs, Ana discovered a lump in her breast. The doctor diagnosed advanced cancer, advised her to schedule surgery immediately, and suggested that she visit her mother in Spain as soon as possible because she might not have another opportunity.

After surgery in January 1993, Ana underwent chemotherapy and radiation treatments from February to November. In July 1994, the doctors discovered that her cancer had metastasized to her ribs and skull. They immediately began a new round of chemotherapy. In December 1996, they declared her in complete remission, which lasted until 2003.

An American oncologist observes that for many patients, cancer is all-consuming:

> Cancer is not a concentration camp, but it shares the quality of annihilation: It negates the possibility of life outside and beyond itself; it subsumes all living. The daily life of the patient becomes so intensely preoccupied with his or her illness that the world fades away. Every last morsel of energy is spent tending the disease. . . . When I asked a woman with a rare form of muscle sarcoma about her life outside the hospital, she told me that she spent her days and nights scouring the Internet for news about the disease. "I am in the hospital," she said, "even when I am outside the hospital." The poet Jason Shinder wrote, "Cancer is a tremendous opportunity to have your face pressed right up against the glass of your mortality." But what patients see through the glass is not a world outside cancer, but a world taken over by it—cancer reflected endlessly around them like a hall of mirrors.[1]

Ana did not allow anything like that to happen to her. Less than forty-eight hours after she received the grim news that she had advanced cancer, she wore a clown costume to a party after midnight Mass in the Opus Dei center where she lived. She could have taken sick leave while receiving chemotherapy and radiation but didn't. She took advantage of the European Commission's flextime policy that permitted her to work extra hours from Monday through Thursday and take off Fridays for therapy. After spending the weekend recovering, she went back to work on Monday. Between 1992 and 1996, Ana made thirteen trips to Lebanon and one to Israel despite the rigors of cancer therapy and the spread of the disease to her ribs and skull. Few of her colleagues had any idea of how sick she was.

---

1. Siddhartha Mukherjee, *The Emperor of All Maladies: A Biography of Cancer* (New York: Scribner, 2010), p. 398.

South and Southeast Asia

In 1996, Ana moved from the Lebanon and Israel desk to become director of the European Union's educational programs in twenty-one countries of South and Southeast Asia. The projects involved programs of European studies in Asia and Asian studies in Europe. During the two years she held this post, she traveled to many countries where Christians were a tiny minority.

In Hanoi, she was deeply moved by the courageous profession of faith of the people who attended Mass in the cathedral. After Mass, they gathered outside to sing a hymn before a statue of Our Lady, Queen of Peace. Ana commented:

> It is impressive to see that they are working-class people. I don't know whether they know how to read, but they have received formation in the faith which shines forth in their piety. What a lesson for me. How often I will recall these Vietnamese brothers who share our faith in a Communist country, who sing with fervor right out in the street in a central square in Hanoi.

In countries like Vietnam, where Christ is little-known, she made a special effort to maintain an awareness of God's presence:

> I have tried—I don't say that I've always succeeded, but only that I've tried—not to forget Him. I have done two things. First, think of my work as a service to the countries and to the individuals I work with, and the people the projects are meant to help. Second, not interrupt the plan of life, the norms and customs of the Work. They make it possible to be aware that God is present.

Ana was firmly convinced of the truth of her Catholic faith, but she was also quick to recognize the virtues of people of other religions. In Thailand, she observed, "Buddhism is present everywhere, and this is reflected even in the character of its inhabitants. They are amiable, human, refined. They try to please you. They are smiling, ceremonious, grateful, and always looking for the spiritual." Her experience in Thailand gave her "the impression of a thirst for God without having yet found him. A sign of openness to the transcendent and an awareness of the vacuum that only God can fill." In her diary, she recorded:

I talked about this one day with one of the people I worked with. In my desire to give him a little bit of the truth that I thought he was looking for, I commented that in my opinion, Thailand seemed ready to receive the totality of the truth. Its spirituality opened it to the divine. They know that the Buddha is not a god, but rather an indication of the fact that there is a supreme and transcendent truth.

In Indonesia, where almost 90 percent of the population is Muslim, she was favorably impressed by the openness she observed. She found that people believed "in one God despite the differences and counting with the differences. Pluralism does not mean for them, as it sometimes does for us, that they don't care, but rather that everything contains good and truth." During her trips to South and Southeast Asia, she was moved by the poverty she saw, especially women street-vendors carrying baskets that were too heavy for them. She found she could not walk a meter without an avalanche of people insisting that she buy postcards, little straw hats, or oranges. Other people wanted to transport her where she wanted to go on their bicycle or their scooter. "It is very sad and makes you want to buy everything to give them a little money." She preferred to buy things rather than give alms. In Jakarta, she bought a little boat from a very old man. When he was not looking, she gave it to a small boy who was passing by. "It is better to buy than to give alms," she observed in her diary, "and in this way both the old man and the boy are happy."

China

In 1998, Ana transferred to the office responsible for the European Union's relations with China. Between 1998 and 2001, she participated in projects involving the training of government officials, scholarships for postgraduates, internships for young people, the creation or enlargement of centers of European studies in six cities, training for primary school teachers, construction of schools in poor rural areas, and the creation of a business school which, at the time, was the only one in China. Despite the diversity of the projects, Ana saw them all as a way of "extending our values which we know are universal: freedom, respect for others, and recognition of the individual." She was convinced, therefore, that "these projects can have a significant impact on the way of thinking and acting of China in the future."

In Lanzhou, the capital and largest city of Gansu province, the European Community was financing the construction of a grade school and teacher training center in a barren, impoverished agricultural area. She was the first foreigner the students had ever seen, and some of them cried when they saw her. She observed, "If you think you are attractive, this will do you good." In a television interview, she stressed that for the European Community, "each person is unique and unrepeatable, that each child who will be helped by the project is a person who justifies all our efforts."

On numerous occasions, she argued against the Chinese one-child policy with officials, youth representatives, and ordinary people she met. In a conversation with a farmer in a poverty-stricken area about the killing of baby girls, she was impressed to hear him say, "It's not necessary to kill baby girls. People here just leave them out in a field, and someone ends up picking them up." Anna reflected, "The people who pick them up are people who live charity perhaps without even knowing the word. People who still have a heart, although they don't have enough to eat. The adoption of Chinese baby girls by people from the West is a true work of charity. It is a case of really saving their lives."

On her first morning in Beijing, the temperature was 5 degrees Fahrenheit (-15 degrees Celsius). She took a taxi at five o'clock in the morning to get to 5:30 AM Mass. When she reached the Church of St. Joseph, she was moved to find more than one hundred people. On Sunday, she went to a church near Tiananmen Square. She arrived as the seven o'clock Mass was ending and found the church packed with more than a thousand people. Many of them stayed for the eight o'clock solemn Mass. "Such faith in a country like China is something that will help me later when I compare it with ours. We can do everything without effort, whereas for them to continue living their faith requires so much sacrifice."

On another trip, she happened to meet the bishop's secretary after Mass. When she told him that she was a member of Opus Dei, he responded that many people in the parish had great devotion to St. Josemaría. They knew about him because a visitor from Macao had brought them cards with his picture and a prayer asking his intercession. In Beijing, she visited the monument where Chairman Mao lies in state. She recorded in her diary: "Of course, I prayed for him and for all those millions of Chinese people who don't know that they come from God and are going to Him."

North Africa and the Middle East

Following the European Commission's usual practice of rotating people every three years, Ana was named head of the office of Geographic Coordination for the Mediterranean Zone in July 2001. This involved responsibility for EU projects in Morocco, Algeria, Tunis, Egypt, Palestine, Israel, Syria, Jordan, and Lebanon. The new position brought with it new challenges. Ana was the first Spanish woman to be named head of a unit of the European Commission. As a woman, she had to prove that she was up to the task. Many of her colleagues had hoped to be named to the position, and the Director-General to whom she reported had a well-deserved reputation as a rigorous and at times difficult person to work for. Ana accepted all of these challenges with her usual smile and good humor.

One of her first trips in her new position was to the capital of Algeria. She flew there only three days after the 9/11 terrorist attack on the United States in an atmosphere of high tension and concern about Arab terrorism. She was told that she could only travel in a bulletproof car accompanied by a driver and armed bodyguard. Walking alone through the city as she usually did was out of the question. There were no tourists in the hotel, only a few businesspeople whose work required them to be there. Anyone less intrepid than Ana would have likely postponed the visit, but she was undaunted by the situation. The concierge of the hotel did not know when Mass might be celebrated and could not call to find out because he did not have the number, and there were no phone directories. Ana decided to go at dawn, based on her experience that, in countries with a tiny minority of Catholics, Mass is usually celebrated very early in the morning. She arrived at the basilica at 6:20 AM only to find it closed, but she learned that Mass would be celebrated at 7:00 in the chapel of a convent attached to the basilica. The congregation was limited to a few Europeans. Ana was saddened by the eradication of what many centuries earlier had been flourishing Christian communities.

One day after Mass in the cathedral, Ana introduced herself to the priest and told him that she was a member of Opus Dei. "Opus Dei," the priest

responded, "people who pray, people who are faithful to the Lord." His opinion was based on having met a member of Opus Dei in Casablanca who
went to the cathedral every day to pray. In her diary, Ana comments, "I do
not know if he would have been able to say that about me. But I was very
pleased with his commentary, with the fact that this was the idea of Opus
Dei held by a priest from a Muslim country with such a small, dispersed, and
solitary Christian population."

From Algeria, Ana traveled to Morocco. The European Community
had financed the installation of a sewer system in an area on the outskirts of
Rabat. There was no electricity or running water, and people lived in shacks
of cardboard and scrap metal. The only transport in the area was wagons
pulled by half-starved mules. Everywhere mountains of garbage were covered
with flies. Ana wondered if she was having a nightmare situated in the dis-
tant past. Never before had she seen such poverty. "I can hardly believe that I
am seeing it, but I am. . . . Poor people! I hope that they find some way of
making it possible for their children to study, to lead a life more in keeping
with the basic dignity that every human being ought to have."

In Tunisia, the European Union was financing the construction of some
six hundred small dams and holding pools to facilitate irrigation. In one village, the village representative told Ana, "We have water, and we have electricity. The only thing we need is a mosque, and that is what we asked the
European Union for." Ana found it difficult to explain why the European
Union would not finance the construction of a mosque.

In Egypt, she took advantage of the fact that non-Muslims were permitted to enter the mosques. Ana did not limit herself to looking around,
but prayed "to the one God, to the one who is capable of leading so many
millions of men and women who pray to him sincerely and devoutly to the
totality of the truth." She was left with the impression of "deep-rooted faith."
She came to understand that many young people were attracted by Islam and
even converted to it "because in Islam they find a conviction that we Christians so often lack."

In Jordan, Ana found the situation of women especially interesting. The
country had invested a great deal in education, and the percentage of university graduates was higher than in Europe. More women than men held
university degrees. Nonetheless, there were very few women in important

government posts and only one minister of the government was a woman. The picture in business and industry was much the same. Most women did not work outside the home after finishing their studies. Many outside observers thought that this must be because work outside the home was not permitted in an Islamic society and that the education women received was going to waste. A French official of the European Union's delegation told Ana that she believed the real reason for the absence of women outside the home was different. In Jordan, family and social life were considered more important than work. Not working outside the home, the official said, was a different way of taking advantage of the education received, not a waste of it. Jordanian women who dedicated themselves to their families did not do so, she explained, because of any prohibition—which did not exist either legally or in fact—but rather because of a conscious decision. This conversation gave Ana a great deal to think about.

Cancer Reappears

Toward the end of Ana's assignment as head of the Geographic Coordination Office for the Mediterranean Zone, in 2003, her cancer reappeared in her ribs. She underwent surgery in 2005 and 2006, but neither the operations nor chemotherapy and radiation therapy stopped the cancer from spreading. In her travel notes, however, she does not even mention the recurrence of her cancer, nor does she show any less interest and enthusiasm for her work and the areas she visited. In 2008, she was forced to take disability, but she argued persistently that although she was ill, she was not disabled. Eventually, she was able to return to work as a consultant, but within a year her cancer had progressed to the point where she could no longer work.

In the seven years between the reappearance of cancer in 2003 and Ana's definitive retirement in 2010, she held several responsible positions. From 2003 to 2006, she served as head of the recently created Quality Control Unit, which was charged with reviewing projects all over the world before the final decision to finance them. In 2006, she was named head of the Unit for Coordination and Supervision of Latin America. This twenty-three-person unit prepared and followed programs and projects all over Latin America as well as coordinating relations with the European Parliament and international organizations interested in the projects. Her work required frequent trips to Latin America, which Ana found increasingly challenging.

The Meaning of Suffering

In 2007, Ana wrote a series of reflections on "The Christian Meaning of Suffering." In the epilogue, she explains,

> Fourteen years ago, I was diagnosed with a serious illness. Since then, I have had to undergo regular and at times painful treatments. In these few lines, I only want to share my readings and some of my reflections, principally with other Christians, but also with anyone who is looking sincerely for the meaning of his own illness or that of his loved ones.

Ana takes as her starting point a paragraph of the *Catechism of the Catholic Church*: "Illness and suffering have always been among the gravest problems confronted in human life. In illness, man experiences his powerlessness, his limitations, and his finitude. Every illness can make us glimpse death."[2] Viewing suffering from a spiritual point of view, Ana writes:

> When we believe that the redemption was carried out on the cross; when we accept and love our own participation in the cross of Christ, we begin a path of conversion. We come closer to God; we grow in virtues; we direct ourselves toward eternal salvation, and we bring happiness to others.
>
> When a Christian encounters the Cross in his life, the Lord may hope that that person goes through three interior stages and that—with his help—he may reach the last. The first consists in resigning oneself; the second in accepting the suffering, and the third in loving it.
>
> When we accept and love our participation in the Cross of Christ, we find joy and peace in suffering, because we know that Christ carries the cross and that our cross is perfectly logical from a supernatural point of view, a small splinter of the wood of his Cross.

In the final months of her life, Ana became completely dependent on others. She could no longer read, make a telephone call, or take care of her

---

2. *Catechism of the Catholic Church*, 2nd ed. (Washington, DC: Libreria Editrice Vaticana–United States Conference of Catholic Bishops, 2000) no. 1500.

personal needs. Her sister thinks that for someone who had always been very independent, this must have been a particularly difficult trial. Ana was able to overcome it thanks to her faith. In her reflections, she writes:

> With faith, the sick person can overcome the feeling, which is perfectly logical from a natural point of view, of being useless or of being a burden for others. In reality, the sick person is more useful than ever. That person is useful to God and "helps" to carry out the redemption. That person is useful to the Church, which is aware of the value of suffering and considers the sick as a treasure and entrusts itself to their prayer. And that person is useful to other people, providing the occasion to demonstrate their affection, to exercise charity, to be generous.

Ana's deep faith and strong character do not mean that she always found her illness easy to bear. In June 2010, almost a year before her death, her sister visited her in the hospital. Suddenly, Ana experienced a moment of extreme distress. She broke down and sobbed, "I'm afraid. I'm not going to reach October. I'm very sick." Embracing her sister, she repeated, "I'm afraid, Blanca! I'm afraid." She quickly recovered, dried her eyes, and attempted to smile. Then she began to excuse herself, "Pardon, pardon me. What a show I've put on!"

At the moment of her death, however, Ana experienced no such fear. She was no longer able to speak but could still understand what was said to her. The person accompanying her asked, "Are you afraid?" Ana shook her head, "No." It was her final communication.

When they received the notice of her death, many of Ana's colleagues in the European Commission were surprised. They had not known she was ill or at least did not realize her illness was so serious. As her sister says, "Considering that she suffered cancer for nineteen years, the fact that her illness passed unnoticed for so many can only be explained in terms of her great fortitude and desire to work and live with optimism. That made her an exceptional person."

CHAPTER EIGHT

Guadalupe Ortiz de Landázuri:
Chemist

G uadalupe Ortiz de Landázuri was a pioneer in many ways. She was one of the few Spanish women of her generation who earned a doctorate in science. She was among the very early members of the women's branch of the Work, directed its first residence for university students, and played a leading role in starting Opus Dei in Mexico.

Early Life

In 1927, when Guadalupe was eleven years old, her father, a professional Spanish artillery officer, was assigned to a base in North Africa where there were no secondary schools for girls. At the time, most Spaniards would not have been concerned about a girl's education. Guadalupe's parents, however, were determined to give her the best education they could, so they enrolled her in an all-boys school. She won the respect of her fellow students not only for her grades but also for her athletic prowess and her daring. She liked to recall that on one occasion, she drank a bottle of ink on a dare. (Years later, shortly after arriving in Mexico, she similarly won the respect of a group of Mexican college students by winning a chili-eating contest.)

Guadalupe began studying chemistry at the University of Madrid in 1932, the year after her family returned to Spain. Most people at the time thought women did not need higher education. In Guadalupe's freshman year, only six percent of Spanish university students were women and hardly any of them studied science. The few women who graduated and began working professionally were expected to retire when they got married. Guadalupe did well in her studies and enjoyed an active social life. On at least one occasion, a friend who was a pilot took her flying in her biplane. During her college years, she had a serious boyfriend, although she sometimes complained to her friends about his perfectionism.

At the outbreak of the civil war in Spain in 1936, Guadalupe's father was charged with treason and condemned to death by the Republican government. Through his connections to high-level Republican officials, her brother, Eduardo, managed to win a conditional last-minute pardon. Their father, however, refused to accept the conditions. Guadalupe, together with her mother and brother Eduardo, spent their father's final night with him in his prison cell. Eduardo recalls that she "did not show signs of emotion, and her serenity gave strength to my mother and, certainly, to me."

All Spanish universities remained closed during the three years of the civil war, but in June 1940, Guadalupe finally received her degree in chemistry. She would have liked to go on directly to a PhD but needed to start work immediately to support herself and her widowed mother. She began teaching chemistry at the French International School and the Irish School in Madrid. Guadalupe planned to get married and have a family but does not seem to have been in a hurry. Although she went to Mass on Sundays and occasionally said the Rosary, religion did not play an especially important role in her life. One day at Mass, however, she experienced a strong conviction that God was asking something more of her, though she didn't know what.

Guadalupe asked a friend for the name of a priest who could advise her and was referred to the founder of Opus Dei. She met St. Josemaría for the first time on January 25, 1944. Years later she recalled that at their first meeting, she had "the clear sensation that God was speaking to me through that priest. . . . I felt a great faith that was a reflection of his. Interiorly, I put myself in his hands for the rest of my life." On March 19, 1944, after making a retreat, Guadalupe asked to join Opus Dei. Two months later, she moved into the Work's only women's center, located on the outskirts of Madrid.

First Years in Opus Dei

When Guadalupe joined Opus Dei, the men's branch was growing rapidly and had somewhere between three hundred and five hundred members, but the women's branch still had only a handful of members. St. Josemaría was convinced that, in the future, the women of Opus Dei would carry out a wide range of professional activities, including research and university teaching. In addition, he envisioned that they would take care of the cooking, housekeeping, and laundry services with the goal of making the Work's centers true Christian homes with the warmth and atmosphere of a Christian family. He called the women who carried out these tasks and the work they did the Administration. In the early years, he asked the few women of Opus Dei to concentrate on staffing the Administration, curtailing for the moment other apostolic and professional activities.

Guadalupe had little talent for homemaking and even less experience. Nonetheless, in September 1945, she moved to Bilbao in northern Spain with three other women to work in the Administration of a new residence for male university students. On this and many later occasions, Guadalupe showed her willingness to contribute to the development of Opus Dei by taking on cheerfully, and even enthusiastically, essential tasks for which she was not particularly well equipped, putting aside for the moment the professional work she had spent years preparing for.

Days after arriving in Bilbao, she wrote to Escrivá: "I'm very happy here. Some days I notice God's presence very much." Referring to the fact that the Blessed Sacrament would soon be reserved in the tabernacle of the oratory, she said that she was "preparing him a new home. Very soon he will come to live with me." A year later, after telling Escrivá about the difficulties she encountered in living the plan of life and how sorry she was about failing many times to fulfill all the norms, she said, "I would like the Lord to be content [with me] and seeing how much he helps me despite everything, I even think at times that he is and that he forgives me."

In March 1946, two years after joining Opus Dei, Guadalupe became the director of the Work in Bilbao. She wrote to Escrivá:

> I am delighted to say that here I am, now acting as the head and tomorrow in the last spot, but always content because I am serving the Lord. Every day I have more confidence in his help and less in my own strength. From the moment in which Nisa [who till then had been the director] told me that she was leaving [for another post in Madrid], I asked him very truly not to separate himself from me for even a moment. With him, I want to

always carry the house on my shoulders and move my sisters to come closer to him.

After two years in Bilbao, during which the apostolate of Opus Dei grew substantially, Guadalupe returned to Madrid to join the governing body of the women's branch of Opus Dei, establish a residence for university women called Zurbarán, and begin her PhD studies in chemistry.

Establishing Zurbarán was not easy. Few of the handful of women members of the Work had themselves studied at the university. The pool of female university students from which residents could be recruited was small and, even in that small pool, there were many characters who would not find it easy to live with other women in a residence that aspired to promote academic excellence and serious Christian life. It would be several years before Zurbarán would be full. This brought with it serious financial problems and meant that the fledgling residence could not afford to be very selective. It would have been easier to start with a girls' school, a teachers' college, or some other more traditional women's institution, but Escrivá wanted the women of Opus Dei to focus from the beginning on the university.

Even more difficult than filling the beds was creating in the residence a welcoming, homelike environment. Guadalupe and the other members of the Work struggled to foster a climate of peace and harmony, but in the beginning, heated arguments broke out frequently, especially over politics. Little by little, however, the environment in Zurbarán improved and more and more students who lived there or in other residences and boarding houses began attending classes of Christian formation and other activities. Many of them turned frequently to Guadalupe for advice about their studies and their spiritual life. Many nights she was up to all hours talking with students.

Starting Opus Dei in Mexico

In 1949, Escrivá asked Guadalupe if she would be willing to head a small group that would start Opus Dei's apostolic activities with women in Mexico. In a letter a few days later, she said, "I am delighted to go, although I don't really think much about it. Just in the mental prayer, I dedicate a little time to praying about it, and from time to time I say a Rosary to Our Lady of Guadalupe praying for everything that I still don't even know about."

Guadalupe flew to Mexico together with Maolia Ortiz and María Ester Cianas on March 3, 1950. Fr. Pedro Casciaro, the head of Opus Dei in Mexico, had met many women, who helped the new arrivals find their way in Mexico. At the end of the month, he preached a retreat for fifty young women, mostly college students. On April 1, 1950, the first women's center, a university residence called Copenhaguen, opened its doors. In addition to being the director of the residence and of Opus Dei's activities in Mexico, Guadalupe enrolled in doctoral courses in chemistry, but, not surprisingly, she did not make much academic progress during the years she lived in Mexico.

At first, there were few residents, but from the beginning the house was full of students who came to study or attend meditations, days of recollection, or circles. At the end of May, the first resident joined Opus Dei as a numerary. Guadalupe earned the affection and respect of the students with her warm character, cheerfulness, and good humor, which often found expression in a deep, hearty laugh. One friend said, "Despite the time that has gone by, whenever I think about her, I hear her laugh. Guadalupe wore a permanent smile. A smile that was welcoming, good-natured, and simple." Another friend says:

> She had a permanent smile. Guadalupe laughed a great deal and was always smiling. I think that this was a result of her complete forgetfulness of self. I never saw her looking serious or worried. She was completely detached from her health, and I didn't see any other issues that affected her enough to keep her from smiling.

Another facet of her personality that facilitated Guadalupe's work as director of the residence and of Opus Dei's other activities in Mexico was, according to one of her collaborators, "always seeing the positive aspects of each person. . . . At times she was somewhat lacking in objectivity because her positive sense made her exaggerate the good found in others."

Closely connected with her optimism was understanding. According to a person who worked with her, "In the difficult equilibrium between being understanding and being demanding, she always inclined toward the first. She understood that in some cases it is necessary to give in for the good of souls. Some people said that she was too understanding, but no one said that she was too demanding in her approach." Perhaps for this reason, according to another person who knew her well, "When she had to correct something, she did so with fortitude, but with such refinement and affection that it didn't feel like a scolding but rather something you appreciated."

Working with All Types of People

Guadalupe related easily to the residents and their friends, who belonged to the highest social classes of Mexico City, but she was equally at ease with uneducated indigenous girls from the surrounding farming communities, known in Mexico as *ranchos*. She hired a number of those girls to come to work in the Administration of the student residence while receiving an elementary education. Their fathers, who often did not even speak Spanish, viewed the big city with deep suspicion but trusted Guadalupe enough to allow their daughters to leave the village to work and study in the capital. Learning to read and write as well as to cook and sew, perfecting their Spanish, and getting to know Mexico City opened horizons these girls could not have dreamed of in their villages.

To visit the *ranchos*, Guadalupe had to travel through dangerous areas, often alone on horseback. Friends suggested that she carry a pistol, but she preferred a knife because she was afraid she might unnecessarily shoot someone at a distance. If it came to using the knife, she explained, she would know that it was clearly necessary. On one of her trips, she got off the bus in a little town and was walking on a lonely road when she realized that a man was following her. She changed direction several times, but he kept close behind. She wheeled around, slapped him, and asked what he thought he was doing. The man fled and Guadalupe continued on her way. The incident did not deter her from making similar trips in the future.

Guadalupe also got to know some Spanish exiles who had fled Spain at the end of the civil war. Among them was Ernestina de Champourcin, a well-known poet whose husband had been the political secretary of the president of the Spanish Republic when Guadalupe's father was executed by the

Republic. The two became good friends, and eventually, Ernestina became one of the first married members of Opus Dei in Mexico.

Montefalco Conference Center

During the first years of its activities in Mexico, Opus Dei held retreats in borrowed houses, usually out in the country. While giving a talk during one of those activities in 1952, Guadalupe was stung by a scorpion. Despite the acute pain, Guadalupe brushed the arachnid aside and continued giving the talk as if nothing had happened. Soon thereafter she developed a life-threatening fever, perhaps due to malaria. Her recovery was slow and difficult.

Both Guadalupe and Fr. Casciaro wanted Opus Dei to have a place of its own that could be used for retreats and other formational activities and as a base for offering education and formation to the peasants living in the environs. A wealthy, socially active family offered Opus Dei a former sugar plantation south of Mexico City called Santa Clara de Montefalco. Until the early twentieth century, it had had vast fields of sugar cane as well as many large buildings in an area enclosed by a high wall. During the revolution that began in 1910, most of the land was confiscated and all the buildings burned down except for a church that formed part of the compound. When Guadalupe visited it for the first time in 1951, the plantation was completely abandoned and overgrown with tropical vegetation. The church was the only building with a roof, and it had no glass in the windows and was infested with rats and bats. Although everything was in ruins and there was neither electricity nor running water, Guadalupe was enthused with the hacienda's possibilities. In a letter after a visit in 1952 when none of the buildings was even remotely habitable, she exclaimed, "How beautiful it is!"

It took several years to finalize the purchase of the property by a non-profit organization that made it available for retreats and other activities. In 1954, the first retreat was held at Montefalco. The participants had to carry in food and water, coal for cooking, sheets, towels, and everything else they needed. At night, before going to bed on cots, they killed scorpions. For the first few years, the only permanent occupants were a caretaker and his family, but in 1956 a group of women of Opus Dei moved in. Two years later, they opened a school for peasant girls from the surrounding towns. By that time, however, Guadalupe had left Mexico.

Directing Opus Dei in Mexico

Guadalupe was a woman of vision and big plans. A Spanish member of the Work who moved to Mexico observed, "We tended to be taken up in solving immediate problems, but Guadalupe was way out ahead of us." Under Guadalupe's leadership, the women of Opus Dei had opened centers in Monterrey and Culiacán by the end of 1951. By the time she left Mexico in 1956, there were eleven centers in different parts of the country.

Just planning all these undertakings—solving the economic and staffing problems they presented, and overseeing their development—was an enormous challenge. But in addition, Guadalupe played a central role in planning the formation of the many women of all social classes who joined Opus Dei. In many cases, she was also personally involved in guiding them spiritually.

All of this was possible thanks to her intelligence, optimism, daring, executive ability, and willingness to delegate responsibility to young women who had only recently joined Opus Dei. But above all, it was due to her unwavering confidence in God and openness to the inspiration of the Holy Spirit. She passed on to the director of one of the centers her own experience:

> The things that happen to you all seem to me very human. Don't worry about them, but try to react and see things more from the perspective of God and the eternal truths. I assure you that the irritating little things that put us in a bad mood disappear when viewed against this background which is so real and so fundamental.

Guadalupe had no desire to occupy leadership positions. Her principal resolution from her retreat in 1954, was "to let others govern. To annul myself little by little so that they take on more responsibility. I have given enough orders." At the end of 1955, she told Escrivá, "Father, I've been the head for many years. Wouldn't it be good to begin to be the feet?" She added, however, "But as you know, here or wherever you put me, I will be happy serving God in the Work."

Living Close to God

During her years in Mexico, Guadalupe continued to grow in interior life. During a retreat in 1955, she wrote to Escrivá:

> It would not be true if I told you that I have sensible spiritual consolations, but I can assure you that there are no ups or downs. I find God almost constantly in everything, with too much naturalness. I think I take things too much for granted. My security that God is on my path, near me, makes me eager to do everything. It makes easy the things that in the past I didn't like to do. Now without even thinking about it, I do them. Father, I do have one concern: does the path I'm on lead to heaven? I find it too comfortable since I almost never have personal problems.

She found, as she told Escrivá in a 1954 letter, that "I think so much about the others that I no longer think about myself." Nonetheless, she feared that although deeply concerned about others, she didn't have enough affection for them. She confessed to Escrivá in a May 1956 letter:

> My struggle is mostly in putting more heart into things, because perhaps my charity is not very deep. A few times my sisters have said so to me. They say that they notice that I am concerned about them but that there comes a moment in which they find a sort of barrier in me, that . . . they don't get all the way into me. Father, I'm not very clear what exactly this means, but I am going to ask God to love him more, and in that way surely, I will also love others better.

Toward the end of her stay in Mexico, she wrote to Escrivá:

> I think this year we have to really move forward spiritually, and I the first. Until now I have prayed for and tried to achieve the virtues we need in the Work (piety, work, joy, apostolate, spirit of sacrifice, etc.). This is what I have also prayed for and tried to achieve for the other members of the Work. But now I see the need to go deeper. By now, there should be contemplative souls in the region, who desire and ask for more spiritually refined things, and who know how to appreciate them. Help me to win this from God. If I'm not made for this sort of thing, may I at least not be an obstacle to others achieving it. May I have God's grace to orient them

and encourage them to travel these paths. May I also have the desire to try them and the humility and patience to understand that God may not want this for me, although I desire it with all my soul.

She recorded in her notebook her desire "to go deep into silence to the point where God alone is. Where not even the angels can enter without our permission. And there, to adore God, to praise him, and to say loving things to him."

In Rome

In October 1956, Guadalupe attended the General Congress of Opus Dei in Rome. The members of the Congress elected her a member of the international governing body of the women's branch, the central advisory. Her new position involved supervising Opus Dei's apostolate with married women throughout the world. She took up residence in Villa Tevere, the Work's Rome headquarters.

The women's branch was growing rapidly and planning to begin activities in France, Uruguay, and Brazil in 1957. One hundred women were living in Villa Tevere, between the members of the central advisory, the people who worked in the Administration, and the students at the Roman College of Holy Mary, Opus Dei's international center of formation for women. The buildings were very crowded, but that did not seem to bother Guadalupe. Although she undoubtedly missed Mexico and the people she had left behind there, she was very happy in Rome, particularly because she was frequently able to see and talk with Escrivá.

She was still settling into her new job when she suffered a severe heart attack on March 6, 1957. She cheerfully accepted God's will and showed no sign of fear. In her notebook, she wrote: "If death comes now, I will go to purgatory for a while—not for anything concrete—and then I will help the Work from above as much as I can."

Gradually she recovered and began to return to normal life, although she still couldn't climb stairs and needed to rest more than usual. Her brother Eduardo, a distinguished professor of medicine at the University of Navarre, suggested that she go to Madrid for surgery. In early July she had two heart valves replaced. At the time, the operation was novel and dangerous, but it went well. A week later she wrote to Escrivá:

> It has been a week of great physical pain but of much moral consolation. I have felt as never before, affection for you, for my sisters, and for all the members of the Work. . . . Once again let me thank you. I do not deserve so much. . . . I will try to behave well and to be courageous. The presence of God does marvels. How you notice it! I want to return promptly and to serve.

After four months in Madrid, Guadalupe returned to Rome in October 1957. On December 27, she began to suffer from pneumonia and atrial fibrillation. Her heart rate became so elevated and her arrhythmia so severe, that the doctor could not even determine her pulse rate. Guadalupe accepted the situation calmly, saying to one of the women who were with her, "Don't worry! Nothing is going to happen, and furthermore, I have everything in order." Little by little, she once again recovered.

Back in Madrid

In May 1958, Guadalupe returned to Spain. Her doctors found her situation puzzling, but eventually concluded that she was well enough to live a normal life if she avoided excessive exercise and slept more than usual. By July, she was able to begin helping out with formational activities for married members in a conference center near Madrid, but not well enough to resume her duties as a member of the central advisory. At the end of the month, she resigned her position and began a new stage of her life. At forty-two years of age and with serious heart problems, she returned to her youthful dream of completing a doctorate in chemistry and carrying out research.

In the fall of 1958, after a summer spent filling in for people who were out of Madrid attending courses of formation, Guadalupe began working regularly at Montelar, a center where some two hundred girls, many from well-to-do families, including the daughter of the US ambassador, learned home economics, and where many of their mothers attended days of recollection. Guadalupe found herself giving classes on practical Christian

life to a group of young girls as well as helping to organize the days of recollection for their mothers. At first, she was concerned that her age would
prove a problem in dealing with students who could be her daughters,
but she soon found that "they trust me and our friendship is increasing,
which makes it possible for me to help them come closer to God and to
the Work."

Many of the students who came to Montelar offered to teach catechism
to small children in some of the poorest areas of Madrid, and the medical students organized a walk-in clinic in Valdebebas, a shanty town whose
inhabitants lacked even the most elementary medical services.

In the fall of 1959, Guadalupe began to live in the Montelar center.
It must have been a strain for a woman over forty years of age who had
serious heart problems to live in a center that was often full to overflowing
with four to five hundred high school girls whom Guadalupe described to
Escrivá as "being very modern looking and having very few serious things
in their heads." Guadalupe focused on "discovering behind their appearance the possibilities of each one." She rejoiced that many of them were
involved in social projects and that they were gradually coming to know
the spirit of Opus Dei. With evident relish, she told Escrivá that "a young
woman from a very well-known family who at the beginning of the school
year was a frivolous little girl came with a marvelous bouquet and blushed
as she asked if she could put it next to the tabernacle." Guadalupe was
delighted that "almost all the girls greet our Lord in the oratory when they
come into the house and make a short visit to the Blessed Sacrament when
they leave."

Guadalupe frequently looked back with some nostalgia on the time she
had spent in Rome close to St. Josemaría and the women who made up the
central governing body of Opus Dei. In a letter to Escrivá shortly before the
Feast of St. Joseph, she wrote that on St. Joseph's day she would

> pray with all my strength to the Lord for you and for all the Work, asking
> a year full of sanctity, of perseverance, and effectiveness. As I do on all
> special days, I will try to spend that day in Rome near you and my sisters,
> recalling what happened in Villa Tevere during the two years that I had the
> good fortune to spend there. Everything that has happened in my life is

wonderful, but having been in Rome is one of the things that I am most grateful for.

By the fall of 1960, Guadalupe was well enough to begin teaching chemistry and physics in the most prestigious public boys' high school in Madrid, Ramiro de Maeztu. Despite the difficulties a woman could expect to face teaching science to teenage boys, Guadalupe proved a popular teacher. She worked at Ramiro for three years, and after the first year also taught chemistry in the Women's Industrial School.

In 1962, Guadalupe became the director of the center where the women who directed Opus Dei's activities in Spain lived. She was not a member of the governing body but was responsible for the day-to-day life of the center. She told Escrivá:. "I try to help my sisters who belong to the Regional Advisory as much as possible. I have a great deal of affection for all of them. We have a good time in family life. In my mental prayer, I ask the Lord what he wants me to say to each one of them."

In 1963, Guadalupe began to combine her activities in Montelar and as the director of the center of the regional advisory with writing her dissertation in chemistry. She worked with great concentration but kept the door of her room open so anyone who wanted to speak to her could do so easily. She could not find a single lab with all the equipment she needed and had to work in several in Madrid, as well as in Valencia, Barcelona, and Bilbao. Her dissertation advisor was a woman who had obtained her own master's in 1932 at the age of nineteen and had gone on to win her PhD and do postgraduate work in Copenhagen. Guadalupe's dissertation was in applied chemistry, focusing on the use of rice hulls to make heat-resistant bricks for boilers and furnaces. She obtained her doctorate in July 1965.

Given her age and the length of the process for becoming a university professor in Spain, Guadalupe had no realistic possibility of getting a position at the university, so she focused on winning a permanent position in the Women's Industrial School where she had had a temporary appointment for four years. In 1968, she received a permanent position at the school, and she would remain there for the rest of her working life. At one point, her colleagues elected her director of the school, which at the time had about one thousand students, but Guadalupe's health was too fragile to permit her to accept the post.

Since the mid-1960s, some women of Opus Dei, encouraged by the Founder, had been working on professionalizing the Administration. From very early in the history of Opus Dei, St. Josemaría had insisted that the work of the Administration was not only vitally important for Opus Dei, (the "apostolate of the apostolates" he often called it) but a professional task that required serious education and training. Nonetheless, because of the rapid growth of Opus Dei's apostolic activities, most of the actual training had been improvised on the job.

By 1968, when Guadalupe became involved, the women's branch was rolling out a four-year degree program for women who would oversee Administrations. It was like home economics in the United States and many other countries, but with a focus on the special needs of Opus Dei centers. Guadalupe taught chemistry with an emphasis on fabrics and their care. To carry out experiments, she made arrangements to use the laboratories of several detergent manufacturers.

Failing Health

As the years went by, Guadalupe found it increasingly difficult to keep up the pace, but she did not slow down. As she wrote to Escrivá: "At times, I think I no longer have the strength that these activities and comings and goings require, but I continue doing them and it seems that the Lord wants me to because they all come out well. I can hardly find a way to say no." In 1973, she was awarded the medal of the International Committee on Rayon and Synthetic Fibers. The same year she privately published a book on laundry technology.

Gradually, Guadalupe's heart problems became more severe. A simple cold or flu could put her into fibrillation which required hospitalization. She could hardly talk after climbing one flight of stairs. For a while, she seemed to respond to medication, and most people were not aware of how sick she was. She did not complain and tried not to let her limitations show. She managed to continue to teach while serving as director of an Opus Dei center.

By the summer of 1975, however, her doctors began to think that the only solution was to replace damaged valves. She traveled to the hospital of the University of Navarre in Pamplona for extensive tests. Shortly before leaving Madrid, she wrote: "I am going to Pamplona to put myself in the hands of those who know, because it's the right thing to do. But I don't believe I will return. I'm not afraid of pain or death. If I'm afraid of anything, it is of not being yet sufficiently mature." On the way to Pamplona, she said to the person who accompanied her: "I am in God's hands. If he wants to cure me, I will be very happy to continue living to serve the Work. Furthermore, after successful surgery, I would be healthy and therefore could do things better than during these past years. But it would give me much joy to see God, to be with him."

From the hospital where she was undergoing tests, she wrote to Escrivá saying that she was praying for him and his intentions and asking him to pray for her "to behave well in whatever God may want of me now." On June 27, her brother Eduardo told her about Escrivá's death the previous day. He said, "One of two things will happen. You may rejoin him soon and see him at the side of God and of Our Lady. Or the Father may ask God to have you stay here. Both paths are good." Guadalupe immediately began to pray for Escrivá and for Álvaro del Portillo who was expected to succeed him. Her brother says, "She was aware of all the dangers of the surgery but accepted it without the slightest doubt, thinking that [if it was successful] she would be more useful to the Work, or if she did not survive the surgery and God wanted to take her life, that would be even better."

Finally, on July 1, 1975, she underwent open heart surgery. On her way into the operating room, she said with a smile, "Don't worry. I don't know if the Father will say to me, 'Guadalupe, come on up here' or 'Stay down there,' Either would be good."

In the first few days following the surgery, she seemed to be recovering well. She wrote to the acting head of Opus Dei, Álvaro del Portillo, "The prayer of my body has been offered, loved, accepted, and lived for the Father and for you. It was, perhaps, the only thing that this daughter and sister could do."

On July 12, in response to Del Portillo's request for much prayer and sacrifice for Escrivá's soul, Guadalupe wrote:

Since I found out on June 27 about the death of the Father, I offered the entire heart operation carried out on July 1 and my collaboration in it. I don't think I retreated at any moment. Quite the contrary, even in the long periods in which I was conscious in the operating room since part of the procedure was carried out under local anesthetic. This offering was made almost constantly as I maintained the presence of Christ, the Virgin, and the Father. I was able to do this naturally before and during the operation and in the postoperative period, which included three days of reanimation, exercises, massages, etc. I have offered my Communion and since the seventh [of July], mass, the daily norms, the three parts of the rosary, and many aspirations, especially: "Jesus, Joseph, and Mary, I give you my heart and my soul." I have offered my cheerfulness and words of affection for everyone as well: doctors, nurses, and all kinds of other people. I don't think that I have asked for anything or complained at all.

During the more than a month she was in the hospital, she made a point of talking with the people who cleaned her room and offered them candy. When they finished cleaning, she always thanked them. A young nurse who was beginning to specialize in cardiology spent many hours caring for Guadalupe. She wrote:

Guadalupe was different from the other patients. . . . She could hardly sleep because of her difficulty in breathing, nor could she make any effort. Nonetheless, I never heard her complain or comment at all about how much that situation must have cost her. I was amazed and did not know what to think. I distinguished clearly between a strong person, who puts up with illness, and Guadalupe, who accepted it in such an extraordinarily serene way.

Thanks to her experience with Guadalupe, the nurse returned to the Church and later joined Opus Dei.

In her notebook, Guadalupe wrote: "I accept death or life, whichever. I will be happy if I go to you soon, but I accept everything, including staying here to serve. . . . Whatever you want. I am serene. I am not afraid. I feel contrition for the good I have failed to do to my sisters. I'm a bit of a clown."

Eventually, Guadalupe was able to get up and even go outside to visit the nearby shrine of Our Lady of Fair Love. Suddenly, however, she suffered a major collapse on July 14. Two days later, on the feast of Our Lady of Mount Carmel, after kissing the crucifix and a picture of Our Lady, she stopped breathing.

Guadalupe was beatified in 2019.

CHAPTER NINE

Isidoro Zorzano:
Engineer

sidoro Zorzano was the first person to join Opus Dei and persevere. He lived his vocation to Opus Dei in the difficult circumstances of the Spanish Civil War and the immediate postwar years.

Early Life

Isidoro was born in Argentina in 1902, the third child of a Spanish couple who had moved there seeking a better life for themselves and their children. Although they did well financially in Argentina, when Isidoro was three they decided to return to their hometown of Logroño in northern Spain.

During his high-school years, Isidoro became friends with Josemaría Escrivá, whose family had moved to Logroño after the bankruptcy of their business. In 1912, Isidoro's father died. Despite this loss, the family continued to be reasonably well-off, and Isidoro was able to gain admission in 1921 to the highly competitive School of Industrial Engineering in Madrid.

Life changed radically for Isidoro in 1927 with the failure of the bank where most of his family's money was deposited. After being a carefree student, Isidoro suddenly found himself responsible for taking care of a financially stressed family. To help make ends meet, he found a part-time job as an accountant and started walking to school rather than taking the bus.

After graduating from engineering school in 1928, he found a job in the south of Spain, first at a shipyard in Cádiz and a few months later at the headquarters of the Andalusian Railroad in Málaga. As an industrial engineer, Isidoro had a brilliant future ahead of him, and several young women in Málaga thought he would be a good catch. But Isidoro felt that he needed to solve his family's precarious financial situation before considering marriage.

Moved by the desperate conditions of Spanish laborers, he began teaching mathematics and electricity in the evening at the Industrial School of Málaga, which trained young men to become skilled technicians. In addition to classes, he offered free tutoring sessions to students who needed extra help.

Vocation to Opus Dei

By 1930, Isidoro had begun to feel that God was asking something more of him. In keeping with the mentality of the time, he thought this must mean joining a religious order. But somehow that did not fit with the ideal he had formed of harmonizing dedication to God, professional work, and care for his family. In August, he received a note from his old friend and classmate Escrivá asking him to see him the next time he was in Madrid. Isidoro knew nothing about Opus Dei but was hopeful that Escrivá could help him see more clearly what God was asking of him.

On August 23, 1930, Zorzano took the train to Madrid, where he would transfer to another train to spend his vacation near Logroño. He went to see Escrivá but found that he was not at home. Rather than going directly to his next destination, he hung around the neighborhood. Meanwhile, Escrivá, who was visiting a sick person, began to feel uneasy for no apparent reason and cut his visit short. On the way home and for no specific reason, rather than taking the most direct route he went somewhat out of his way and ran into Zorzano on the sidewalk. Isidoro immediately told Escrivá about his concerns and they agreed to meet and talk at length that afternoon.

Isidoro explained his situation, and Escrivá told him about Opus Dei, which involved a full dedication to God without abandoning one's profession or place in the world. Isidoro joined Opus Dei immediately. That evening he continued his trip with a sense of peace and joy. As he wrote, "I feel completely comforted now. I find my spirit invaded by a sense of well-being and peace that I have never felt before."

When Isidoro joined Opus Dei, he had little religious education, not much interior life, and only the sketchiest idea about the spirit of Opus Dei. He clearly needed to be in close contact with the Founder, but that was not to be because his job required him to live in Málaga. For several years, his contact with Escrivá would be limited to letters and occasional trips to

Madrid. Within the limits imposed by distance, St. Josemaría took advantage of every opportunity to help Zorzano develop a more robust interior life. In a letter written in November 1930, for example, he encouraged him: "Look. To be what we and our Lord want, we have to lay the foundations before all else in *prayer* and *expiation* (sacrifice). To pray. Let me repeat, never omit your meditation when you get up. And offer every day as expiation all the annoying things and sacrifices of the day."

At first, Isidoro received Communion only on Sundays, and not even every Sunday, because he often organized Sunday hikes in the nearby mountains. He was able to get to Mass in nearby villages, but the schedule of the trains hikers took to the starting points of their hikes, combined with the rules then in effect about the Eucharistic fast, made it impractical to receive Communion.

Initially, Isidoro seems to have focused on taking part in as many apostolic activities and social works as he could, but gradually he came to understand better the primary importance of mental prayer and the sacraments. By the end of 1932, he was receiving Communion every day. Soon he was also giving formation and guidance to a new member of the Work, Josemaría González Barredo, who was teaching in the town of Linares, about 150 miles (250 km) away.

With the opening of the first Opus Dei center in Madrid in 1933, the Work's need for money increased sharply. Isidoro sent a large percentage of his salary to the center, to the point of leaving his bank account virtually empty.

As Spain drew closer to civil war, the railroad shops where Isidoro worked became increasingly radicalized. Isidoro's fairness, sense of justice, and concern for his workers and their families won the respect and even the affection of most of the men who worked under him. Many Anarchist and Communist workers, however, viewed practicing Catholics as dangerous political opponents. Isidoro might be just, considerate, and even kind, but his Catholicism triggered their antipathy. One day in the shop, a crude sign appeared: "Death to Isidoro." Isiodoro's reaction was: "We need to pardon [those who made the sign] because they don't know what they are saying."

During the 1935–1936 school year, Isidoro decided that he needed to move to Madrid so that he could receive more intense personal formation, help run the DYA Academy and Residence, and give a hand with the formation of the young members of the Work. A final reason for moving was the extremely radicalized political environment in Málaga generally, and specifically in the railroad shops, which made life unpleasant and posed a real personal threat to Isidoro. On May 22, 1936, Isidoro requested leave from the railroad, and on June 7 he arrived in Madrid. He found in the DYA Academy and Residence an environment of fraternity, work, and good humor that contrasted sharply with the violence and tension in the streets. On June 17, DYA purchased a new building. Isidoro helped with the move, which was completed by July 13.

The Outbreak of the Spanish Civil War

Four days later, parts of the Spanish army rose against the left-wing government. Although the authors of the uprising had in mind a quick coup, the uprising failed in most major cities and Spain soon found itself in a civil war that would last almost three years and cost five hundred thousand lives.

In Madrid, as in most other areas where the military uprising failed, the attempted coup triggered a political, social, and economic revolution led by Socialists, Anarchists, and Communists. The Republican government, in a desperate effort to put down the uprising, distributed arms to militia groups associated with Socialist and Anarchist trade unions. They quickly took control, and the government temporarily lost all effective control of the streets. Militia groups confiscated property, ranging from factories to private automobiles, burned churches and other church property, and assassinated those they considered political enemies, including approximately seven thousand priests and religious. In Madrid, during the civil war, some seven hundred priests and religious were assassinated, more than 40 percent of the total living in the capital at the outbreak of the war. Almost all these assassinations took place in 1936, mostly in August. At that time, being a priest, or simply being known as an active Catholic, meant mortal danger.

Isidoro was not well-known in Madrid and having been born in Argentina would provide him some protection, but he was vulnerable because left-wing workers in Málaga sent a denunciation complete with pictures to their comrades in Madrid. He decided to hide out in his family's apartment. The Argentine Embassy gave the Zorzanos a sign to put on the door of their apartment which said that it was under the protection of Argentina. This provided some limited protection. For approximately two months Isidoro stayed at home without setting foot outside.

Opus Dei's Go-Between

At the end of those two months, Zorzano had lost quite a bit of weight due to the scarcity of food in Madrid. He had changed his haircut and had purchased dark prescription glasses. His appearance had changed enough that he was no longer in much danger of being recognized as the man in the picture sent from Málaga. He had obtained a birth certificate from the embassy showing that he had been born in Buenos Aires and an armband with the colors of the Argentine flag. Together they might be sufficient to convince militia patrols to let him pass, but if he were arrested, they would not do him much good. For a year after he emerged from hiding, he was not able to get an Argentine passport because Argentina issued them only to men who had done their military service in Argentina.

When he emerged from the house, Isidoro began to act as a liaison between St. Josemaría and the other members of the Work. In retrospect, it is clear that by this time, the systematic execution of priests and other Catholics had largely come to an end. The danger of being imprisoned for being an active Catholic, however, was still great.

At the time, Isidoro probably felt he was in danger, not only of being imprisoned but of losing his life. He willingly ran those risks, however, to contribute to the survival of the newborn Opus Dei by fulfilling the role of liaison given to him by the Founder. Escrivá, for his part, seems to have overestimated how much protection having been born in Argentina conferred on Isidoro and consequently underestimated how precarious his situation was.

During the fall of 1936, St. Josemaría hid out in a private insane asylum run by a friend. Isidoro visited him virtually every day to receive his support and guidance, bring him wine for celebrating Mass, keep him informed about the situation of other members of the Work, and receive messages to pass on to them. He also began to visit frequently the members of the Work who had been imprisoned. A few mothers and wives of political prisoners visited them from time to time, but almost no men were willing to run the danger of entering a prison to visit a political prisoner. Hernández Garnica, whom Zorzano visited almost every day in prison, recalls: "At a time when no men went to visit prisoners in jail because it was too dangerous, he visited me. He came repeatedly to the San Antón prison and did all he could to get me released on grounds that I had a kidney problem." When Hernández Garnica was transferred to a prison in Valencia, Zorzano wrote to the members of the Work there urging them to see what they could do to help him.

Isidoro also went frequently to visit Hernández Garnica's family to give them news and try to console them. Hernández Garnica's mother says, "When we told him that he was running great risks, he said he was not afraid because he was an Argentine citizen. But we all knew that many people had lost their lives despite being foreign."

Isidoro also frequently visited members of the Work who had sought asylum in foreign embassies. This too involved considerable risk, since the militia units that guarded the embassies looked with suspicion on visitors. Vicente Rodríguez Casado had found asylum in the Norwegian Embassy. He recalls that Isidoro

> talked with enormous confidence in God and with great naturalness and simplicity about what the Lord would do through the Work very soon if we were faithful. My faith grew enormously in contact with his. I had not lost my faith, thanks be to God, and I had complete security. But seeing him and hearing him, my faith, which was abstract, became concrete, and ideals became realities.

When Rodríguez Casado tried to impress upon Zorzano the danger involved in visiting the embassy so frequently, Isidoro simply "smiled and told me that if we use the means, God could not fail to assist us."

Zorzano also visited Álvaro del Portillo, the future Prelate of Opus Dei, in the Mexican Embassy. Álvaro says:

> We spent a long time talking about the things that were important to us: the situation of the Father, and that of all the rest of the members of the Work. . . . I recall his strikingly supernatural vision of so much tragedy, his great confidence in God, and the naturalness and simplicity with which he expressed his hope. I also recall his security that if we were faithful God would soon bring forth great fruits of salvation, of souls, and of peace through the Work. All this did me a great deal of good.

In addition to visiting the members of the Work who were in Madrid, Zorzano tried to locate and correspond with those who were in other parts of Spain. They sent their letters to the Founder through Isidoro. Because of censorship, all the correspondence had to be carried on in a sort of code that arose spontaneously among them. Thus, for instance, they referred to Escrivá as "the Grandfather," the Work as "the Grandfather's business," Our Lord as "Don Manuel," and the Blessed Virgin as "Don Manuel's mother."

The Legation of Honduras

In mid-March 1937, Zorzano took St. Josemaría and his brother Santiago from the insane asylum where they had been hiding out to the Legation of Honduras, where several members of the Work had found refuge. From then on, Isidoro visited the legation frequently. He brought not only information about the other members of the Work but also the small amounts of food and other supplies that he could assemble, including the wine Escrivá needed to celebrate Mass every day. Isidoro also took advantage of his visits to seek advice from Escrivá and to receive assignments from him.

Isidoro's most important function was to serve as the conduit between the Founder and the other members, who very much needed his support and encouragement. During those months, Escrivá preached meditations frequently to the members of the Work who were with him at the legation. Immediately after each meditation, one of them wrote down as best he could the main ideas. Isidoro collected these texts which he used for his own mental prayer and made them available to the other members in Madrid. For a time, he brought the texts with him when he visited Vicente Rodríguez Casado in the Norwegian Embassy, but when the militiamen who controlled access to the embassy began searching visitors more rigorously, he decided he could no longer do so. Instead, he memorized the texts and recited them to Vicente. He also began to share them with José María Albareda, a soil scientist in his mid-thirties who gave signs of a possible vocation to Opus Dei.

In his letters to the members of the Work outside Madrid, Isidoro included short texts from Escrivá. In May 1937, for instance, he passed on to Francisco Botella in Valencia what the Founder had written to him:

> You give me the impression of being discouraged. I find that you are crest-fallen, annoyed . . . and tired. I can't recognize you. If you are children, children insist stubbornly when they meet obstacles until they overcome them, and encounter great satisfaction from achieving their goals [despite the obstacles]. If you are men, men grow in the face of obstacles and smile. . . . They convert into a manly sport what was a painful duty and always end up satisfied whether they achieve their goals or not (which doesn't really matter).

In June 1937, he wrote again to Botella:

> My grandfather [Escrivá] never stops repeating the refrain "joy with peace." His words seem to go straight to the heart. What we have to do is use all the means at our disposal in all of the tasks entrusted to us. Whether things turn out well or poorly is not terribly important. The outcome will always be for the best, provided that we let ourselves be guided by Don Manuel [Our Lord].

A few weeks after the Founder took refuge in the Legation of Honduras, the Argentine Embassy told Zorzano that since he had been born in Argentina, he was eligible for evacuation to another country. Madrid continued to be bombarded, finding food was increasingly difficult, and Zorzano continued to be at risk of being arrested and thrown in prison. The prospect of escaping from all of this was extremely attractive, but Isidoro realized that Opus Dei and its founder needed him in Madrid.

Zorzano consulted Escrivá about what he should do. Escrivá, who continued to underestimate the dangers to which Isidoro was exposed, sketched out the advantages of staying in Madrid but encouraged Isidoro to act with "the greatest freedom." Zorzano normally did not act without considering matters at length. In this case, however, after talking with his relatives, he decided quickly to remain in Madrid. He did not even explain to St. Josemaría that he did not have papers showing that he was an Argentine citizen and was, therefore, at greater risk of being arrested and perhaps executed than Escrivá seemed to think. St. Josemaría was overjoyed at his courage and generosity: "I did not expect less from you, Isidoro. Your decision is what Our Lord undoubtedly wants."

In early April 1937, Juan Jiménez Vargas, a member of the Work who was serving in the Republican Army, decided that Escrivá needed him in Madrid. He deserted from his brigade and went directly to Isidoro's home. He recalls that "despite the danger to himself and his family of giving shelter to a deserter at that time, he did not show the least fear or indecision." Zorzano went to Jiménez Vargas's home to search for civilian clothes and managed to arrange for him to take refuge with Escrivá in the Legation of Honduras.

During the early months of 1937, in addition to his ongoing efforts to stay in touch with the other members of the Work and encourage them to remain faithful to their vocation, Zorzano dedicated himself to three major tasks: trying to arrange for an embassy to evacuate the members of the Work in the Legation of Honduras; preparing the paperwork to claim damages to DYA's property from the Spanish government; and finding food and other items for the members of the Work and their families.

Attempts to Arrange Evacuation

Like most people, Escrivá and the other members of the Work had originally assumed that the war would be relatively short. As they saw it initially, the problem was simply to survive until the war ended and they were able once again to take up the apostolates of Opus Dei. As 1936 gave way to 1937, however, it began to appear that the war might drag on indefinitely. Escrivá and the others became increasingly anxious to escape from Madrid and reach the Nationalist zone, where they would be free to carry out their apostolate openly.

By early 1937, more than 10,000 people had found asylum in an embassy or consulate in Madrid. In January and February 1937, the Argentine Embassy evacuated some 300 refugees to whom it had granted asylum. In March, the Mexican Embassy evacuated 600 persons. Between March and July 1937, several European and South American embassies succeeded in evacuating some 3,000 refugees.

During the spring of 1937, diplomatic evacuation appeared the best way for members of the Work to escape from Madrid. The most obvious course was for the Legation of Honduras, where they had received asylum, to arrange their evacuation. There were, however, serious difficulties. The head of the Honduran diplomatic mission was only an honorary counsel, and the Honduran consulate did not have the rank of an embassy but rather the lesser status of a legation. More important, the government of Honduras had broken diplomatic relations with the Spanish Republic and recognized Franco's government. Despite these obstacles, for a time the members of the Work continued to hope that the Honduran legation would be able to evacuate them.

At the end of April, the government of the Republic refused to grant visas to the Honduran consul and his family. Escrivá did not immediately give up all hope of being evacuated through the good offices of Honduras, but he began to urge Zorzano to find another solution and to find it quickly:

> "It is essential to keep on top of things to the very end . . . [because] just a delay in the paperwork can delay the success of the project, and even impede it. I think I'm speaking clearly. Don't leave things for tomorrow. Today!!! I don't care whether it is Chile or China! That's all the same to me. But do something."

Working through whatever contacts he could find, Isidoro tried to interest the embassies of Chile, Turkey, Panama, and Switzerland in evacuating the members of the Work, but without success. Escrivá continued to urge him and the other members to leave no stone unturned, but he also told them: "I am very pleased with you and more pleased with the One who allows you to encounter difficulties, humiliations, and hassles. This means things are going well."

In early June 1937, the Republican government announced that in the future it would allow only women, children, and the elderly to be evacuated. This put an end to any lingering hopes that the members of the Work could escape from Madrid through diplomatic channels.

Food and Supplies

As the war dragged on, food became increasingly scarce in Madrid. Zorzano struggled to find food and distribute it to the members of the Work and their families. He received some supplies from the members living in eastern Spain where food was more available. Packages also arrived from a family in the little town of Damiel, about a hundred miles south of Madrid. A member of the Work in Madrid who was employed in the offices of a prison was able to buy some food in the prison's commissary. Isidoro himself was able to purchase some items in the commissary of the Argentine Embassy. For some months, he also went to militia barracks with false documents and drew rations. As the scarcity of food increased, however, officials in the barracks began to suspect that something was wrong and arrested a friend who had helped Isidoro, so he had to abandon this source.

Isidoro sent whatever he could obtain to the Legation of Honduras, to other members of the Work in Madrid, and to the families of the members of the Work in Madrid, but the quantities he could assemble were pitifully inadequate. Most of the packages he received weighed only about two pounds (one kilogram). The little food he was able to get was limited to garbanzos and other beans (often insect-infested), potatoes, olive oil, and condensed milk. Nonetheless, in a city where milk, fresh vegetables, meat, and fish could be purchased only with a doctor's prescription and where food of all kinds, including bread, was in very short supply, Isidoro's efforts helped to lessen the threat of starvation.

Reparations for Damages to DYA's Property

Toward the end of April 1937, Escrivá learned that one of the officials of the Legation of Honduras had filed a claim against the Republican government for damage to property he owned in Madrid. Escrivá immediately thought that the DYA Academy and Residence should also file a claim. Isidoro was the logical person to undertake this task because he was president of the nonprofit that owned the building, was relatively free to move around Madrid, and could request the support of the Argentine Embassy.

Together with Sainz de los Terreros, Isidoro immediately set about drafting a claim and making a list of the items that had been stolen or destroyed. It soon became clear that the Argentine embassy was not getting involved, among other reasons because Isidoro had not fulfilled his compulsory military service.

Nonetheless, Isidoro worked diligently to prepare a claim. He sent copies of the documents he had drafted to Pedro Casciaro in the hope that he might be able to interest the British Embassy in supporting the claim since Pedro's grandfather was a British citizen. He also briefly considered trying to involve someone he thought was from Chile in the hopes that the Chilean Embassy might back the request, but it turned out that the person had lived in Chile but was not Chilean. He tried getting a Bolivian and a Paraguayan involved, but these efforts were also in vain. Escrivá encouraged Isidoro and the others involved in the project to keep trying. Isidoro took this not simply as encouragement, but as a directive he should obey, even though Escrivá indicated that he understood the efforts might fail: "Whether you achieve anything or not, what tranquility for us all to know that we have done everything possible to defend the patrimony of DYA."

Failing Health

Zorzano's health gradually deteriorated, undermined by lack of food, cold, and the many concerns that weighed upon him. Psychologically, he suffered from the tension caused by frequently being caught running errands out in the streets during bombardments. His determination to carry out faithfully all the assignments Escrivá gave him also weighed on him. Many of the tasks, like arranging the evacuation of the refugees and convincing the government to pay for the damages to DYA's building, were virtually impossible to carry out, but Isidoro suffered when his efforts failed. In a letter to Casciaro in June, he commented, "Recently, we don't succeed at anything. If we are asked to take care of something, it turns out that we fail."

By late summer 1937, Isidoro was down to approximately 105 pounds (48 kg). He was so weak that after walking a short distance he had to sit on a bench to regain his strength. He attributed his ability to keep going forward despite all these difficulties to the Eucharist. Most days he was able to attend Mass in a nearby apartment. At the end of Mass, the priest gave him consecrated hosts so that he could distribute Communion to other people and receive himself if the next day he could not make it to Mass. He noted in his diary: "It is something very impressive to carry Our Lord, to be converted into a monstrance. It is a magnificent way of being constantly aware of his presence because of the precautions that you have to take to carry him with the dignity the King of Kings merits."

Director of Opus Dei in Madrid

Isidoro learned in spring of 1937 that in Barcelona it was possible to engage men who had been smugglers in peacetime to guide groups across the Pyrenees

Mountains into France. From there, it would be easy to cross back into the Nationalist-controlled part of Spain. The trek through the mountains would be arduous and anyone caught in the attempt would be executed, but it seemed the best available option.

By the end of September, preparations were complete. Escrivá, six members of the Work, and Tomás Alvira, who would eventually become the first married member, made their way to Barcelona, established contact with a smuggler, and finally made their way through the Pyrenees Mountains into France and from there into the Nationalist zone of Spain. Zorzano stayed behind in Madrid as the director of the eight members who for one reason or another had to remain.

Isidoro worked diligently to alleviate the isolation of the members of the Work stuck in the Republican zone. He frequently visited those he could reach, wrote to others, and encouraged them to write to each other. For a time, he visited every day those who were living in Madrid, because "we feel more and more each day the need for this union to cure the deficiencies of the isolated life we have lived until a short time ago." During these visits, they talked primarily about the Work. "We are so concerned about it that we barely talk about the events of the war."

Isidoro transmitted to others, and particularly to other members of the Work, his sense of prayer. He wrote to Paco Botella for instance: "Now that we face so many difficulties, we should spend more time with D. Manuel [Jesus] and tell him about absolutely all our little things. We should make him our confidant and demonstrate to him, in every way that we can, our love and affection." As a way of promoting a sense of unity among the members of the Work, Isidoro suggested:

> Although we are separated, we can do something together that will unite us more, namely we can all recite the Preces [brief prayers composed by St. Josemaría and recited daily by members of the Work] at a fixed time, for example, eight in the evening. What do you think? United, not in a single place, but by the same spirit.

The three members of the Work who had remained in the Legation of Honduras because it would be too dangerous for them to emerge began to press Isidoro to allow them to enlist in the Republican Army and attempt to cross the front lines to the Nationalist zone. Isidoro stoutly rejected their requests, stressing "the advantage of waiting without exposing yourselves to dangerous adventures in which the risk is extraordinarily high and the possibility of success merely hypothetical." In response to their insistence that they needed to get to a place where they would be free to do the apostolate of Opus Dei, he responded, "Are you sure that you are less useful where you are?"

In mid-June 1938, the refugees insisted again, even though they had recently learned that someone who had left the Honduran consulate, enlisted in the Republican Army, and tried to cross the lines had been killed in the attempt. They were astounded when Isidoro responded, "With the help of Don Manuel [Our Lord] I have thought carefully about your projects. . . . I think that you can carry them out and that Don Manuel and Doña Maria [the Blessed Virgin] will answer your desires, which we share."

What the refugees did not know, and what Isidoro did not reveal until he was on his deathbed years later, was that praying before a crucifix he had received from Our Lord the assurance that the project would be successful and had even learned the date on which the group would cross the lines. (Escrivá had also learned in prayer the date of their arrival in the Nationalist zone.)

Between when they left the Legation of Honduras and when they were shipped to the front, the former refugees spent several months in Madrid. During that time, they were in constant contact with Isidoro. According to Del Portillo:

> Whenever possible we went to his house or we got together in a boardinghouse on Goya street. There we made our prayer and talked about the things of our family. During those months, Isidoro did us a great deal of good with his conversation, with his dealings with us, and above all with his example. His spirits were always the same. He always had the same confidence in God and the Work. And he always had a cheerful gravity and naturalness.

Many days they went together to the barracks to which the three former refugees had been assigned by the army. They sat on the ground to share the scant rations they were given and talk. On feast days of the Blessed Virgin, they celebrated by distributing their rations to the poor as a way of "following the Father's custom of giving something to the poor on Mary's feast days."

One day after eating, they began commenting about the disasters and advantages of the war. One of them recalls that

> Isidoro began to draw up a list of the good things that the war had brought us and was bringing us. He saw it in a completely supernatural way, as a magnificent opportunity that God was providing us to sanctify ourselves. Full of joy he enumerated the virtues—above all, charity and fraternal union—that under those circumstances and through the grace of God we were growing in. I recall that when we got home we were full of joy and interiorly gave thanks with our whole heart to God for all the gifts he was giving us.

The End of the Civil War

By the beginning of 1939, it was becoming obvious that the war would soon end with a Nationalist victory. The major question was whether the Republic could negotiate some type of agreement or would be forced to surrender unconditionally. In early 1939, the government of the Republic arrested a hundred young Spanish men who were also citizens of other countries, on grounds that they were simply trying to avoid military service. Isidoro was among those picked up.

He was held for a day before being instructed to go every day to have his passport stamped. For five days in mid-January, he took refuge in the Argentine Embassy. When he left, embassy personnel threatened to withdraw Argentina's protection if he insisted on remaining in Madrid. Isidoro, however, decided to stay because he was needed there by his own family, by the members of the Work, by the families of the members, and by friends. At the end of March 1939, heavy fighting broke out between Republican forces that wanted to surrender and those that wanted to continue fighting. This further weakened the Republic, and on March 28 Nationalist troops occupied Madrid. It was the end of a 982-day nightmare during which Isidoro risked his life in the service of others. They had been days of isolation and of hunger in which he sowed serenity and good humor despite the lack of any natural reason to be cheerful. His recourse to Our Lord and Our Lady, and his loyalty to Escrivá, had maintained him.

Working for the Railroad and as Administrator of Opus Dei

At the end of the civil war in spring 1939, Isidoro went back to work for the railroad as head of the Office of Research on Rolling Stock and Locomotives, but based in Madrid, not Málaga. He worked there until the fall of 1942, when illness forced him to retire.

Isidoro had learned from St. Josemaría the importance of doing his work as well as possible because he was offering it to God. One of his colleagues at the railroad recalls that he "always stood out for the exemplary way in which he fulfilled all his duties, even in little things, because nothing that he needed to do seemed to him of little importance." He was among the first to arrive at the office and rarely took off time at midmorning, as did most of his colleagues, to go to the bar for a cup of coffee or a glass of beer.

Zorzano's immediate supervisor was ill-tempered and hard to get along with, but Isidoro accepted his outbursts with a smile. He was not, however, afraid to defend his subordinates if he felt that his supervisor was treating them unfairly. He took great interest in those who worked for him and tried to help them develop their professional skills. When someone was unable to carry out a task, he did not take it away and give it to someone else, but rather coached and taught the person until he learned how to do it. He also helped the people who worked for him to prepare for the competitive exams on which most promotions depended.

He was equally open to employees of all political persuasions. One of his workers had been purged as a "Red," but subsequently cleared. Most people avoided him, perhaps out of fear that in the highly charged atmosphere of Franco's Spain they might themselves be considered suspect. Isidoro not only did not keep his distance from him but helped him find a second job so he could supplement his income. At Isidoro's death, the people who reported to him signed a declaration saying that he "was known as a saint because of his extreme goodness."

Starting in July 1939, Zorzano's schedule called for him to work from seven in the morning to two in the afternoon. He had to rise very early by Spanish standards in order to be able to do his morning meditation and hear Mass before going to work. On the other hand, this schedule made it possible for him to dedicate afternoons and evenings to his responsibilities as General Administrator of Opus Dei.

Among his first tasks as General Administrator was overseeing the installation of a new university residence in several rented apartments on Jenner Street in Madrid. The task was complicated by the lack of money and shortages of almost everything in post-civil war Madrid. Isidoro spent a great deal of time going from shop to shop looking for furniture, housewares, and even food for the residence.

For help in solving the many problems he faced as Opus Dei's administrator, Isidoro often turned to the Blessed Virgin. Shortly before his death, talking to a young man who had just joined Opus Dei, he told him about earlier times.

> We didn't have a house nor clothing nor anything at all; just love and faith in the most holy Virgin who, little by little, helped us overcome the difficulties. Those of you who are younger have come across the Work already underway and even flourishing. All of this that you see is the fruit of Our Lady's great love for us. We have to love her with our whole soul, with a love infinitely greater than all the loves of the earth. How well she has treated us!

Between his professional work and his duties as administrator, Isidoro was extremely busy, but he found time to accompany Escrivá and other members of the Work on trips to other cities where they could meet students and explain Opus Dei to them. He also took advantage of every opportunity to get to know the young men who joined Opus Dei after the civil war and to pass its spirit on to them.

St. Josemaría told the members of the Work in the recently opened center in Valencia that he had asked Isidoro to visit them "so we could learn to do things right." During his visit, Isidoro repaired various things in the house and taught them how to do the accounts and how to live poverty in very small things; for instance, using pieces of paper that already had something written on one side. He urged them to correct even small mistakes in the accounts, not because a couple of *pesetas* were important, but because the spirit of Opus Dei requires showing love of God by doing small things well. He was careful never to wound them and praised what they had done well, or at least their goodwill.

Despite being the oldest member of the Work, Isidoro tried not to stand out. He rarely talked about things he had done during the civil war. He consulted Del Portillo, the Secretary General of the Work, about many issues, even though Del Portillo was younger and had joined Opus Dei after he did.

Final Illness and Death

In the fall of 1940, Isidoro moved to a newly opened center in Madrid. The house was large and handsome but in ill repair. During the winter of 1940–1941, the heat did not work. Isidoro suffered from the cold and from other health problems. Although was already very thin, he lost weight and had little strength. He began to find going up the stairs exhausting. In July 1941, he was diagnosed with Hodgkin lymphoma and given two years to live. Although he was in considerable pain and unable to sleep, for a year he was able to continue working and carrying on a normal life, including fulfilling his duties as Administrator of Opus Dei and taking responsibility for furnishing another new center in Madrid.

Just before Christmas 1942, Isidoro made a retreat preached by Escrivá. After a meditation on death, he remained in the oratory. Thinking that he was alone, he said softly, "Lord, I'm ready." Shortly thereafter, he entered a clinic. Escrivá told him that he had days or at most a few months left to live. His immediate reaction was a look of repugnance, but he soon reacted and asked Escrivá what he wanted him to take care of from heaven and what he should pray for.

In the clinic, he wanted only books that talked about God. When visitors came, he sometimes turned on the radio, but once they left, he turned it off. He had to force himself to eat, but he did so "thinking of the many needs of the Church." His doctor told other patients about Isidoro, and concretely about "his attitude toward death, his courage in the face of pain, his remarkable patience and his constant smile."

One doctor frequently told him that he was getting better. At first, Isidoro pretended to believe him, but finally, he said,

> I very much appreciate your good intentions, but there's no point in trying
> to deceive me. I realize that for a long time now there's been nothing you

can do for me. I am in God's hands and very content. . . . There can be no doubt that it is the Lord who gives me this peace and this joy. No doubt he is the one.

Toward the very end of his life, he confided to another member of the Work:

Our obligation is to fulfill the duty of each moment. My only duty is to suffer. . . . I don't have to worry about anything else. I suffer a great deal. It is remarkable how much you can suffer. At times, it seems you can't suffer more, but the Lord gives greater strength. What a joy to think that one is useful. Suffering with supernatural spirit is how we have to move the Work forward. Pain purifies. The longer the trial, the better. In that way, we will purify ourselves more.

Isidoro did not request special attention. The doctor in charge of the clinic says that he does not recall Isidoro ever calling for him to come. If a nurse was taking care of him and he heard a call bell ring he would say, "Why don't you go see what they need? I can wait." By the end of his life, the nurses found it impossible to understand what he was asking for. After bringing him several things that were not what he needed, they would say that they were sorry but could not understand him. He remained very calm and showed no sign of being upset.

Isidoro died on July 15, 1943.

Isidoro's cause of beatification was opened by the Archdiocese of Madrid in 1948. In 2015, Pope Francis approved a decree declaring that Isidoro had lived the virtues in a heroic manner.

CHAPTER TEN

❧

Montserrat Grases:
Teenager

M ontserrat Grases had been a member of Opus Dei for a little over a year when she died of bone cancer at age seventeen. During that brief time, she gave a stunning example of love for God and others and of accepting joyfully the suffering God sent her. Three short prayers which she prayed frequently sum up her spiritual life: "I am a daughter of God." "Whatever you want. When you want. As you want it." And "Omnia in bonum" (Everything is for the good).

Childhood

Montse was born in 1941, the second child of a middle-class Barcelona family. She was the oldest girl in the family, which eventually grew to include nine children. Her parents, both of whom belonged to Opus Dei, strove to create what St. Josemaría described as "a bright and cheerful Christian home," where the children learned to pray and to love God in an atmosphere of freedom and trust. Montse's father frequently said to the children, "Tell me what happened. I don't mind your having broken something. I do want you to always be sincere and to tell the truth, no matter what."

Montse was an average student but quite athletic. During summers spent with the family in Seva, a small town in the mountains about forty miles north of Barcelona, she bicycled, swam in the river, and went on hikes with friends. She loved dancing the traditional Catalan Sardana and was a vigorous tennis player.

Especially as a young girl, Montse was easily provoked and her older brother enjoyed getting a rise out of her. As time went by, she gradually overcame her tendency to be annoyed. She was a natural leader and organizer, but she preferred doing things she knew her friends enjoyed rather than things she personally liked. Several of her friends noticed that "she gave way easily."

One of her closest friends describes her as "very spontaneous and open." "Everyone," she says, "found her attractive. Her simplicity and joy attracted people. She was very optimistic, and therefore she was pleasant to be with." The same friend found that "she was attentive to the smallest things that interested others. She was concerned about the problems of others."

Another person who knew her well recalls that

> her defining characteristic was knowing how to live for others. She was one of those generous people who always offered to help you with everything. Did something need to be carried? Montse carried it. Did someone need to be helped? Montse helped them. You could count on her for everything. . . . She was generous, very generous. She helped you in everything she could and she did it . . . without making herself noticed. She knew how to do and disappear. . . . This attitude might seem natural in an older person, but I was struck by finding it in a girl as young as she was. She was attentive to the big things and little things. For example, if there

weren't enough chairs in the room for everyone, she went out, got a chair, put it in place, and then sat down.

First Contact with Opus Dei

When Montse was thirteen, her mother took her for the first time to Llar, a center of the women's branch of Opus Dei which offered girls training in household skills like sewing, ironing, and cooking, as well as classes in French, English, and piano. Montse was one of the youngest girls at the center, but she quickly made friends and fit in easily. In addition to the classes she attended, she looked forward to informal get-togethers in which she spent time with the other girls. On weekends and holidays, the girls often went on short excursions. Montse especially enjoyed hiking in the nearby mountains.

The chaplain of the center preached meditations on Saturday evenings, and from time to time the director of the center or one of the staff members gave a talk on virtues and practical Christian life. According to one of her best friends, Montse "made the spirit of Opus Dei her own, and soon became enthusiastic with the idea of being holy in the midst of the world, of sanctifying work and helping others along the path to sanctity." She joined a group of girls who taught catechism classes to children in a shantytown.

Montse invited many of her friends to attend activities at Llar. In the fall of 1956, she attended a retreat preached by a priest of Opus Dei. During the retreat, a friend asked her if she had ever thought she might have a vocation to Opus Dei. Montse was startled and annoyed and stopped going to Llar. Both her mother and the girls at the center respected her decision and refrained from calling her or inviting her to activities. After a few days, however, she decided to return.

Her older brother Enrique's decision to enter the seminary and begin studying for the priesthood made a deep impression on Montse. She began to think more about how she could come closer to God. With the help of the meditations and talks at Llar, and with the personal guidance she received there, she began to develop an interior life of prayer and mortification in small things. For example, one day, she said to her friend Rosa Maria, "I like to look at everything. I walk down the street, and I look. I pass in front of a bookstore, and I look. I see a dress store, and I look. I've been told that I could mortify myself in these little things." A week later she told Rosa Maria that she was meeting with some success in not looking at so many things. At about the same time, her knee began to hurt. She mentioned it to her parents, but neither she nor they thought it was anything serious. She thought of it as one more thing she could offer to our Lord.

In November 1957, Montse again attended a retreat preached by a priest of Opus Dei. When she came back from the retreat, her younger brother noticed a change in her:

> She tried to avoid quarreling. She no longer got so upset about the ridiculous little things that used to really get to her. And if we still fought, she tried to put a quick end to it. She even began to act as a peacemaker among the children when some conflict arose. At roughly the same time I also began to notice new ways in which she lived charity. She began to serve as a volunteer nurse at the Red Cross hospital and to visit and console a friend of hers who was very ill. Montse had always been cheerful but now her cheerfulness was more noticeable and above all more constant.

The retreat affected Montse deeply and gave her the strength and inspiration to rein in and direct her personality. Before, her brothers had loved to tease her, but now she stopped losing her temper and simply remained quiet when one of her brothers or sisters called her a name or pulled some other prank to get her upset.

Joining Opus Dei

During the November 1957 retreat, her friend Rosa, who was crippled by polio, suggested once again that she consider in her prayer whether God might be calling her to Opus Dei. A few days before Christmas, after praying about it for some time, Montse told her mother that she thought she had a vocation to Opus Dei. To respect her freedom and that of their other children, neither her mother nor her father had told them that they belonged to Opus Dei. Even then, when Montse was considering her vocation, they said nothing about their own vocation so as not to influence her decision.

Her mother suggested that she talk it over with the priest she normally saw for confession and tell her father. Montse was not eager to tell him, but eventually she did. He responded:

> "Look, Montse, the only thing I can say is that a vocation is a marvelous gift that God gives us. It supposes a decision that we have to meditate on very carefully in the presence of God. The only thing your mother and I can do in this case is to pray. Since we are so close to Christmas, all three of us can pray to the Child Jesus so that he makes you see clearly what your vocation is. What do you think?"

Montse's main objection to joining Opus Dei was the fear that she might not persevere. Her friend agreed that she could not know for sure but urged her to put her trust in God. If he was calling her, he would give her the grace she needed to persevere. After thinking and praying about it a bit more, Montse told the director of Llar that she wanted to join the Work. Opus Dei's statutes provide that from a legal point of view, Montse would not be able to become a member until she was at least eighteen years old. In the meantime, she could begin to live its spirit with a sense that she was responding to God's call. Despite her youth, the director was convinced that her decision was mature, carefully thought out in the presence of God, and free. So, she told her to go ahead and write a letter to the head of Opus Dei, telling him of her desire to join. Her letter was very brief and to the point:

> Father,
>
> My name is Montse Grases. I am still very young, but I have been coming to Llar for a long time, and little by little I have gotten to know the Work which has ended up filling me with enthusiasm. Not long ago, I made a retreat in Casteldaura which was decisive for me.
>
> I ask you, Father, to admit me as a numerary member of Opus Dei. My parents know [what I am doing] and are very content.
>
> Your daughter asks your blessing.
Montse Grases

As soon as she got home, she told her parents that she had joined Opus Dei. "Well, we too are members of the Work," they responded. Montse, her mother recalls, was exploding with joy and gratitude to God. Her father offered a toast to his daughter, and the three of them sang a song: "The fields have been opened up. Love opened a furrow, and the world became a path for the sower's desires. Be faithful. It's worthwhile to follow the sower down his clear path through the fields, sowing love."

A Normal Teenager

Montse's life continued much as before. Mass at Llar in the morning, classes, homework, helping her mother around the house, basketball, excursions. Her knee continued to hurt, but at the time neither she nor her parents thought it was anything serious. Her mother recalls: "Everything about her life was always very small because the love of God is full of little things done for love. Everything was very small, like that pain in her knee that wouldn't go away and that couldn't be localized. Sometimes it was higher up, other times lower." Montse didn't let the knee problem interfere with playing sports, although it hurt. "I may be lame," she said, "but I'll continue playing."

During Montse's first months of life as a member of Opus Dei, she did not stand out from the other young members of the Work in her center. In the diary of the center, she is rarely mentioned, and then only in passing. Looking back, however, the director of Llar concluded that from the moment Montse asked to be admitted, "The Work was her entire life." She adds: "Her life in in the Work during the first months developed peacefully. Like everyone else, she had her struggles, her small failures and difficulties. But she was always someone of great interior beauty, sincere and transparent. She understood everything very easily. Her happiness and her love for the vocation were a joy to see."

Montse invited many of her friends to Llar and prayed that they might come closer to God and possibly receive a vocation to Opus Dei. As one of the members of Opus Dei at Llar observed:

> From the very first moment, she showed desires to do apostolate. Later, [these desires] grew enormously. She felt a great desire to help all of her friends. . . . She took pleasure in giving herself to others, and she was happy when she saw that her friends were content, especially when they grew in the interior life and discovered the possibility of greater generosity with God.

Montse's knee did not improve with time, and the specialist her family took her to see was unable to diagnose her condition. By Easter, she had lost her appetite and was having trouble sleeping because of the pain, but she continued to get up on time and live a normal life. She found it difficult to accept the limitations her condition imposed on her. When the doctor suggested that she get up later, she was unhappy because this made it hard for her to help her mother with household chores. In May, she went with some other young women from Llar to visit a shrine of Our Lady. They were going to walk, but the director of the center suggested that Montse go in the car with her crippled friend Rosa. Montse kept insisting that she could walk. At one point she said, "I can go walking like everyone else. I'm not a cripple!" She immediately realized that she might have hurt Rosa's feelings, got into the car without further protest, and said, "Pardon me, Rosa. I said something stupid because the important thing is not to be physically crippled but to be interiorly crippled, to have little charity and to say things that hurt others."

In late June 1958, Montse went to the hospital for a biopsy. She told her mother that she was afraid of being alone in the operating room. Her mother responded that once, when she had had an operation, she had felt very alone until she began to pray, but then she felt great certainty that God was at her side giving her courage and strength. She urged Montse to pray. When Montse was recovering from the anesthesia she kept repeating, "You were right, Mama. You were right."

Bone Cancer

The biopsy revealed that Montse had Ewing sarcoma, a rare form of bone cancer that mostly affects people between the age of ten and twenty. Today treatment is quite effective, but in the late 1950s Ewing sarcoma was incurable. Radiation was used to reduce swelling and pain but did nothing to cure the disease.

Montse's parents decided to tell her at first only that she had a tumor, but not to talk about cancer and not to hint that there was no cure. Her mother wrote to St. Josemaría asking him to pray that the Lord might "make her see and accept God's will."

In the summer of 1958, thirty sessions of radiation therapy temporarily reduced the swelling and pain in her leg and permitted her to enjoy the summer in Seva with the rest of the family. She continued to swim and bicycle and took part in a play put on by the children summering in the area. The whole time though, she kept asking her parents and the director of Llar what exactly was wrong with her. They hinted at the potential seriousness of her condition but did not tell her openly that she had incurable cancer. One day, the director of Llar mentioned that some tumors degenerate into cancer. Montse continued to be serene, and asked, "But if it is the Lord who gave me a vocation, why wouldn't He give me health?" "Certainly," the director responded, "But you are ready for everything, aren't you?" "Yes, of course," Montse replied, "although I'm very afraid of suffering and the doctors frighten me. But if God sends me more suffering, as you say, God will help me very much, as you all will."

As Montse continued to suffer and learn to put into practice the spirit of Opus Dei, the director of Llar noticed that "she was growing in the interior life. She asked me how to live little things better, grew in her devotion to the Virgin, and showed great sincerity in everything. She spoke with great simplicity."

In the face of Montse's persistent questions about her condition, her parents told her that they would talk with her at the end of the summer when they returned to Barcelona. The evening they returned, Montse insisted that they talk immediately without putting things off to the next morning. Her parents told her clearly that she had cancer. Her first response was to say that perhaps they could amputate her leg. When her father replied that the doctors said that would not help, she momentarily put on a face as if to say, "What a shame." Then, without saying anything, she went to her room, knelt before a picture of Our Lady of Montserrat, and prayed briefly saying, "Whatever you want." Then she sat down and examined her conscience. Her mother decided to spend the night with her, fearing that she would not be able to sleep after receiving such terrible news. She poked her to move over and make room. Montse asked what she was doing. "I'm going to sleep with you." "What luck!" Montse commented in a jovial tone of voice. She rested her head on her mother's shoulder, and in a few seconds fell asleep.

The witnesses differ on how clearly she understood her condition at first. Her parents think that from the beginning she understood clearly that she was going to die. Others who were close to her think that at first she still expected to recover. At a minimum, she understood that she had cancer and

that it was very serious. As her mother comments, that makes her initial reaction all the more remarkable:

> I recall perfectly her expression. Just pursing her lips. Her eyes did not
> fill with tears or anything else. Nothing! Nothing! How supernatural!
> *Supernatural*. I thought about it before employing that word, but it is the
> appropriate one. What could I say otherwise? How unnatural? Or how
> abnormal? No. She always acted normally and naturally.
>
> It was evident that God was comforting her. Because suddenly all her
> dreams were taken away. Everything. . . . From that moment on she
> couldn't convert any of her dreams into realities.

The next morning, Montse went to confession with a priest of Opus
Dei. One person who saw her right afterward recalls noticing that she had
cried, but the priest recalls that she reacted "with the deep joy of someone
who has abandoned herself entirely in the Lord's hands." After confession,
she went to Llar. Seeing that Lia, the director, was busy, she said that she
would like to talk to her when she was free and asked what she would like
her to do in the meantime. Lia asked her to iron some oratory linens.

While ironing, Montse sang a Mexican song: "When I was living happily without thinking about your affection, you wanted me to love you, and
I loved you madly. And I will continue loving you even after death. Because
I love you with my soul, and the soul never dies. I love you with my soul and
the soul never dies."

Hearing her sing so cheerfully, Lia thought that perhaps she had not
understood what her parents had told her. But seeing that Lia had been
crying, Montse asked her, "Have you been crying, Lia? Well, you know
that I know everything, including that I have to die soon because Papa told
me yesterday."

"Then what, Montse?"

"I am ready. I went to Confession and I am very content. The priest told
me that I am lucky because soon I am going to enjoy God. At the beginning,
I didn't see it that way, but now yes, and I am very tranquil and very content.
I have great peace, and I love the will of God. Remind me about that in case
I forget. I want to do the will of God. This is the second time that I give
myself to God."

"Mama tells me to ask Isidoro for a cure," Montse continued. "But what do you think? I get very mixed up. Sometimes I think that I want to be cured. Other times I think that if the Lord wants this, it is because it is His will. When I find myself mixed up like that . . . I tell the Virgin that she should arrange everything as she wants. Don't you think that's the best?"

After telling Lia about her conversation with her parents she said, "Mama thought that I would say something to her, but I couldn't think of anything. I felt a lump in my throat, and I could only think that I had to be strong."

Lia recalls that Montse said she had a hard time coming to grips with the idea of dying because she said she wasn't in any pain. She added that she accepted pain as a "purification for going to Heaven," and if God wanted to take her to heaven, "I am ready," she continued.

"Now what are you praying for?" Lia asked her.

"I pray that the will of God be done. That way I will also be much more tranquil," Montse responded.

Montse and Lia talked about the death of St. Josemaría's sister Carmen, who had died of cancer two years earlier. Lia said that she had suffered a great deal and that she had been a very holy woman. Montse asked Lia for help from all the members of the Work. "I want to be as courageous as she was," she said.

When Lia asked her what she had thought when her father explained things to her, "she told me that she had picked up a crucifix, kissed it, and said 'Serviam' I will serve you Lord. I will be faithful.'"

Montse said that the next day she was going to write to the Father asking him to pray for her and telling him that she was going to offer everything for Opus Dei. But then her eyes filled with tears as she asked, "So now I can no longer be a Numerary member of the Work?" Her face lit up when Lia told her that of course, she could be a numerary.

Lia comments, "I saw that she had great peace. As if she had suddenly matured. I even told her that we had been thinking about her going to Paris to start Opus Dei there. 'But look, Montse,' I said to her, 'from now on we are going to pray for that undertaking although you're not going to be able to go.'"

After being told that she had cancer, Montse registered for classes and began attending them. She avoided talking about her illness and tried to live a normal life without becoming the center of attention. One day, when her mother saw her spending a lot of time trying to choose between two new dresses, she began to think that Montse must not realize she wasn't going to wear the new dress for long. She commented to her, "Your father is convinced that you will be cured. I sometimes think so also. What about you?"

Montse answered with a peaceful smile, "I never think about it." Her mother took this to mean that Montse had abandoned herself entirely in God's hands.

On October 2, the thirtieth anniversary of the foundation of Opus Dei, Montse went to the anniversary party at Llar, but soon began to suffer serious pain and felt ill. Not wanting to upset anyone, she left quietly and made her way home. She knew her parents were planning on going to a movie and didn't want to them stay home to take care of her. She smiled as she came in the door and began to set the table, but soon had to ask her sister to take over for her. When her mother found her lying down in her room, Montse tried to assure her that she was fine and that there was no reason for them not to go to the movies, but soon the pain became so bad that she could not contain her tears. Naturally, her parents stayed home with her.

As her health deteriorated, Montse struggled to come closer to God. Of course, she had her ups and downs because, as St. Josemaría wrote, the interior life is "to begin . . . and to begin again." For Montse, an ongoing struggle was to pray well during the two half-hour periods she dedicated to mental prayer each day. She noted in her examination of conscience one day in October 1958, "I find it hard to be united to God." A few days later: "Prayer: Better in the morning, but I lost about ten minutes with distractions." Toward the end of the month: "Prayer: I find it very difficult because I don't know what to say to Him." Sometimes she was able to say, "Prayer. I made more of an effort, and it went better." But then, "Prayer. Quite bad. I was distracted."

Meeting St. Josemaría

In November 1958, Montse made a short trip to Rome, fundamentally to see the Father. Her family decided that she should go alone because if her mother accompanied her, it would be natural for her to stay with her mother in the hotel. If she went alone, she would stay in a center of the Work.

Montse decided to bring high heels for meeting the Father, although she could barely get them on because of swelling.

On the way to Rome, the plane encountered thunderstorms and bounced around a great deal. Montse prayed many Acts of Contrition, thinking she might die at any moment. Members of the Work met her at the airport and took her to a center near Opus Dei's central house, Villa Tevere. In preparation for her visit, they had turned a ground-floor sitting room into a bedroom so that she would not need to go up and down stairs. The next morning, Encarnita Ortega, the worldwide head of Opus Dei's women's branch, came to see her and take her to St. Peter's Basilica.

The following day, Montse met the Father. He asked her about her family and about what she had seen both in Opus Dei's central house and in Rome. He urged her to pray for health and to promise God that if he granted it, she would always be faithful. At the same time, the Father said, she should tell God that she fully accepted his will. He added that he wanted her to recover and would pray that she did, but that he too accepted God's will. He gave her a rosary, a holy card, and a medal. Before the visit ended, he asked someone to take a picture of Montse with him, Don Álvaro del Portillo, and several other members.

During her brief tours of the city, Montse was impressed with the beauty and grandeur of Rome, but she kept a sharp eye out for bottle caps to bring to her younger brother for his collection and bought small presents for the other members of the family. She attended an informal after-lunch get-to-gether with young women of the Work from many different countries who were studying in Rome. A number of them sang songs from their countries, and Montse joined in singing a Catalan song.

Both during the gathering and the rest of her stay, Montse tried to cover up her pain, but when Encarnita asked her if she was in much pain she answered simply, "Yes. It's as if a furious dog was biting me all the time." She added that she was terrified of pain, but convinced that "if I am faithful in what God asks of me every day, he will give me His grace." The young woman in the room next to hers had told her that if she couldn't sleep, she should come and talk, but she didn't want to wake her up. So, after tossing and turning for a long time, she got up, danced a bit in front of the picture of Our Lady in her room, lay down again, and promptly went to sleep.

Visiting Rome and meeting St. Josemaría were highlights of Montse's life. In later days, when she was suffering a great deal and alone with her mother in her room, she would often say, "What a wonderful thing, Mama, those days."

Concern for Other People

The day after returning home, Montse was supposed to stay in bed, but when a visitor came, she got up to show her all the things she had brought from Rome. Her visitor commented later, "This happened to her a lot. At times, she was very tired, but when charity required something, she reacted as if she didn't find it hard at all." When friends from Llar and other friends came to visit, she talked, sang, played cards, and prayed with them. She tried to encourage everyone, including older people who came to visit her, to be close to God and bring others close to him. According to one of her best friends, "She took great pleasure in giving herself to others, and she was happy when she saw that her friends were content, especially when they grew in the interior life and discovered the possibility of greater generosity with God."

Often, she was in pain and felt sick when people came to visit, but despite the effort it cost her, she kept a smile on her face. When she knew friends were coming, she tried to fix herself up. If they commented on how pretty she looked, she responded, "That's because I fixed myself up to look pretty when you came." One day some cousins and friends came to visit. Montse's mother suspected that she would find their visit exhausting. When another girl who was a close friend dropped by, Montse's mother suggested she ask the other visitors to leave if it seemed Montse was in a lot of pain. But Montse seemed so cheerful and upbeat that the girl didn't say anything until the visitors finally left on their own. As soon as they had closed the door, Montse exclaimed, "I can't take it anymore! I can't take it anymore! I can't take it anymore!" and threw off the blankets that were weighing on her leg. On another occasion, when her mother asked her if she felt like seeing two girls who wanted to visit, she responded, "Mama, we're not here to do what we feel like. Tell them to come in."

Her doctor recalls: "I never saw her sad or bitter or depressed. All of my visits were lively, cheerful, upbeat, without any trace of sadness, despite the seriousness of the illness she suffered." When someone suggested she stop telling the doctor that she was well, she responded, "He's doing all that he can. There's nothing more he can do. And telling him I'm having a bad time just makes him suffer." She resisted asking for painkillers because they made her too sleepy to spend time with her friends. She didn't want to lose the opportunity to enjoy their company and occasionally encourage them to go to Llar or to pray more. When visitors asked if they could do something for her, she habitually said no, but then sometimes she added, "Well, if you want to know something that would make me very happy, it's that there is a retreat coming up and I would be delighted if you went."

Llar, like many other centers of Opus Dei, celebrated a novena in preparation for the Feast of the Immaculate Conception on December 8. Montse attended the novena every day, although she had to lie down briefly after arriving at the center. After the novena, she stayed for a while to talk to the girls who had come.

As Christmas approached, she decided to ask for a coat to wear outside, because she thought that would signal to her parents that she was still hopeful about being able to go out again. At the same time, she was careful to choose something that one of her siblings would be able to use when she was gone.

Looking back on the many hours she spent with Montse during her illness, Rosa Pantaleoni, who had been crippled by polio, says:

> I'm a very sensitive person. Seeing others suffer makes a deep impression on me. But Montse carried the cross in such a way that I never felt sorry for her. I never left her house sad. I recall that my parents said they couldn't understand how I could spend entire afternoons with her and return so cheerful. It was very difficult to explain the atmosphere that Montse created around her, and that her family fostered: an atmosphere of detachment, of the gift of self, the love of God, and of human affection such that all the negative aspects of pain went unnoticed.
>
> It was very difficult to explain the joy that was found in that room. No one will be able to understand how we were happy. I still do not understand the joy with which I went to that house and the joy with which I left it, considering how horrible all that was from a human point of view. At

the time, I couldn't tell anybody about these things because no one would understand. No one would understand that there could be an environment of so much joy. . . . Now when I think about it, all of that seems impossible to me. I don't understand how I could spend so many hard moments at her side and yet the two of us could be happy. Perhaps it is that at her side I learned, with the example of her life, what our Founder taught us: that what truly makes a person unfortunate is attempting to take the cross out of life, and that encountering the cross is to encounter Christ, to encounter Love. . . . At her side, I learned to . . . Love. I don't know if that's quite the right word, but I don't find another. I learned to love her illness and my own.

Final Months

Gradually, the swelling in Montse's leg grew worse and she developed open sores. Changing bandages became a long, painful process, but she managed not to complain. On one occasion when her father was holding her up outside of bed so that the bandages could be changed, she asked him to dance with her.

She was anxious not to have her illness throw a pall of sadness over the family. From time to time, Montse asked her family to sing. One day, while other family members were singing, her father pretended to be reading the paper so she wouldn't notice his tears. Seeing that he was not singing, she said, "Papa, I can't hear you. I want you all to be happy."

As the months went past, Montse was filled with a desire for heaven and began to ask people to talk to her about it. Her mother liked to talk with her about heaven, because when she did Montse smiled. One day she told her mother she wanted to go soon. Her mother responded, "Yes, but when God wants it." Montse remained silent for a moment and then said simply, "Fine." That was a condensed version of a prayer she said often: "Lord, Whatever you want. When you want. As you want it." On another occasion, when her mother told her that she thought she might fall asleep and wake up in heaven, Montse said, "But if it's like that, we won't have time to say goodbye!" Her mother knelt beside her bed, and they embraced.

After receiving the anointing of the sick, she said, "I have such desires to go. When will it end?" Her parents responded that perhaps the Lord wanted her to help him by suffering some more. "In that case, she said, "a few days more don't matter. Or what the Lord wants." Three or four days before her death she said to the director of Llar, "Lía, how slowly all this is going. I would never have thought that it was so difficult to die. But in any case, you know I'm very content. Apparently, the Lord still needs me."

Shortly before Montse's death, her parents told her that she might die the next day. She exclaimed, "Is that true Mama, that I'm going to go now? Do you understand? Heaven forever! Do you understand? To Heaven! I'm going to Heaven!"

"Yes, my daughter, you are going and you will be very happy. But how we will miss you when your little brother Rafita grows up or when Enrique is ordained!"

"But, Papa! I will see it all from heaven, and from there I will pray for all of you."

Still, at times Montse experienced fear and doubts about whether she would go to heaven, a trial that God permits in the lives of many holy people. A week and a half before her death, she made her last note from her daily examination of conscience: "Lack of peace and anxiety. As if I were alone." She asked Lia, "Do you really think the Lord wants me in heaven? Sometimes I suffer a great deal from temptations that come and go. But if you tell me I will go to heaven, I believe you. I believe you . . . Tell me! Repeat it again and again! 'I will go to heaven. I will go to heaven. I will go to heaven.'"

Even during the intense suffering of her final days, she continued to focus on others and be concerned about their spiritual well-being. Just two or three days before her death, she talked with a visitor in detail about his family. When two friends came to visit, she urged them to go to Llar. One of them wrote in her diary that day: "At that moment life had full sense. You, Lord, were there. It was necessary to live for you, much more directed toward you, completely for you. With you, life had a real meaning, without you, it lost all sense. It's strange to find the sense of life through death."

A nonbelieving friend who visited her in her final days was disconcerted by Montse's ability to take an interest in him and his family in such difficult moments:

I was very moved by her sentiments. I faced a reality that was disconcerting for someone incapable of seeing things from the supernatural point of view. That young girl was behaving with the naturalness that always characterized her as if she was not a prisoner of what I knew she had and that was making her suffer so much. I went away disconcerted. "This girl is dying," I thought, "and the only thing that interests her is how I am doing and how my family is doing, how things are going for us." Turning toward home, I thought, "I don't understand it. She has a rotten leg, and she knows it perfectly well, and yet she continues to act as she always has, without becoming sad. I really don't understand it."

The friend's bewilderment would be the beginning of his conversion.

Montse struggled not only to smile and appear cheerful but to really be happy. In her examination of conscience, she took note of days when she was "a little down." On other days she was able to say, "I have struggled a great deal to be happy and content," or "Joy despite everything, yes." Joy did not come easily. One day she noted, "In the morning, dejection. Then I overcame it with joy." A few weeks before her death she observed, "Joy, good, but need for still more."

Montse's final words were, "I'm so happy, so happy. I am so content."

The cause for Montse's beatification began in 1962. In 2016, Pope Francis approved a decree confirming that she had lived the virtues to a heroic degree.

CHAPTER ELEVEN

Pepe Serret:
Businessman

P epe Serret was an executive and the father of a large family. He stood out for his cheerfulness, his concern for other people, and his generosity in fostering apostolic activities.

Early Life

Pepe Serret was born in 1941 in the village of Vallfogona de Balaguer in the Catalan province of Lleida, northwest of Barcelona. His father died when he was five, and he was raised by his older brother, who was a farmer. Vall-fogona had a one-room schoolhouse and one teacher. Very few of the students went on to high school. The teacher, however, convinced Pepe's older brother that he would benefit from further education, and Pepe joined a group of five other children who prepared for high school. At fifteen, he moved to the nearby city of Reus. There he lived with an older sister and finished high school. A year later he enrolled in the School of Engineering Technology in Tarrassa, where he would obtain the equivalent of an American associate's degree.

"An average student with average abilities who put in an average effort," is how one of his fellow students recalled him. He liked cards and the movies and occasionally skipped classes. Another classmate concluded that "study was not his thing. He did it more by willpower than by desire. In our conversations, technical topics rarely came up. On one occasion he came to my house and saw that I was reading a technical book. He asked me with surprise, 'Do you read that sort of thing? Is it possible?'"

One of Pepe's coworkers at his first job confirms that

> although he had done technical studies, he was not really a technician. He didn't like to talk very much about derivatives, integrals, etc. He preferred to interact with people. His strength was more in the area of administration and direction of businesses, the organization of a business, dealing with people.

During his student days, Pepe went to Sunday Mass, said the Rosary, and made an occasional visit to the Blessed Sacrament. He also attended meetings of Catholic Action. One of his colleagues reports that after getting his first job Pepe continued going to Mass and "suffered if he saw that some of his friends did not go to Sunday Mass." He recalls, "On more than one occasion, he asked me if I had gone to Mass and did all he could to help me."

First Steps in Business

In 1962, Pepe completed his degree and got his first job in an electronics factory. Although he was hired as an engineering technician, the company's philosophy was that new hires should learn the business from the bottom up. Pepe began working in the stock room as a laborer, pulling a cart around the factory to deliver parts. At the same time, he began a three-year night program to obtain a bachelor's degree in business administration at the Esade school in Barcelona.

Pepe had already fallen in love with his future wife, Roser Sima, but between work and classes, they had very little time to see each other. Pepe offered to drop his classes to have more time to spend together, but Roser encouraged him to finish. They were married in April 1965, when Pepe was twenty-four. Their first daughter was born in 1966. Eventually they would have eleven children.

In 1968, Pepe found a new job directing the construction of an industrial slaughterhouse. The project did not go well financially, and Pepe ended up paying part of its debts with his own money before quitting. In 1970, Pepe got a job building and operating a new industrial dairy operation in León, a pleasant small city, where the Serret family made many good friends. Professionally, things went well for Pepe. He succeeded in forming a good team at the dairy and made sure they were well-paid. Many Sunday afternoons his family picnicked with colleagues on the banks of the river. As the children grew older, he took them to old-age homes and hospitals to visit and care for the sick and other people in need, to brighten the people's lives, and to help the children become sensitive to the pain of others.

In 1977, when Pepe was thirty-six, the owners of the dairy's parent company, who were approaching retirement age, decided to name him the manager of their entire company. This involved moving to Mollerussa, a town of about seven thousand inhabitants in Pepe's home region of Catalonia, about eighty-five miles west of Barcelona. The next year, Pepe enrolled in a part-time program of General Direction of Businesses at the IESE, a Barcelona business school connected with Opus Dei.

Supporting Two Schools Connected to Opus Dei

Two years after moving to Mollerussa, Pepe and Roser decided to enroll their boys in Terrafirma, a school where religious education had been entrusted to Opus Dei. This decision proved a turning point in Pepe's life. He had had some contact with Opus Dei during his student days and at IESE Business School, but nothing much had ever come of it. Like all schools connected to Opus Dei, Terrafirma placed great emphasis on parents' involvement in the education of their children and in the life of the school. This made a lot of sense to Pepe, and he soon found himself involved in a wide range of activities at Terrafirma. He became close friends with the headmaster, who discovered Pepe was someone he could count on.

Through the school's programs for parents and contact with members of Opus Dei who worked there, Pepe and Roser gradually became familiar with the spirit of Opus Dei and learned to put it into practice. In addition, a friend invited Pepe to attend classes, talks, days of recollection, and retreats organized by Opus Dei. Despite the demands of an important job and a large and growing family, Pepe managed to make time for these formational activities and began to receive personal spiritual guidance from a priest of the Work. More importantly, Pepe put into practice the things he learned about sanctifying his work and family life. At about the same time, Roser began attending Opus Dei's formational activities for women.

In June 1979, Pepe and Roser heard that a small group of parents wanted to start a school for girls similar to the Terrafirma school for boys. The task was a daunting one. There was little demand for quality education for girls in the largely rural area and many of the families with boys in Terrafirma were already finding it challenging to support that school, much less take on financial responsibility for another project. Pepe and Roser were undeterred by the difficulties and immediately enrolled three of their daughters in the new school, which at the time existed only on paper. Within a few days, they recruited another six girls, made a generous donation toward the purchase of land, and persuaded some friends to contribute. It is worth noting that Pepe was, at this time, a well-paid executive of a modest-sized company, but he was far from wealthy and already had seven children, the eldest of whom was thirteen.

Although Pepe did not hold any official position at the nascent girls' school, he soon found himself deeply involved in fundraising and planning. The school faced many serious difficulties. The Spanish government was slow in delivering promised construction aid, and the banks were pressing for payment. One person who worked closely with Pepe on getting the school started recalls many economic crises which "provoked at times expressions of despair." Pepe would immediately respond, "Have faith. Things will work out if we use our heads and make the effort." A parent who attended many of the early organizational meetings recalls that

> among the group promoting the school, there were some with a lot of interest but with few ideas. Others had many ideas, but they were not practical. Some were optimistic, others pessimistic. The meetings seemed interminable. Pepe intervened briefly but he got right to the point. He understood the financial aspects of that ambitious project very well and was optimistic. He transmitted calm and full confidence in the project. With a certain amount of humor, he got us all to agree.
>
> Addressing a meeting of parents in which some were concerned, others worried, and some furious, Pepe explained clearly and briefly the situation. Economically, he said, things couldn't look much worse. But the project was a reality that was moving forward. And that's what they had all joined for. It was worthwhile looking for a solution to the economic problem. He stepped to the blackboard and filled it with numbers showing that the school could be a success, and with God's help, it would be, although that would mean a new sacrifice on the part of everyone. Pepe's calm, optimism, and sensible approach spread among the parents and the school was able to continue moving forward.

Once the school was established, Pepe joined a four-person steering committee. The committee met once a week at 8:00 AM. In Spain, that was a very early hour, but it was the only time he could make available. In addition to working for the school, Pepe made several large contributions, which he insisted remain anonymous.

The headmistress describes him as "very pleasant to work with. In addition to being a very hard worker, he had great humanity and an optimistic sense of life. He always arrived with a smile and a conciliatory and peaceful attitude. His was the peace of a man who is not looking for anything for himself, the peace that comes from a constant attitude of giving."

In his committee work for the school, Pepe showed extraordinary detachment from his ideas and projects. On one occasion he invested a great deal of time in preparing a marketing plan to increase enrollment. Before rolling out the plan, he asked the opinion of another father of one of the girls in the school. He responded that the project looked good for a manufacturing company, but that it did not seem appropriate for a nonprofit educational institution. Pepe immediately saw that the critic's position was well-founded and abandoned his plan without lessening his dedication to recruiting more students.

As his involvement with the girls' school showed, Pepe was both optimistic and apostolic, but he was also a realist. He became involved in helping another school that had been operating for twenty years but was meeting great difficulties because the market for the kind of education it offered was drying up. After studying the situation, Pepe concluded that the only solution was to close the school. A short time later it was, in fact, forced to close.

Pepe did not limit himself to helping projects which would benefit his children. A friend talked to him about several family agricultural schools in the area, promoted by members of Opus Dei. Based on a French model, they offered the sons of local peasants a sound general education and technical training in agriculture. He hoped to recruit Pepe to help solve the problems they were facing but "expected him to respond with a detailed list of his innumerable tasks. He was super-occupied and there were very few blank spaces in his calendar. Nonetheless, he took out his notebook and asked, 'What needs to be done?'"

In April 1980, Pepe concluded that God was calling him to join Opus Dei. The director of the Opus Dei center encouraged him to continue attending Mass, saying the Rosary, and spending time in mental prayer, but suggested that he wait a bit to confirm that he had a genuine vocation. In the meantime, his wife, Roser, joined the Work. Although Pepe was somewhat irritated that Roser had been allowed to join Opus Dei while he had been advised to wait, he celebrated her vocation by taking the entire family to the most famous Marian shrine in Catalonia, the Benedictine Monastery of Montserrat. A few weeks later, the director of the center gave Pepe the green light, and he also joined Opus Dei.

In 1980, the Serrets moved from their apartment to a house on the outskirts of Mollerussa with a sizable garden and a basement. They installed a small swimming pool in one corner of the garden and remodeled the basement into a large living and dining room for family and friends. They built an entrance to the room directly from the garden. This made the space accessible without having to go through the rest of the house, so the schools their children attended could use the pool and the living room for recreational activities.

Working with and for Nestlé

In 1985, the owners of the business Pepe had been running since 1977 decided to sell a 50 percent interest in their company to Nestlé, which was one of its principal customers. In a sign of extraordinary confidence, they asked Pepe to work out the details of the deal. Pepe needed to protect the interests of the sellers and satisfy the demands of Nestlé. The task was made even more delicate by the fact that he expected to continue working in the business over which both parties would have a significant measure of control. The head of Nestlé in Spain wrote:

> If he was able to maintain the difficult equilibrium demanded of him, it was because he always aimed to do what he understood was best for the business, leaving to one side the legitimate but individual interests of different people, including his own personal interests. He understood the business as the joint effort of all those who through it not only earn their living but to a very important degree find their personal fulfillment.

Thanks to Pepe's efforts, the deal went through, and he continued to run the company.

Over time, the executives of Nestlé in Spain got to know Pepe well. In 1992, after working with him for seven years, they decided to offer him a position as the director general of one of Nestlé's Spanish subsidiaries, Coffee Products SA. The new position represented a major change for Pepe and the family. He had to leave the dairy industry in which he had great expertise and many contacts and move to the coffee industry where he had neither experience nor contacts. It also involved the transition from being the head of an independent company to leading a division of a giant multinational.

For the family, it meant moving about fifty miles from Mollerussa, a village of less than ten thousand inhabitants, to Reus, a provincial city with almost a hundred thousand inhabitants. The children—the youngest of whom was just beginning school—would have to change schools. Despite the challenges involved, Pepe and Roser thought the opportunity was too good to pass up.

Of course, the Serrets would also need to sell their house and find a new one large enough for a family with eleven children. An incident during the negotiations for a new house in Reus reveals much about Pepe's character. He had persuaded the seller to reduce the asking price but probably could have negotiated a further reduction. At one point, however, he told his agent, "Don't press any harder. It may be that this good woman needs the money."

Personality

One of his collaborators describes Pepe as a complex personality who combined different characteristics. He was

> enthusiastic and impulsive, with a great desire to live and enjoy every situation. I discovered he was a romantic and a dreamer. And also, a personality with many contradictions. Contradictions because he easily went from a dreamy romanticism to positions that were practical and Cartesian. He could be a rebel for whom there were no barriers and a few minutes later be methodical, disciplined and with great self-control, He was contradictory and stimulating, generous and enthusiastic, impulsive, and sociable.

There may have been conflicting features in Pepe's personality, but one constant was that he was a happy, optimistic person who always had a smile on his face and often a song on his lips. Many people recall his cheerfulness and his smile. An engineer who was a good friend commented shortly after his death, "I imagine his soul with the smile that was always on his face, but which came from his soul, introducing himself to some angel or saint as 'Serret of Mollerussa' and interceding for the entire church (because we all fit in his heart) and, especially, for those closest to him."

The Serrets sang a lot, both during car trips and after meals, because Pepe liked to sing and thought that singing brought the family together. But Pepe didn't sing with only the family. On the frequent occasions when the family had guests for dinner, songbooks often came out because, in the words of a family friend, "Pepe was overflowing with happiness and wanted us all to participate" in his happiness.

Pepe was intensely loyal. An engineer with whom he was friends for many years does not recall "ever having heard him speak badly about anyone." Rather, he says, "If there was something he thought was not right, he said it face-to-face to the person, in a manner that was full of affection and good manners." When it would have been easy to criticize public figures or people with whom he had business dealings,

> He didn't speak badly about anyone. On the contrary, he took advantage of the occasion to speak well of those who had done something good. When someone had done something harmful to him or his friends, he was respectful and refined with them. If he had to express a judgment, he focused on the business dealings or the public event in question, but he did not judge the persons.

Pepe was faithful to his word, punctual to appointments, and fulfilled the obligations he took on. Often after eating in his home with some other families, if the conversation went on at length, he "disappeared" for a little while to fulfill some commitment.

He had, according to a colleague at Nestlé, a concern for creating unity. "He tried very hard to bring people together so that, knowing each other better, their personal and professional relations might be smoother and more fruitful." He also knew how to control his temper. A neighbor, who became a good friend, reports that in the twelve years he had known him, "I never once saw him angry, and I can testify that there were times when he had good reason to be so. Not one inappropriate word nor one complaint. He always forgave and smiled. It was a pleasure to be with him."

Many accounts seem to suggest that Pepe did everything effortlessly, but that was not true. A person who met with him frequently, although they were not close friends, says that what most impressed him about Pepe was "his smile and his tiredness." He continues:

I don't know if it is correct, but the picture that I have of Pepe is of a man who was tired. . . . Perhaps it is because I usually saw him at the end of the day, only a little before the late Spanish supper and sometimes at the end of a long professional trip. In any case, although you saw in him the fatigue of someone preparing to go home after a long day's work, it was always accompanied by a smile.

Working to Create a Bright and Cheerful Christian Home

The Founder of Opus Dei often urged its members to try to make their homes "bright and cheerful." The Serrets took that message seriously and put it into practice very successfully. Pepe and Roser avoided arguing in front of the children. He habitually addressed her in Catalan as Roser, but if he noticed that things were getting out of hand he would address her as Rosario in Spanish, signaling that it was time to drop the subject and take it up later when the children were not present.

The cheerful atmosphere of the Serret household didn't just happen spontaneously or without effort. Pepe and Roser worked hard at maintaining it, whether there were guests or not. If Pepe saw one of the little ones upset, he would stand in front of him and say, "A smile for the press," with the gesture of taking his picture. He wouldn't give up until he managed to get the child to smile. If one of the older children talked back or reacted angrily or with an ill temper, instead of rebuking him or her he usually smiled and said, "It's really difficult to behave well, isn't it?"

Pepe also worked hard at keeping the house neat and pleasant. He did not consider that his professional position and his many occupations exempted him from pitching in at home. Someone who came over to help the Serrets move into their house in 1992 noticed that he could never help with sweeping because Pepe always had the broom in his hand.

One might think that in a family with many children and many guests, the children might feel neglected or abandoned, but that was not the case. One of them later commented, "Dad was not like other fathers. He was with us and paid attention to us." A teacher who got to know the family well confirms this observation:

He knew his children perfectly. He knew their virtues and their defects and so he knew how to deal with each one in the best possible way. Each one was "his favorite." With one he sang, with another he did a crossword puzzle, with another he watched soccer, with another he wrote a letter to the newspaper, with another he played, with yet another he worked in the garden.

The Serrets learned in Opus Dei the importance of giving their children a great deal of freedom, but if a child committed to doing something, Pepe insisted that he or she follow through on the commitment. If, for instance, a child asked to be woken up early to study, Pepe gave them no peace in the morning until they got up and opened their books. If necessary, he stayed with them while they studied. Another thing Pepe insisted on was that the children respect their mother. If one of them interrupted her, he would intervene energetically, insisting that the child let Roser finish what she was saying.

A businessman who originally got to know the family through his own children recalls being impressed with Pepe's great

> esteem for his children and the friends of his children. You immediately noticed the atmosphere of freedom and joy that characterized the house. He knew how to educate his children in freedom and responsibility. He wanted other people to be happy and made his own the slogan, "Always cheerful to make other people happy." He lived that and knew how to transmit it to his children. When I went to his house, I noticed the cheerfulness. Every member of the family greeted you with a smile on their lips.

The children were very much at ease with Pepe. A teacher in the school that his sons attended was impressed with "the naturalness with which his children acted in his presence. They never acted with fear of a possible correction from their father."

One year at Christmas time, the family went to visit the nuns at a convent in whose chapel they sometimes went to Mass. One of the nuns observed: "The simplicity with which the children told jokes and explained situations caught our attention, as did the affection with which their parents and older brothers and sisters encouraged the little ones."

Especially in the later years of his life, Pepe earned a good living, but he tried hard to put into practice St. Josemaría's advice about living with the spirit of the father of a large and poor family. He got ten years of service out of a van before finally trading it in. At one point, the family's TV was sixteen years old. Many of his colleagues spent large amounts of money on luxurious briefcases, but for many years Pepe used the inexpensive one he had acquired shortly before his marriage.

He taught his children to treat people with humble jobs with particular respect, especially if they were in service professions. Pepe himself went beyond respect to show them affection and friendship. A man who worked for him as a part-time gardener says he was so moved by the news of Pepe's death that he wept a great deal. He remembers Pepe as "a very good person. He was always in good humor, and he had a lot of affection for me. . . . He was the best person I have ever known. I have dealt with lots of people, but no one like him."

A Home Overflowing with Guests

The Serret family was extraordinarily open to guests. They frequently invited friends of the family, friends of the children, or teachers from their schools for lunch or a snack. More strikingly, Pepe often invited business colleagues, clients, and suppliers to his home. So many people came for lunch, dinner, or a snack, that one day the five-year-old asked his mother, "Mama, why don't we open a restaurant?"

"What makes you think of that, Kiko?"

"So many people come to eat at our house, that we could charge them and make a lot of money."

The reason there were so many was that people enjoyed visiting the family. As a teacher at the boys' school remarked: "It was really pleasant to be in their home. While you were leaving, you were already thinking about coming back. The atmosphere of their home was cheerful, open, and welcoming. There was nothing rigid about it."

When the addition to the house in Mollerussa and the swimming pool were finished, Pepe called the director of the nearby Opus Dei center which carried on activities with high school boys and told him, "We have built this for you so that you can fill it with kids. During the summer, you can come to swim. Roser will give you a snack and you can have a very pleasant afternoon. The more kids the better."

A Christian Businessman

The business world in which Pepe moved was often harsh, and at times cutthroat. Nonetheless, he was strictly honest in his business dealings. A colleague at Nestlé says that he was "able to combine harmonically his rigorous moral principles with great business ability." A government official who dealt with Pepe says that he always "put into practice what was required by the legislation in whatever area we were dealing with." Pepe went beyond honesty. He was, in the words of a business school professor,

> a man of clear ideas, who spoke clearly. When you asked him something or proposed something to him, he answered directly with simplicity and without beating about the bush. He said what he thought. He approached business, family, or matters of friendship with a smile and interest, but also very concretely, ready to collaborate if he should or could. If he could not, he told you so clearly and you always knew how far you could go.

According to one of his subordinates, "he was well respected. In negotiations, he would disarm the other party by the simplicity of his approach." One colleague has described his negotiating style as "exhaustive and combative," but at the same time "very honorable." In one particularly difficult negotiation, after three hours of analyzing the situation marked by heated arguments, Pepe finally said, "Look, I've come to understand that you are right, so how do you want to do this?"

When circumstances demanded it, he could be tough and even harsh. When a supplier announced a serious delay in providing certain machinery, Pepe "did not fail to express very clearly his opinion about our company, its way of honoring agreements, and about its representatives." Even in circumstances like these, however, Pepe usually ended up as friends of the people involved.

In more normal circumstances, according to a regional distributor for his company's products, "His way of negotiating was not cold or numerical.

He mixed into the dynamics of negotiation an uncommon human factor. The transaction became something secondary which gave it a characteristic flavor rarely found in the commercial world."

A young man who was just beginning his career when Pepe became his client says:

> I suppose that he could have utilized his greater experience to gain advantages from our professional relationship. Others certainly would have attempted to do so. . . . [But with Pepe, it was a question of] instruction, advice, dealing as among equals, and negotiations that were just and honest. . . . He also tried to help me with good advice on personal matters. Although we didn't always agree on how to think about them, that was never an obstacle to our relationship being daily more frank and cordial.

Friendship and Concern for Colleagues

If Pepe was friends with many suppliers and clients, he was much better friends with the people who worked with or for him. One of his colleagues at Nestlé reports that after work meetings, "he would ask me to swing by his house so he could cut some roses in the garden for my wife." Another colleague, who reported to Pepe, recalls how after a hard day's work "he would come to my office and say, 'Let's go take a look at the sea.' Almost like two high school boys, we would set off to take a walk through the port, conversing animatedly, and letting the time go by almost without realizing it."

Pepe took time to get to know his colleagues and those who worked for him, and he had a real interest in helping them develop and become better human beings. A student who worked with him one summer recalls that he "showed me how beautiful it can be to work with real interest and the satisfaction that we can take from things well done." A colleague recalls with gratitude advice he received from Pepe: "Before doing something, think about it carefully, and then take full responsibility without ever lying. If you think you have to deform something, don't say it at all. It is better to be silent than to lie in business."

Given Pepe's large number of friends, his friendships could easily have been superficial, but he put his whole heart into them. On one occasion, a friend of the family was diagnosed with a serious and possibly life-threatening illness. Pepe learned the news late at night. Despite the hour, he immediately called to ask the woman's husband for more details. Before her husband picked up the phone, Pepe began to weep inconsolably. The husband's efforts to tranquilize and console him failed to calm his weeping. All he managed to say at the end of the call was, "Count on me for everything!"

Ability to Overcome Disagreements

One of Pepe's outstanding characteristics was his ability to be friends with people who did not agree with him. In a book of recollections put together shortly after his death, this is a recurring theme. A friend from León recalls that his father and Pepe became good friends even though they had very different political and religious ideas and argued a lot. A friend from Lleida recalls that he and Pepe discussed politics from time to time but never reached any agreement. That, however, did not lead to clashes. "Pepe chuckled and we ended up with a good taste in our mouths." The son of the owners of the business in which Pepe worked for so many years recalls that the first time they met, it was clear that they disagreed about many things, but that "made the conversation even more fascinating. From that first conversation of ours, there arose a stimulating disagreement about how we approached many questions." A young person who worked with him on a project realized that they had very different views about some important topics. "Because I didn't yet know him sufficiently," he reports, "I was afraid that these differences would sour our relationship, but that never happened. Not only did he never have a bad expression on his face, but his words always had a tone of good humor." A long-time friend describes him as

> pleasantly stubborn when he did not share the way of thinking of another person. He argued explaining all the reasons why he saw a particular problem in a particular way. But his "adversary" didn't get angry because he

noticed in his way of speaking that there was friendship and affection. When it seemed to him that there was nothing further to say . . . he quickly changed the topic, perhaps with a joke. Sometimes after a while, the topic would come up again but in a lighthearted way which dissipated any tension that there might have been. This way of acting was the fruit of his affection for people and the distinction he made between people and the ideas that they were arguing about.

Even when things went beyond a difference of opinion and involved competing interests, Pepe had a remarkable ability to pursue his company's interests while cultivating friendship with his competitor. On one occasion, Pepe's company and a competitor were both trying to extend their influence in areas that the other company considered its own. The head of the competitive company recalls that this logically

led to major clashes with Pepe. . . . Nonetheless, curiously, as we got to know each other better, our friendship deepened, and each of us came to understand the point of view of the other business which logically wanted to grow in a market that was ever harsher and more competitive. . . . We also met in other more relaxed circumstances, for example on trips organized by a company that sold to both of us. In those moments, outside our harsh business meetings, Pepe showed himself as he really was, throwing off his mask of being the director general, and appearing as a man with great humanity and sincerity.

A Trusted Advisor

Many people benefited from Pepe's advice in a wide range of situations. Naturally, in the business context, he was often called upon to help solve problems. Even in areas in which he had accumulated considerable expertise, he stopped to think carefully before giving advice or making important decisions. One of his colleagues recalls an occasion when the business was having sales problems. They analyzed them at length in the board meeting but could not find a solution. Only three or four days later did Pepe give him four sheets of paper with suggestions of what he thought would be the best solutions.

Even outside the office, people often turned to him for advice on professional matters. Here too, Pepe took the time to consider matters carefully. A friend recalls an event that occurred during a retreat. As they were going to their rooms at the end of the first day of the retreat, he asked Pepe's advice about a professional topic that was very important to him. The conversation lasted until four in the morning. The following morning, they ran across each other again in the hallway. Pepe gave him ten pages that summarized the facts and explained his point of view about the question they had been discussing in the middle of the night.

People also sought his advice on personal and spiritual matters. His eldest daughter observes that when a person communicated some concern to him, he broke it down and helped them to see the positive aspects and the advantages that they could derive from the situation. Above all, he reminded them that the situation was also the will of God. "Anyone who had recourse to him," she concludes, "never went away without good advice, without a good solution to the problem. Deep down people always left with a sense that the problem no longer existed. The problem became easy to overcome because he made you see it from a different perspective."

Pepe took an interest in other people's problems even when he did not know them well. One day a friend invited him to go with him to a bakery that a friend of his had recently installed in a new neighborhood of the city. Pepe immediately realized that the business was not going very well. He asked the owner if he had considered selling milk in addition to bakery goods. Selling milk, he suggested, would give him more revenue and solve a problem for area housewives who didn't have any place nearby to buy milk.

Bringing Others Closer to God

Especially after he joined Opus Dei, Pepe was anxious to bring other people to God. The most important part of his apostolate was the example he and Roser gave. In most cases, we will never know what impact their good example had, but there are some exceptions. Perhaps the most striking involves a recently married couple who lived across the street from the apartment the

Serrets rented when they first moved to Mollerussa. Through the window, they could see what was going on in the Serrets' home. It seemed to them "a carnival." They counted heads and realized that there were seven children. They commented to each other, "That's crazy. Seven children!" Deep down, both of them suspected that all that hubbub must be fun, but they continued saying to each other, "That's crazy." They investigated and found out who their neighbors were. If they had been surprised by the fact that the Serrets had seven children, they were astonished when they found out that Pepe was a successful executive. They soon became friends with the Serrets and began to visit them frequently. Today they have seven children and continue saying, "It is 'crazy' but truly attractive."

A colleague from Pepe's days in León recalls:

> Everyone in the business knew that he went to daily Mass, whenever possible first thing in the morning. It didn't matter whether he had been able to go to bed early or, for whatever reason, had gone to bed very late. In either case, Mass at the beginning of the day was the first thing for him. He gave an example of constancy and firmness in his religious convictions. On business trips with colleagues, Pepe would frequently invite them to say the Rosary with him.

During a Baltic cruise arranged by a supplier, he was careful to find out before embarking when there would be Mass on Sunday in a little town near Helsinki. As the day approached, he told everyone when the Mass would be celebrated, and many people accompanied him to Mass. On another occasion, Pepe learned that after a professional dinner, the program called for going to a nightclub with a lewd floor show. With light-handed good humor, he convinced the dinner participants to go to the opera instead.

He did not limit himself to giving good example. He made an effort to talk with people about their personal lives and their relationship with God. One day, a person he had met only recently accompanied him to his office to pick up some documents. Pepe took an interest in how his work and his family were going. Although the person said things were going well, it was obvious from his tone of voice that they were not, and Pepe began to talk with him about family life. When they were leaving the office, he picked up a very well-wrapped box that someone had left for him. He opened the box and saw that it contained two bottles of very fine French champagne. Pepe, who appreciated good champagne, took one of the bottles and gave it to his new acquaintance, saying, "Do you remember the advice I just gave you? Well, it will get better results if you put it into practice accompanied from time to time by a bottle of good champagne."

Having people over to the house for lunch, dinner, or a snack provided many opportunities to talk with them about family life. Pepe kept a book he called a "Diary of Encounters." At the end of dinner, he asked guests to write something. When someone asked him why he did so, he responded that it made people think and that this prevented them from making critical comments and spreading rumors as people are inclined to do after dinner. "While they are thinking and writing," Pepe said, "they don't say foolish things."

He often bought more than one copy of spiritual reading books because he knew he would end up giving them away. He usually took advantage of his plane trips to do some spiritual reading. When he finished, he often talked to the person in the seat next to him about what he was reading. At the end of the trip, not infrequently the book changed hands and his seatmate left the plane determined to consider the meaning of his life more seriously.

Life of Piety

From the moment he joined Opus Dei, Pepe took very seriously his commitment to grow in the love of God, take advantage of the formation Opus Dei offered him, and bring others closer to God. At the beginning of his annual retreat in 1983, he made a list of resolutions about how to make the retreat well: "First, dedicate all my time to the retreat; second, spend as much time as possible in the company of the Blessed Sacrament; third, make good use of my time; fourth, work at being silent; fifth, have recourse to Our Lady of Fatima." During his retreats, he made resolutions to carry back home with him. For example, after a talk on apostolate during a retreat, he wrote a list of twenty-six people for whom he would try to offer prayer and mortification to bring them closer to God.

He tried both to put his heart into the norms and customs that make up the plan of life of a member of the Work and to find personal ways in which to express his love of God and devotion to Our Lady. He and Roser had a tastefully chosen picture or statue of the Blessed Virgin in many rooms of their home. On Saturdays, the day the Church dedicates especially to Mary, he would cut flowers in the garden and ask one of the children to put a flower in front of each image of Our Lady in the house. If he was going to be out on a Saturday, he did this on the preceding Friday.

He prayed the Stations of the Cross every Friday and during Lent every day. He liked to read and reread St. Thomas More's *History of the Passion* and St. Josemaría's *The Way of the Cross*. He carefully annotated both and took them with him when he was traveling. Although raising eleven children cannot have been without stress, Pepe does not seem to have faced any especially difficult situations in his life. He tried, however, to find Christ's cross each day in his intense work, in the fulfillment of his family obligations, and in the effort to forget about himself and give himself to others.

He also practiced mortification at meals. When he took business guests out to eat at a restaurant, he would help them choose the best dishes, but he would often limit himself to a single fried egg. A friend and business colleague recalled: "We spent many hours together at the table and I was impressed by how little food he put on his plate while making sure that the others had enough to eat. He lived temperance and had adopted the practice of not having dessert. He said, 'You can't live without eating, but you can live without dessert.'"

Death in a Car Crash

The Serrets were still just getting settled in Reus when on January 24, 1993, for no particular reason, Pepe and Roser spoke at length about heaven and about death. Roser recalls him saying: "You'll see how happy we'll be in heaven, all of us together. Can you imagine how happy we'll be?" The next day, Pepe traveled by plane to Madrid. During the return trip from the Barcelona airport, a car going in the opposite direction jumped the median and crashed into Pepe's car, killing him.

Pepe was buried in the little town where he had been born. Hundreds of people came to the funeral. One of them said, "Seeing the affection with which he treated me, I always thought I was one of his best friends. But that day, seeing so many people weeping because of his loss, I saw clearly that Pepe's heart was so big that hundreds of friends fit in it."

CHAPTER TWELVE

Toni Zweifel:
Foundation Executive

Toni Zweifel, an Italian-born aeronautical engineer, spent his entire working life in Switzerland. He established an international foundation that supports numerous social activities in developing countries.

Youth

Toni Zweifel was born in 1938 in San Giovanni Lupatato, a small town in northern Italy about sixty miles west of Venice. His father, Giusto, a non-practicing Swiss Protestant businessman, owned and operated an embroidery firm which, at its peak, had a thousand employees. He also created a fashion business and two textile firms located in Switzerland. Eventually, he purchased agricultural estates, vineyards, and a marble quarry. Toni's mother, the daughter of a wine merchant, had been educated in a convent school. She worked hard at raising Toni and his sister in the Catholic faith despite suffering from ongoing mental health problems. In later life, Toni would sometimes repeat simple prayers he learned from her, such as, "Beautiful angels in heaven, watch over me forever."

At the beginning of World War II, Giusto sent his family to neutral Switzerland, where Toni learned the Swiss-German dialect. At the close of the war, the family returned to San Giovanni Lupatato, where Toni attended the public grade school. During middle and high school, he rode his bicycle four miles to Verona and back every day. Although he attended a science high school, Toni also acquired a solid command of Latin and English. In later life, he would pick up French and Spanish.

During middle and high school, Toni made a point of stopping in church frequently to spend some time praying before the Blessed Sacrament.

When he was about fifteen, it seemed that his parents were on the verge of divorce. Toni promised God that if he solved their problem, he would go to church to pray for at least a few minutes twice a week for a whole year. His parents worked out their difficulties, and Toni began trying to fulfill his promise and kept a record in a notebook of the days he went to church. At the end of the year, he realized he had not succeeded and began again. (He finally fulfilled his promise the year he joined Opus Dei in 1962.)

In the fall of 1957, Toni enrolled in the five-year mechanical engineering program at the Swiss Federal Institute of Technology, the MIT of Europe, popularly known as Zurich Poly. He drove to Switzerland in the red MG convertible his father had given him as a high school graduation present.

During his years at the Zurich Poly, Toni's religious practice dwindled down to attending Sunday Mass. As he approached his final year, he seemed to be well on his way to achieving his life goals of professional success and founding a family. He had a position assured as his father's successor at the head of a large and prosperous family business, and he was actively dating a professor's daughter who seemed like an ideal wife. Nonetheless, he felt called to something more. As he later told St. Josemaría, "I had to go further, love truly, overcome my self-centeredness for love, choose and commit myself."

Early Days in Opus Dei

A turning point came late in the 1960–1961 school year when a Spanish student invited Toni to visit the apartment where a small number of Opus Dei members were living. Toni liked the people he met there, but their efforts to start a university residence near the Zurich Poly seemed crazy: *They're foreigners, Catholics, and have no money. . . . Furthermore, student residences don't seem to be financially viable here*, he thought. Nonetheless, he accepted an invitation to move into the residence even though he was already comfortably settled for his final year at Zurich Poly in a studio apartment.

In an interview that formed part of the admissions process of the Fluntern Residence, Toni insisted that he needed a quiet single room to concentrate intensely on his studies. The director of Fluntern responded that the residence would try hard to create an environment conducive to serious study, but that all the residents would have shared rooms and would be expected to take an active part in the life of the residence rather than concentrating exclusively on their studies and other private activities. Toni agreed and took his commitment to contribute to the life of the residence seriously. From the start, he tried to respect the residence's schedule and participate in the daily life of the house, renouncing his own tastes and getting involved in activities he initially found unattractive, like playing soccer.

In the residence, Toni became familiar with Opus Dei's message about seeking sanctity in daily life and developing an interior life of prayer and sacrifice. Gradually he began to pray more, see his studies as something he could offer to God, and show greater concern for other people. At the end of 1961, he returned from a retreat preached by an Opus Dei priest with a strong sense that God was calling him to be an apostle in the world and to dedicate his entire life to him. On March 19, 1962, he joined Opus Dei as a numerary member.

A priest who had known Toni well observes that when he met him a short time later,

> I found him transformed. He was a different person. What was most noticeable about him was the great joy he radiated. Those of us who had known him before thought of him as someone who did not smile easily. But now he just couldn't stop smiling. It was a smile that came from the heart, one that didn't depend on circumstances or moods. From then on, I could see that his inner world was surprisingly stable. It came from his absolute certainty that he was doing what God wanted.

From the moment Toni joined Opus Dei, he made a serious effort to develop a deeper interior life based on the sense of being a son of God. He generously made time in a busy schedule to put into practice the plan of life of a member of Opus Dei, trying to dedicate to mental prayer, the Rosary, and the other norms the times when he was most alert. Toni also worked hard at developing and practicing the moral virtues, the qualities that make someone a good human being, whether or not they are Christian. He practiced the cardinal virtues like justice and fortitude as well as the small virtues that make life pleasant for others like punctuality.

Perhaps because he came from an affluent background, he made a special effort to practice Christian detachment in big things and small. For many years he lived in a very small room that was cold in winter and hot in summer. He purchased advanced, high-quality office equipment for the foundation he founded, but he insisted that it be well cared for so that it would last many years. Similarly, he purchased good-quality clothes that wouldn't go out of style quickly and took care of them, so he didn't need to replace them often.

Several anecdotes concerning cars illustrate his detachment. All his life, Toni liked cars, especially sports cars. On one occasion, he was very much looking forward to getting a ride back from a retreat in a participant's two-seater Porsche 928, but when he realized that a young man who also loved fast cars would enjoy the ride, he cheerfully suggested that he take his place. After he joined the Work, he traded the red MG convertible his father had given him for a dull, but much more practical, minivan. From then on, he took such good care of his car that he only needed to replace it twice in his lifetime. But despite how well he cared for the car, he didn't hesitate to let other people borrow it.

Toni was attentive to the demands of justice, including honesty in his business dealings. On one occasion, when he was looking to purchase a house in Zurich, he found a suitable, well-located one. The broker offered a good price, provided that Toni participate in a tax evasion scheme on the sale. Toni immediately refused and ended contact with the broker.

A Busy Engineer

Immediately after his graduation in June 1962, Toni began working at Contraves AG, a leading Swiss aerospace firm, where he researched the aerodynamics of rockets. In the year and a half he worked there, he established a reputation for bringing people together and solving problems. One of his colleagues recalls that despite Toni's youth and lack of experience, when there were disagreements between different groups, he "was able to defuse the situation and resolve the question by his calm, open way of setting out the arguments."

In addition to holding a demanding full-time job, Toni took on more and more responsibilities at the Fluntern residence. Among other things, he organized a series of talks attended by eighty first-year students on "Preparing for Work." It brought together students, professors, and businessmen to talk about different jobs and roles.

To have more time to dedicate to the residence, in January 1964 Toni resigned from Contraves and took a part-time position as a research assistant to Professor Max Berchtold at Zurich Poly. Cutting back on his work as an engineer only a year and a half after graduating from one of Europe's top technical schools cannot have been easy, but Toni cheerfully made this sacrifice for the sake of Opus Dei's still incipient apostolate in Switzerland.

After Toni's death, Professor Berchtold wrote:

> As a scientific coworker, for long years I had the opportunity to appreciate his great human qualities allied to extraordinary professional competence. He successfully carried out each task I entrusted to him, sparing no effort, and devoting every care to it. In conversation, he always won over the other person with his serene, modest, and diligent approach. Working with him left me with a shining example of an unforgettable friendship.

In 1965, Toni became the director of the Fluntern residence, a position he held for eight years. An engineer who got to know Toni well during the early years of his tenure as director of the residence stresses Toni's "balanced personality." He did not show irritation or annoyance and had a "positive, joyful, serene attitude." This led many residents and other people who visited Fluntern to seek his advice on all sorts of questions. If he was not sure, he'd say, "We'll see," and people felt sure he was going to study the matter in depth. Despite his privileged background and intelligence, he was, according to the same engineer, "able to put himself at the other person's level and be friendly and approachable. I don't mean that he was easy-going. . . . Patient, understanding, gentle, yes; but at the same time demanding."

Despite the need for more residents, Toni made clear to prospective residents that a lot was expected of them. A doctoral student in chemistry who was considering moving into Fluntern recalls Toni telling him, "This residence will be a challenge for you. You'll be living with people who practice their faith and commit themselves to really loving God. You'll have to study hard and seriously. You'll have to take on some small task of service for the others."

In addition to overseeing the day-to-day functioning of the residence, including food service and cleaning, Toni spent a lot of time talking one-on-one with the residents, listening to their difficulties, urging them to study hard but also to contribute to the atmosphere of the residence and take part in its activities. To open the eyes and hearts of residents and their friends to the needs of others, he frequently invited them to go with him to visit poor people or hospital patients. He also encouraged believers and others who seemed well-disposed to take advantage of the formational and devotional activities the residence offered.

A resident who eventually became a priest and professor of theology recalls:

> The first impression I got of him was of a young man who was a competent professional, passionate about his work as a mechanical engineer but also about lots of other things. . . . He stood out for his good humor, infectious cheerfulness, simplicity, and modesty. He was very keen on sports, sociable, and generous with his time toward anyone who needed help, whether with work or anything else. He had an excellent reputation and won the esteem of all the residents. It didn't take me long to see that, besides all the things he did (his research work at the Poly and managing the residence), he had a daily plan of religious devotions that he followed conscientiously and naturally: Mass, prayer, Rosary. I realized that this was where he got the strength to do everything in such a selfless spirit and with so much good humor.

In 1968, Toni's father, who had already given a house to Toni's sister, gave Toni a large house in Zurich, quite close to the residence. Toni made this house available to be used as the Work's headquarters in Switzerland, where the members of Opus Dei's regional governing body lived and had their offices.

The year 1972 brought big changes in Toni's life. He left the Fluntern residence and became the director of the center which housed Opus Dei's regional government, taking on responsibility for the day-to-day functioning of the center. In addition, he began to organize Opus Dei's retreats, evenings of recollection, and weekend conferences for married men and others who were already established in their jobs. That same year, he gave up his position at Zurich Poly and began two projects that were destined to have an international outreach and that would occupy much of the rest of his life. One was an international aid foundation for disadvantaged people all over the world; the second was an international conference center.

The Limmat Foundation

Over the years, Toni had become aware that many worthwhile social projects failed altogether or remained small for lack of money and management expertise. In part because of his family background, Toni knew people who had plenty of money to give to good causes, but who did little or nothing with it because they weren't sure where to direct their efforts. He decided to create a foundation to serve as a bridge between these two worlds.

The Founder of Opus Dei, who was deeply concerned with providing education to the poor and raising their standard of living, encouraged Toni to launch this new initiative. The Limmat Foundation (named for a river in Zurich) was born in March 1972. Initially, the foundation was quite small. From the beginning, however, it had a clear philosophy of concentrating less on material help than on enabling people to increase their knowledge and develop their talents so that they could solve their own problems and those of their communities. This focus and clarity of purpose contributed greatly to the foundation's later growth.

Rather than directly running programs, Limmat tried to identify and help local groups who knew the field and were hard-working, honest, and eager to serve the common good. From the beginning, Toni conceived of the new undertaking as an "umbrella foundation," which not only connected local projects with international donors, but also provided other foundations with know-how, administrative structure, and fundraising capabilities so that they could better carry out their activities with lower staffing and administrative costs. To facilitate carrying out a wide range of projects, the Limmat Foundation established specialized sub-foundations (*Sonderpatronate*) which could benefit from the main foundation's expertise and administrative structure while enjoying a wide degree of autonomy—a novel approach in the world of Swiss philanthropy.

Over time, Toni formulated five programmatic principles to guide the foundation:

1. Projects are planned and carried out by local groups that are on the ground, well-qualified, and rooted in the local culture.
2. Priority is given to supporting institutions that promote professional development and job-skill training, particularly in rural areas.

3. Special attention is given to the advancement of women and ensuring that their role in society is fully valued, while also trying to see to it that children receive appropriate nutrition, healthcare, and education.

4. As projects develop, the local communities must progressively take more and more responsibility for them.

5. Local partners must finance at least one-third of the project's total cost.

The director of the Zurich office of the United Nations Industrial Development Organization (UNIDO) was impressed by how this approach helped Toni and the Limmat Foundation achieve an environment of genuine cooperation and disinterested work, avoiding the danger of transplanting foreign values to developing areas. He stressed that this was possible because Toni and his collaborators always assumed good intentions in their local partners, no matter how different their ideas might be.

During the sixteen years that Toni headed the Limmat Foundation, it financed hundreds of remarkably diverse projects in thirty-six countries on four continents, thanks in part to a substantial grant from the Federal Republic of Germany for training programs helping disadvantaged people in poor countries. This enabled Limmat to support twenty projects to be carried out in collaboration with schools and organizations that were already working for the humanitarian and professional training of people in nine Latin American countries, Kenya, and the Philippines. With the help of a grant from the Swiss Authority for Development, Cooperation, and Humanitarian Aid, Limmat was able to help El Alto, a school in Colombia, enlarge its facilities and acquire new teaching equipment for programs for mothers from impoverished rural families. Some years later, a grant from the same Swiss source enabled Limmat to support a project for skills training for special-needs youth in the Philippines.

The foundation supported the Italian Boys Towns, originally founded to care for orphans after the Second World War. It helped the schools for Jewish refugees run by ORT, a major international Jewish charity. Limmat also subsidized an orphanage for Buddhist and Christian orphans run by Buddhist monks in Bangladesh, where Buddhists comprise less than one percent of the population.

Some of the undertakings Limmat supported were collective apostolic activities of Opus Dei, such as the Condoray training center for women in

Peru or the ELIS technical high school in Rome. Another apostolic undertaking of Opus Dei supported by the Limmat Foundation was the Kibondeni Training Center on the outskirts of Nairobi. Kibondeni aims primarily at
improving the standard of living of young women from low-income families
The center equips them with the knowledge, skills, and attitudes needed to
secure employment that makes them self-reliant and meets their needs and
those of their families. Limmat successfully solicited major financial help for
Kibondeni from the Belgian government.

Toni was convinced that "many current crises have their roots in the crisis of the family. . . . In today's growing void of ideas, parents and children
are influenced by ever-changing role models, and it is becoming more and
more difficult to distinguish between real progress and fads." Moved by this
concern, in 1977 Limmat began publishing a magazine entitled *Familie und
Erziehung* (Family and Education). Two years later it sponsored an International Family Congress in Zurich, which brought together 350 married
couples from fifteen countries.

In addition to focusing on specific projects, Toni devoted time and
energy to developing Limmat's personnel. This was especially important
since he deliberately kept the staff small. A distinctive aspect of his manage-
rial style was his practice of delaying reaction to less-than-critical problems
and situations, letting time pass and taking care of several points in a single conversation. He habitually considered in prayer what he was going to
say before correcting anyone or making an important suggestion. One of his
closest collaborators describes his approach:

> He would take out a piece of paper from his notebook where he had noted
> down four or five things he wanted to talk to me about, and in a calm and
> very friendly way he shared them with me. . . . He always left me a way
> out so that I could explain things in case he had misunderstood what had
> taken place or the problem had already been sorted out in the meantime.
> [This way of behaving] implied a great interior struggle: waiting before say-
> ing things in order to say them calmly, in a long-term context, after reflect-
> ing carefully about them not only from the human and professional point
> of view but also in God's presence. . . . His system also made good use of
> time. Instead of spending a lot of time pointing out things to be corrected

singly, just one meeting was enough to deal with several different matters. The way Toni did it made me very grateful.

Toni had the humility and common sense to realize that his approach to a question was not always the best one. The person whom he prepared to be his successor recalls that when they had differing opinions, "he did not reproach me or set out to prove me wrong. Quite the reverse. He asked the reasons I had for my point of view and always asked himself whether maybe it was he who was mistaken."

Because of his duties as the director of the Opus Dei center where he lived, Toni often reached the foundation office later than others. As he went past each office, he had a friendly word for the person working there. One of his collaborators recalls that when Toni came in, he used to say to himself, *The joy of the house has just arrived.* To ensure that relations in the office were not only amicable but fair, he adapted to the needs of his small organization the guidelines of Zurich Poly for salaries, raises, bonuses, and hours of work.

Toni's work at the Limmat Foundation impressed people at the highest levels of international philanthropy. Klaus Schwab, who had known Toni as a student and who eventually became president of the Davos World Economic Forum, said, "The way he devoted himself to social projects through the Limmat Foundation, which was so important for mankind, always seemed to me admirable, and should be a model for each of us."

After a while, Toni realized that what he had developed in the Limmat foundation could be exported to other affluent countries to contribute toward the advancement of poor parts of the world. In January 1988, he organized an international seminar for experts from not-for-profit organizations in Belgium, Germany, France, Italy, Spain, Canada, and the United States. This was the origin of a network of organizations similar to the Limmat Foundation.

Toni's work in creating and developing the Limmat Foundation continues to bear fruit today. Currently, there are sixteen foundations grouped under its umbrella, each benefiting from the infrastructure it provides to make possible their specific activities in over thirty countries. Many of the current projects focus on training teachers and coaches to help special-needs children, street children, and children displaced by conflict and civil war.

International Conference Center

The other major project to which Toni dedicated years of his life was the construction of an international conference center.

The conference center would host retreats, workshops, seminars, and summer courses focused on Christian teaching and ethics training for men, women, and young people from all three Swiss linguistic groups as well as from other countries.

Despite his many other duties, Toni turned his attention enthusiastically to the project. After completing a preliminary study, he established a nonprofit association to promote and manage the future center, *Verein Internationales Tagungszentrum* (VIT). Its first president was Professor Edgardo Giovannini, the former rector of the University of Fribourg. VIT located property in the municipality of Schongau and obtained the approval of the town council, the department of land management, and the building permits office. On September 14, 1978, the association purchased a fifteen-acre (six-hectare) plot at public auction.

Things appeared to be moving forward smoothly until mid-January 1978. Suddenly, their plans began to fall apart due to infighting between local political groups and what eventually became a nationwide media storm against Opus Dei. On January 13, 1978, a major Zurich newspaper published an article criticizing three members of Opus Dei who were religious education teachers in secondary schools in the Zurich canton. The newspaper attacked the teachers for their support of Pope John Paul II's teaching on abortion, contraception, and other family issues. The bishop of the Diocese of Basel (of which Schongau forms part) continued to express his support for the conference center, and for a few months things seemed to be moving forward despite the attacks.

On April 11, 1979, Swiss national television aired a prime-time program attacking Opus Dei's activities in Zurich and the proposed conference center. At this point, one of the two main factions in local politics seized on the issue to attack its opponents and convinced a journalist to dedicate a special feature to the project in a major national newspaper. This triggered a media firestorm that lasted a year. Looking back forty years later, and without being familiar with the characteristics of Swiss society and media of the late 1970s, it is hard to understand how hundreds of articles, radio, and television programs could have been dedicated to covering Opus Dei—which had a very small presence in Switzerland—and to an as-yet-to-be-built conference center, in an out-of-the-way village with 340 inhabitants. That, is, however, what happened.

Encouraged by the adverse media the project was receiving and by the local political group that had taken up the cause, in July 1979 many Schonau inhabitants signed a petition demanding a referendum on the proposed change of the use of the site. Toni spent the day of the referendum (March 2, 1980) at his office preparing a press release. People who saw him that day were impressed with his serenity, which they attributed to his trust in God and to the fact that he was more interested in doing God's will than in the success of a project to which he had dedicated so much work and enthusiasm. Ninety percent of the eligible voters turned out. One hundred thirty-nine voted for the project, and two hundred thirty-nine against it.

Rather than complaining or rebelling, Toni calmly turned to salvaging what he could from the project. By mid-June, he had succeeded in selling the land for what the foundation had paid for it, although this did not recover the time and money spent studying the project and trying to defuse the media campaign against the conference center and Opus Dei. This experience contributed greatly to Toni's personal growth in holiness, teaching him to work for God's glory alone and to be united to Christ in failure as much as in success.

Toni decided he had an obligation to defend the rights and reputation of VIT and Opus Dei. He lodged complaints for defamation, seeking rectifications from the magazine and the newspaper in which the most egregious attacks and falsehoods had been published. The magazine quickly agreed to publish a rectification but dragged matters out until December 1982. When the rectification was eventually published, it was accompanied by comments from the editors presenting themselves as the victims. Toni decided nothing further could be done on this front and calmly accepted this unsatisfactory outcome without complaint. The legal case against the newspaper dragged on for nine years. Eventually, Switzerland's highest court found that the paper's allegation that Opus Dei had hidden behind VIT was false but did not consider the statement defamatory.

Bringing Friends Closer to God

From the time when he joined Opus Dei until his death, Toni spent many hours with friends, coworkers, and relatives. He especially enjoyed swimming and hiking in the mountains with them, but he was also there for them in their joys and sorrows. He encouraged them to take their Christian faith seriously, to receive the sacraments frequently, and to get to know the Church's teaching.

Many of the people with whom he came in contact ended up turning to him for advice in different areas of their life. A law student who was torn between trying to have an academic career and going to work in development aid in South America approached Toni for advice. Toni stressed that this was a decision that only the student could make since no one else knew him anywhere near as well as he knew himself. He urged him to

> weigh up the different possibilities calmly, serenely, and dispassionately, not letting yourself be ruled by your feelings. Ask God to enlighten you. If you conclude that the best thing for you is to go to South America, then go there in good conscience. But realize that once you've made up your mind, that decision is made. It may happen that some years from now, you could be faced with a situation where you have to make a fresh decision. Take the decision again, at that point, after having considered everything carefully, but without imagining that you made a mistake before or did something stupid. That would be pointless. Take your new decision without feeling your life is already determined by the decision you made before.

In addition to one-on-one conversations with friends, relatives, and colleagues, Toni organized a series of monthly classes for bankers and other people from the world of finance on living the faith in daily life. One of the participants, an evangelical Protestant who eventually became Catholic, recalled the classes as "stimulating" and "unforgettable," and said they played an important part in his long process of conversion. Toni also frequently invited people to attend the evenings of recollection, retreats, and other formational activities organized by Opus Dei.

Many people reacted positively to Toni's efforts to help them take their faith more seriously. A businessman, for instance, who worked with Toni on a charitable project, accepted his recommendation to sever his relations with a company that bought and sold human embryos and from then on sought his advice about other important decisions. During Toni's illness, a young doctor who had known him during his years in medical school came to visit him frequently, at first simply out of friendship and compassion. As time went by, he began to visit more frequently, fascinated by the strength and conviction with which Toni urged him to marry the girl he was living with. When they had a baby, Toni stressed the importance of having the infant baptized and eventually persuaded the couple to get married in the church.

Others, however, rejected what they considered Toni's inflexible attitudes in matters of faith. Toni regretted losing friends, but rather than getting angry or feeling personally wounded, he calmly accepted this as an inevitable consequence of people's freedom and part of the cost of following Christ.

Final Illness and Death

In February 1986, at forty-eight years of age, Toni was diagnosed with advanced leukemia which would lead to his death three and a half years later. In the days following his diagnosis, Toni was confined to a hospital bed, subject to aggressive and often painful therapy with all sorts of complications and side effects. For a time, he was too weak to work. At first, he was saddened by the prospect of spending the rest of his life as an incurable invalid, unable to work, and probably destined to die young, but he soon recovered his characteristic joy and cheerfulness.

Toni did everything he could to recover and return to work. Periods of hospitalization in which he continued working as much as possible from his bed alternated with returns to the office. After several bouts of unsuccessful conventional chemotherapy, he agreed to an experimental therapy with extreme side effects, which he bore without complaint. He strove to put into practice the advice that the Prelate of Opus Dei, Blessed Álvaro del Portillo, gave him: to nurture hope for a total cure, and hope for heaven if that was what God wanted.

In his final months, he often said that his life had been a love story and that he had fallen hopelessly in love with God. Throughout the long period of his illness, Toni strove to work as much as he could, to keep up his life of prayer, and to bring as many people as possible, including his sister and brother-in-law, closer to God. As he told the Prelate of Opus Dei in a letter: "Because of my situation, I was able to go straight to the heart of things and talk about God openly. This period has been very intense. I have so many reasons for being grateful, deeply grateful!"

Toni died early in the morning of Friday, November 24, 1989, after receiving Holy Communion. One of the two members of the Work who were accompanying him recalls his final moments:

> I took his right hand so that he could "feel" our prayer. After a while, I felt him trying to withdraw his hand. With the hand that I released, he waved us goodbye, fully conscious and smiling. I took his hand again and asked him to greet the Founder of Opus Dei in heaven and to ask him to intercede for us. He then opened his eyes to show that he had understood; he looked at the picture of Our Lady on the wall facing him, exhaled noisily, and began to inhale. There was a slight noise as though something had closed. Toni was no longer breathing. Everything had happened very gently. It was six-thirty in the morning. There were just the two of us, Antonine Suarez and I, on either side of the bed. We were deeply moved by the peaceful way he had left us.

Toni's process of beatification and canonization was opened in 2000.

CHAPTER THIRTEEN

Ed Dillett:
Plumber

E d Dillett had been working as a plumber for thirty years when he became the third married man to join Opus Dei in the United States. Over the following two decades, he quietly but effectively spread the Work's message of holiness in daily work to many friends, relatives, and fellow workers.

Early Life

Ed Dillett grew up in a small Wisconsin town some 250 miles northwest of Milwaukee. Shortly after graduating from high school in 1925, he moved to Milwaukee, where he became an apprentice plumber and won the Golden Gloves welterweight boxing championship. At age twenty-four, Ed became a master plumber and started his own plumbing company.

At first, business was slow, and he had to go door-to-door asking people if they needed any plumbing work done. Soon, however, he was making good money and purchased three houses that he intended to rent out. His venture into real estate was ill-timed, however. As the effects of the Great Depression grew worse, his tenants were unable to pay their rent, and the bank foreclosed on his properties. Soon, his plumbing business also failed.

With no work as a plumber and no prospect of finding any, he joined the Civilian Conservation Corps, one of the New Deal's projects to relieve unemployment by hiring single young men to carry out conservation projects on federal land. Ed was sent to northern Wisconsin to cut brush, clear stumps, construct fire lanes, and plant pine trees. His cheerfulness and leadership qualities won him the camp's annual Fellowship Trophy.

Shortly before leaving Milwaukee, Ed had fallen in love with Myra Prze-worski, the daughter of a coal miner who had been killed in an explosion. Many weekends, to spend time with her, he "rode the rails" on the top of boxcars to and from Milwaukee. He would wait until a train had cleared the rail yard but was still moving slowly enough for him to grab the ladder and climb up to the top of a boxcar, where he tied himself down with a wide leather belt. He could have easily been injured or arrested and thrown in jail, but, fortunately, he had no mishaps.

Marriage

After one year in the Civilian Conservation Corps, Ed returned to Milwaukee and proposed to Myra. A year and a half later, on May 25, 1936, they were married. They rented the upper floor of a two-story house that had no plumbing except a sink in the kitchen and a shared toilet in the basement. Instead of paying rent, Ed installed bathrooms in their flat and in the ground-floor flat where the owner lived. On November 27, 1937, their first child, Jim, was born.

Shortly after his marriage, Ed once again started his own plumbing company, doing everything himself, from installing pipes to sending out bills. Business improved as the economy recovered toward the end of the 1930s.

By the late 1930s, Ed was attending daily Mass, and he and Myra soon began to say the Rosary every evening. He joined the Holy Name Society and became more involved in the parish. He also tried to bring his friends and coworkers closer to God on a one-on-one basis. One day, for example, while Ed and a plumber he had hired were driving to work in Ed's truck, Ed asked him, "Where do you go to church, Joe?"

"I haven't been to church in quite a while, Ed, why do you ask?"

"Oh, part of it is curiosity and part of it is I'm very interested in trying to help fellas get closer to God." The next morning, Ed said he had been thinking about their conversation in the truck the previous day. "If I made you uncomfortable, Joe, I didn't mean to."

"No, not really," Joe said, "Your question about where I went to church was a good one. The thing that really made me think is what you said after that: something about your interest in helping me get closer to God.

Sometime, Ed, I'd like to talk to you more about that, okay?" As time went by Joe returned to practicing his faith and he and Ed talked frequently about God.

World War II

At the beginning of World War II, Ed was drafted by the Army to work as a plumbing foreman on the construction of a defense plant in Milwaukee. The job involved seventy-two-hour workweeks and supervising a crew of men, few of whom had any previous plumbing experience. Once the plant was completed, Ed shifted to maintenance of the machines used to produce turbochargers for bomber aircraft.

Ed and Myra both followed the war news closely. But while Ed was elated to hear about effective US bombing raids, Myra was troubled by the killing of innocent civilians. Ed understood her concern but felt an obligation rooted in faith. "I know what the fifth commandment says honey, but I know it's morally right that we need to help those enslaved by a dictator. Hitler is a dictator who is not just enslaving the German people, he's killed hundreds of thousands of Jewish people. We, as Catholics, can't just sit and let that happen; God wants us to intervene."

The Immediate Postwar Years

At the end of World War II, Myra tried to convince Ed to take a job as a union plumber with a large firm and a steady income, but he was determined to reestablish his own business. He started a new company called Dillett Plumbing. In the economic boom that followed World War II, the business prospered, and Ed hired several other men.

In January 1947, Milwaukee was hit by an enormous blizzard that blocked the doors of the Dillett's home, but that did not prevent Ed from getting to Mass. He crawled out a second-story window and skied down the side of the twelve-foot snowdrift piled against the house. The church was locked when he arrived, but he knocked at the rectory door and the pastor agreed to celebrate Mass if he would serve. It was the first time he had ever served Mass and he was deeply impressed: "I have never been that close to the altar when the bread and wine become the Body and Blood of Jesus. It was an experience I'll never forget." His son comments, "For Dad, the Mass was something he treasured, and it was the highlight of his day every day."

Ed continued trying to bring others closer to Christ. One day he asked the owner of the gas station where he brought his truck to be repaired, "When's the last time you went to church, Red?"

"Been quite a while, Ed. Not sure God wants me to go to church. Last time I went, someone broke into the station and stole half my tools. I think God was trying to tell me something about taking care of business."

"Well, Red. Let me explain it the best way I can. God has a plan for all of us and goals beyond our business. He wants us to be happy with Him in heaven when we die. And we're all going to die. Let's say you're very successful in business and make a lot of money and leave God out of your life. All the money you make won't matter when you face God on Judgment Day. Do you ever think about it in that way, Red?" "

"I guess I don't ever give it a whole lot of thought, Ed. Maybe I should."

"I say you should," Ed responded with a smile. "In the meantime, I'll pray for you, and I hope you will give God's plan a lot of thought and then decide to go to Mass regularly. Okay?"

Ed had accepted the job of retreat chairman for the Holy Name Society at his parish. With prayer and gentle persuasion, he convinced over forty men to attend a parish retreat at a nearby monastery.

As the immediate postwar boom petered out, Ed's business ventures ran into serious problems. He had formed a partnership with his brother-in-law to purchase a mechanical trenching machine to dig sewer trenches and footings for buildings. The new company, D.S. Construction, soon began to face stiff competition from firms with newer and more efficient machines. In 1949, Ed built a new building to house his plumbing business and a hardware store. The hardware store that rented space from him failed within a year, and D.S. Construction was also forced to dissolve. Eventually, Ed had to sell the building as well. He had also purchased a farm, partly out of concern that the United States might find itself at war with Russia. Ed rented the farm to a large family and agreed that they could live there rent-free for a year in exchange for work on the buildings. The family was glad to have free housing but did little work on the property.

The Dillett family and their seven children badly needed a larger house. Although Ed's businesses were not going well, in 1953 he built a four-bedroom ranch. The family moved into the new house in 1954 but had a hard time making ends meet and had to cut back on food and clothing. Nonetheless, they continued making substantial contributions to their parish and several Catholic charities.

About this time, Ed learned that his oldest son, Jim, was being bullied in school. Rather than going to the school to protest, Ed taught Jim to box. The bullying stopped and after a while, the bully came to Ed for boxing lessons.

A Totally New Life

Ed and Myra first heard about Opus Dei in 1955. Many young people learn about Opus Dei through their parents or other relatives who are supernumerary members or cooperators. The Dilletts learned about Opus Dei through their eldest son, who was a senior at Don Bosco High School on the south side of Milwaukee.

In February 1955, two members of the Work visited the school to invite seniors to make a retreat at Woodlawn residence in Chicago, the first center of Opus Dei in the United States. A priest of Opus Dei, Father Ray Madurga, drove Jim and several other boys back to Milwaukee after the retreat and took advantage of the occasion to visit the Dillett family. Ed and Myra were fascinated by what he told them about Opus Dei, and not long after, they both joined the Work. Ed was the first married male member of Opus Dei in Milwaukee, and the third in the United States.

Both Ed and Myra came closer to God after joining Opus Dei. They each found time for daily mental prayer and began reading the New Testament and other spiritual books regularly. They both tried to bring friends and relatives closer to God, not only with their example but with their conversation and gentle persuasion as well. Of course, Ed had tried to do this before he joined Opus Dei, but now he had a clearer sense that he had been called by God from all eternity to do so. In addition, he had a specific message to deliver: that his friends and relatives were also called by God, not just to be upright and nice, but to pursue holiness in and through the activities that made up their everyday lives.

Their son Jim says, "It was as if they were beginning a totally new life." Externally, very little changed in Ed's life. He continued working as a plumber. He was already attending daily Mass, saying the Rosary, and practicing many of the other customary Catholic devotions that make up the plan of life of a member of Opus Dei. Throughout his life, he had tried to bring friends and colleagues closer to Christ and had instinctively practiced the "apostolate of friendship and confidence" that members of Opus Dei are called to carry out with their friends and colleagues.

Why then does Jim say that joining Opus Dei was the beginning of a totally new life for his parents? Ed did not keep spiritual diaries or write other accounts of his life. From the notes he took during retreats, it seems clear, however, that the new element in his life was a sense of being called not just to be a "good Catholic" and get to heaven—but to be a saint. He understood, as he put it, "We are all called to be saints." He also learned that sanctity requires an interior life, which he saw as a "direct, interior conversation with God and not with self." He became convinced that "the center of the interior life is the Mass and the Blessed Sacrament," and that "personal prayer is a must."

Ed learned that God was calling him to live an interior life of prayer and seek sanctity precisely through his daily life and ordinary work. He discovered in Opus Dei that he could grow in love of God not only by going to Mass and saying the Rosary better, but also by fixing faucets, installing furnaces, and unclogging sewer lines as well as he could for love of God and his customers. He became more aware that his work was a service to others and an integral part of God's plan for him. During one retreat, he wrote: "Christ did ordinary work to show us ordinary work is good. We must imitate Christ in our ordinary work by doing it as perfectly as possible. Let us start by putting Jesus at the head of all our human activities."

Spreading the Message of Opus Dei

Ed hoped his oldest son would become a plumber and join him in the business, but at first Jim was not interested. Instead, he joined the Army Reserve. In April 1958, however, when Jim completed his active duty in the Army Reserve and moved back home, he asked his father if his offer of a plumbing apprenticeship was still open.

Ed was happy to have him. He took advantage of the occasion to confide that he'd been praying for him a great deal. Not so much that he would become a plumber, but that he would come closer to God through his work, whatever that might be.

> Jim, I really think plumbing is a great way to get closer to God; I know it's been that way for me. When I do a plumbing job, I try to do the work as well as possible. I know it's not perfect, but it's as good as I can make it. That's pleasing to God since He created us to work, and He wants us to work out our salvation through our work.

The Dilletts were eager to tell their friends and relatives about Opus Dei. Shortly after Ed and Myra joined the Work, Myra's sister Helen and her brother-in-law Ted also joined. Several other men whom Ed invited to attend evenings of recollection eventually became supernumerary members of Opus Dei. One of them, George Sell, became a particularly close friend. When he died several years later, Ed grieved deeply for him. He remarked, "I'm really gonna miss him, but I'll see him in heaven."

Ed helped set up the first Opus Dei centers in Madison and Milwaukee, Wisconsin. During the summer of 1955, he went to Madison on weekends to help install plumbing in the property which would become Randall House residence. The following year the archbishop of Milwaukee gave Opus Dei a substantial two-story brick house located on the south side of the city, close to Ed's home and many of the other people who had recently joined Opus Dei or attended its activities. Ed and other supernumeraries and their friends worked on the house during evenings and weekends after they finished their jobs. One of them, who was a pattern maker and had a complete woodworking shop, made the altar for the new center. A few years later, activities in Milwaukee had increased to the point that more space was needed. There was plenty of room in the basement, but its ceiling was low. Ed recruited several friends to help him solve the problem by digging out the floor of the basement by hand. He also volunteered to help install plumbing at Petawa residence, the first center of the women's branch of Opus Dei in Milwaukee. Amid all these activities, Ed continued to be deeply involved in his parish, where he taught Catholic catechism classes for students attending public schools.

A Failing Business

Once again, Ed faced serious financial difficulties. In retrospect, it was clear that Myra had been right when she urged him to work as a union plumber with a regular salary, rather than try to run his own business. He was forced to fire all his employees and try to carry on single-handedly. The business was not profitable enough to pay the taxes and mortgage payments on the large home Ed had built, and they were forced to sell it. They built a smaller home in a less-expensive neighborhood. It was far from completed when they had to hand over the keys to their prior home and move into the new, smaller building. For several months the Dilletts camped out in the house amid the noise and dust of construction.

Although Ed tried to remain cheerful and optimistic, struggling with a failing business and working against the clock to finish the new house with little money made him less patient and more easily frustrated. Fortunately, the housing market picked up the following spring, and business began to improve. After attending a workshop with other members of the Work, Ed returned home much more upbeat and hopeful. He had even more energy and more spring in his step.

By 1959 however, Ed had to face the reality that he could not earn a living working for himself. The decision to close the business was especially difficult because his son Jim had recently taken out a loan to buy a new house and he would earn much less working for someone else as an apprentice. Ed took a job working for a large company building a factory. He had to work outside through the exceptionally cold and snowy winter of 1959–1960, but working for someone else did bring with it a steady paycheck and a workday with regular hours. It also brought freedom in the evenings to spend time with family and friends rather than doing paperwork.

In 1966, Ed moved to one of the largest plumbing companies in Milwaukee, which prefabricated a lot of piping assemblies in their shop, bringing them to the job sites for installation. Ed worked in the fabrication shop, running a large threading machine. The job was dull, but Ed did it as well as possible for the love of God. Because he worked alone cutting and threading pieces of pipe, he had a lot of time to pray. He talked to Jesus constantly during the day, asking for many intentions, including the apostolate of Opus Dei. At lunchtime, he would try to direct the conversation away from the dirty jokes his fellow workers liked to tell and sometimes steered it toward spiritual topics. Some of his fellow plumbers accepted his invitations to attend evenings of recollection.

Family Life

Myra had never driven a car, but Ed wanted her to learn so that she could drive herself to the women's center of Opus Dei, which was on the other side of Milwaukee. Most men would probably have thought twice about trying to teach their fifty-year-old wife how to drive, especially with a stick shift. Ed did not hesitate. At the first attempt, Myra found clutch and accelerator coordination too difficult. Ed patiently encouraged her. Myra was so short that she had to use a cushion on the seat to see over the steering wheel, and the pedals were almost out of reach; but with Ed's encouragement, she succeeded in learning to drive.

There was a playful element to the Dilletts' family life. On occasion, Ed would pick Myra up and sit her on top of the refrigerator. She was too short to get down on her own, and he would ask her if she was going to behave herself. Only after she said yes would he gently take her down. One year at Ed's birthday, Myra decorated the cake with candles that relit themselves as soon as they were blown out. Myra laughed hysterically at his efforts until he started taking the candles and turning them upside down into the cake's pink frosting.

Ed did not believe in spanking or hitting the children, but he was a fairly strict disciplinarian, who tried to fit the punishment to the offense. When one of the children talked back to his mother who had asked him to clean the kitchen floor, for example, Ed announced that he would have to scrub the floor on his hands and knees every day for the next week.

Ed's love could be tough when necessary. On one occasion, one of the boys moved out, rented a room over a bar, and began drinking although he was below the legal age. After he had several small traffic accidents, Ed saw him one day in the bar and called the police, who arrested both him and the bartender. He then proceeded to bail the boy out of jail. They were estranged for a time, but eventually they were reconciled and grew so close that they frequently stayed up late into the night talking.

In addition to numerous financial setbacks and the death of an infant son, Ed and Myra suffered other disappointments. One of their children was divorced after five years of marriage; two entered religious life only to decide later that it was not for them; and one of their two children who joined Opus Dei eventually did not continue. Although they were disappointed, they tried to overcome their disappointment and provide their children with the emotional and financial support they needed.

Sickness and Death

In 1969, Ed suffered a mild heart attack, but he continued working at his physically demanding job. In 1972, a more serious heart attack forced him to retire. His heart stopped six or seven times, but each time he was resuscitated. In response to his son's question about what it felt like, he responded, "I was scared, really scared, but I didn't feel a lot of pain. I knew I wasn't ready to meet God, and there was a lot more I needed to do."

When Ed was finally able to leave the house three months after the attack, he exclaimed, "I'm so glad I can finally get to Mass every day; it's such a joy!" During his prolonged recovery, Ed sometimes talked with his children about heaven:

> Heaven is so great it can't be described in human terms. God has prepared a place for us who are faithful that we can't even imagine. Jesus himself said, "Eye has not seen, ear has not heard, nor has it entered into the heart of man what God has prepared for those who love him."[1] I'm so glad God has given me more time to get ready to meet him.

After a while, the doctor told Ed he could do some work as long as he broke it into short periods with frequent breaks. He started some projects in the Opus Dei centers in Milwaukee as well as at his son Mike's home. The project at Mike's home was a fairly large one, but Ed commented, "I hope

---

1. The words Ed quoted are not from Jesus himself but from St. Paul in the First Epistle to the Corinthians.

God gives me time to finish Mike's house, but if he doesn't, it'll be his will. The important thing is I'm going to be ready when he calls, whenever that is." When his eleven-year-old grandson volunteered to help him with some painting, he got more paint on the glass than on the wood. When Ed came to inspect his work, he said, "Wow, Dan; you're doing such a good job and going so fast I think we're going to let you take the rest of the afternoon off." After that, he found other kinds of work for Dan to do.

On September 24, 1975, Ed arrived for work at Mike's house with his toolbox. That day he was going to lay concrete blocks in a foundation trench he'd dug two weeks earlier. He'd work for twenty minutes and rest for ten. At one point, Mike's wife, Linda, heard her dogs barking although it didn't seem to be at anything in particular. She found Ed sitting there with his head bent forward and called him, but he failed to respond. He had died, as he had lived, serving others with his professional work.

CHAPTER FOURTEEN

Ernesto Cofiño:
Pediatrician

D r. **Cofiño**, the first physician in Guatemala to specialize in pediatrics, supported numerous social and educational projects, including some sponsored by other members of Opus Dei. He focused especially on improving the situation of indigenous children, many of whom at the time lived in dire straits.

Early Life

Dr Ernesto Cofiño first learned about Opus Dei in 1953. He was fifty-four years old and had long been the leading pediatrician in Guatemala. Born in 1899, he studied medicine at the University of Paris, where he specialized in pediatrics under Professor Robert Debré, the foremost French pediatrician of his generation and one of the founders of modern pediatrics.

When Cofiño returned from France to Guatemala in 1929, Guatemalan doctors still treated children as small adults. Pediatrics was not even recognized as a specialty in the country. The early years of his private practice of pediatrics were an uphill struggle, but he eventually became the wealthiest families' pediatrician of choice. Among his private patients, however, there were always many children of poor families whom he treated gratis, frequently paying for their medicine out of his own pocket.

In 1935, Cofiño won an appointment at the medical school as its first professor of pediatrics. He frequently attended international congresses and spent a year as a guest of the United States State Department working at Duke University and the Mayo Clinic. In 1949, he and his wife spent six months in France, Belgium, and Holland studying recent advances in pediatric social work.

Cofiño's vision of pediatrics went well beyond therapy. He stressed preventive medicine, hygiene, and improvement of social conditions, especially for the native population, which suffered from discrimination, poverty, lack of education, and malnutrition.

From 1939 to 1960, Ernesto was the director of pediatric medicine in the country's leading hospital. He was very demanding of himself and of those who worked with him. Other medical directors arrived at ten or eleven in the morning, but he arrived at 6:30 AM and insisted that everyone who worked in his department arrive on time. As a young man, Cofiño could be quite harsh in correcting mistakes. Over the years, however, his wife, Clemencia, gradually helped him learn to treat people more kindly.

In the 1940s, with the support of the Lions Club, Cofiño established a residential care facility for children with tuberculosis in the small town of San Juan Sacatepéquez. For many years, he spent weekends with his family in a small country house nearby and dedicated most of the weekends to caring for the patients, primarily children of poor indigenous families. In addition to providing medical treatment, Cofiño poured out affection on the children. At Christmas, he regularly dressed up as Santa Claus and distributed gifts.

In the 1950s Cofiño led a government-sponsored national tuberculosis vaccination campaign. He was also named director of the national government-sponsored orphanage. Originally, the institution had been private but had been taken over by the government. It was woefully inadequate in every way. The buildings were in terrible condition, and the orphans were malnourished and received virtually no education. When they reached the age of eighteen, they were turned out on the street with no skills, and often turned to crime as the only way of surviving. Cofiño completely transformed the institution. He established small-scale living units in place of sprawling dormitories, upgraded educational programs, and created an environment in which the children were treated with respect and affection. When the orphans reached adulthood and left the orphanage, Cofiño gave them a key to the front door so that they would have a place to go in difficult moments.

Before Cofiño's arrival, families interested in adopting were not screened to ensure that the children would be well cared for. Some orphans ended up as little better than slaves of the families who adopted them. With the help of his wife, who had a degree in social work, Cofiño instituted a modernized program of adoption and foster care focused on the needs and well-being of the children, rather than on the whims of potential adoptive parents.

Encountering Opus Dei

God played a very small role in Cofiño's life as a young man. In his own words, his "dealings with God came down to a social religion of weddings and funerals." After his marriage in 1933, he began to attend Sunday Mass with his wife. Shortly thereafter, he met a priest, Fr. Rossell, who would become archbishop of Guatemala in 1939. The two became good friends, but for many years Cofiño continued to show little interest in religion.

In the early 1950s, however, he began to feel that God was asking something more of him. He asked Rossell to recommend a priest who could guide him. The archbishop introduced his fifty-four-year-old friend to Father Antonio Rodriguez, a recently ordained, twenty-six-year-old Spanish priest of Opus Dei who had just arrived in Guatemala to begin the Work's apostolate there.

Cofiño had always seen his profession as a service to others but was amazed to discover that his work and the rest of his daily life could be an encounter with God. With Fr. Rodriguez's guidance and support, he rapidly began to develop an intense Christian life. In 1956, he joined Opus Dei as its first married member in Guatemala. Twenty-five years later, on his eightieth birthday, Ernesto observed that his vocation to Opus Dei "changed the entire panorama of my life, without taking me out of the place I occupied in life. God's call, the vocation, is a living light that makes you see the meaning of your life."

His youngest son observes:

> He gave himself to God in Opus Dei with all the strength of his heart, with what was deepest in his soul, with all his enthusiasm. . . . The last decades of his life were years of plenitude. . . . He discovered a deeper, more supernatural sense in work. It was no longer enough to carry it out well from the human point of view. He had always done that. Now he could convert it into prayer, into praise to the Creator, into love of God.

Despite being almost sixty years old when he joined Opus Dei, Cofiño aspired—and struggled—to grow in virtue, correct his defects, and develop an interior life of prayer and dialogue with God. His effort to live the spirit of the Work also led him to treat his wife, children, and siblings with greater refinement and charity. His wife commented to Fr. Rodriguez, "I don't know what you have done with my husband, but it is marvelous."

With the passage of the years, he met with some success in controlling his temper and in being more flexible. During Cofiño's visit to an elderly woman to ask for a contribution to an Opus Dei center, the woman began reminiscing about her life. Cofiño cut her off, saying he had to go. After they left the house, a friend who had accompanied him on the visit pointed out that the woman was lonely and needed to talk. A few days later Cofiño visited her again and let her run on at length about her memories.

Living in God's Presence

In the final hours of 1969, when he was approaching seventy years of age, Cofiño wrote an extensive note which gives us an insight into his relationship with God. Looking back over the past year, he concluded that "the agreeable and favorable events as well as the ones that were unfavorable, painful or simply annoying" all contributed to "showing me the constant presence of God in the expressions of his Will." He thanked God above all for the "difficult or annoying moments and events, which are the ones that bring me closer to the Lord." "You, Lord, were very close to me. Each morning when I awoke, my first thought was for you and then a conversation with you about events, resolutions, or problems. Meditation and thoughts and then, every day, almost without exception, you came to me. You were the nourishment of my soul."

Looking forward to the new year, Ernesto formulated resolutions:

> We are children of God. I am a son of God. I should repeat that to myself many times throughout the day. Although it may seem incredible, it is true: I am a son of God. Through his divine will, he deigns to come to me and to make my misery worthy of receiving him. He brings me closer to himself. He makes me participate in his divinity.

To live in keeping with the dignity of a child of God, Cofiño resolved to fight against

> whims, meanness, pride, sensuality, neglect, and inconstancy. . . . With, your help, Lord, I will be able to move forward, to pick myself up, and begin again. . . . As a child of God, I will try to fill my life with love as you have taught me to do. To love everyone without distinction: those who are pleasant, to thank them for the pleasure they give me, and those I find unpleasant because they give me an opportunity which I have not sought out, to mortify myself. I will try to see only what may be understandable, and perhaps justified, in the conduct of those who might be cruel or unjust to me.

Turning his attention to apostolate, he continued, "There are many, very many, along the edge of the road, waiting for a word, a helping hand that shows them your way. There are many, very many, who are thirsty and longing for a drop of water, of the water of Life with which you have filled me."

He concluded his reflections with an aspiration to Our Lady which he had learned from the founder of Opus Dei. "*Cor Mariae Dulcissimum, iter para tutum*" (Most sweet heart of Mary, prepare a safe way).

Throughout his life, Cofiño lived soberly, spending little on himself and generously helping others. When he learned that a young doctor, who had not yet succeeded in establishing himself in a practice, was working as an unpaid volunteer in the orphanage, he endorsed his monthly paycheck over to him and assured the young physician that until he could establish himself financially he would give him half his salary as director. At one point, he mortgaged his house to be able to help a former student buy a home. Ernesto could have easily purchased a mansion, but to the end of his life he continued to live in the first house he had bought after his marriage, and with the same furniture. He bought only one or two new cars in his lifetime. The rest were secondhand. He gave generously to his children, the church, the apostolates of Opus Dei, and many people in need. An index of his concern for the poor is that toward the very end of his life when his mind was failing, he would become agitated and frequently ask his nurse if he had delivered a check to people in need.

In 1963, Cofiño's wife died unexpectedly of a cerebral hemorrhage. Their youngest child was only nine years old at the time. Later in life, that boy reflected: "After her death, my father could have turned in on himself, focusing on his sufferings and mourning her absence. But he thought about us and fought against his own sorrow. He understood that his children, and especially I who was still a child, needed his joy and his smile."

Ciudad Vieja

At about the same time that Cofiño joined Opus Dei, Fr. Rodriguez approached him and several other professional men about creating a university center with a residence. At the time, Guatemalan universities were overcrowded and understaffed. Students had few opportunities to meet with the professors outside of class, and the level of academic instruction was low. There were few places where students could interact with others outside their field or meet leading figures in the professions, culture, the arts, and public life. The proposed university center would not be a mere dormitory. In addition to providing an environment conducive to serious study, it would help enrich students' college experience. Although it would not have a formal instructional role, the center's goal was to be in some ways like one of the colleges of Oxford. Fr. Rodriguez proposed that Dr. Cofiño and the other men he initially approached along with their friends take responsibility for the financial, organizational, and technical aspects of the project. Opus Dei would help them give a Christian orientation to the undertaking. Cofiño, who had a rare gift for inspiring enthusiasm for his projects, began recruiting friends for the board. "This university center is such an important and indeed decisive project," he told them, "that I have decided to dedicate to it all the salary I receive in one of the hospitals I work in."

The first meeting of the board had to be postponed because the president of Guatemala had been assassinated and the whole country was under a state of siege. Nonetheless, the project moved forward quickly. By summer 1957, the board had located a possible site: a large house in a neighborhood called Ciudad Vieja, from which the center would eventually take its name. The location had many advantages. Among them was one which could not be taken for granted at the time in Guatemala City: it was on a paved street.

The rent was high, but by soliciting the support of friends and taking out personal bank loans they were able to sign the contract and pay the first month's rent in August 1957. From that date until shortly before his death in 1991, Ernesto viewed the project as his personal responsibility.

To help furnish the house, he asked friends to donate furniture they no longer needed. When he learned that the authorities had shut down a clandestine casino, he and his wife purchased at auction some green velvet curtains which they thought would work well in the future oratory of the center. "This is really sanctifying the world," he commented, "because those curtains are going to go from the roulette room to the best place you could imagine."

In January 1958, the first resident moved in. The board had calculated that the center would be economically self-sustaining with twelve residents. In the first year, however, there were only six residents, a number of whom were unable to pay the full fees. Cofiño and the other members of the board soon realized that they would need to find donations not only to pay the rent, but also to create a scholarship fund so the residence could accept students from poor families.

Samuel Camhi Levy

One of the people Cofiño approached for scholarship money was Samuel Camhi Levy, a Sephardic Jew born in Izmir, Turkey, who had emigrated to Guatemala in 1924 with no money. He had barely established a small business when the Great Depression of 1929 drove him to the verge of bankruptcy, but over the years he had become very wealthy. Since his painfully poor youth, he had been determined that if he ever made money, he would use it to help poor children and young people.

Levy responded generously to Cofiño's request for scholarships, and the two became such good friends that Levy's children began to call Cofiño, "Uncle Neto." The two men shared a passion for cooking and frequently fixed family dinners together. Levy soon became involved not only in Ciudad Vieja but in several social works promoted by Cofiño and other members and friends of Opus Dei. When Cofiño was working with a small group of people to establish a school for working-class students that would be called Kinal, Levy lent them a building. In 1963, Levy was contacted by Junkabal, a girls' school situated in perhaps the poorest neighborhood of Guatemala City. The school was a few hundred yards from the edge of a massive dump where destitute families lived in shacks built on top of the junk and spent their days combing through it in the hope of finding something they could use or sell. Junkabal was in such serious financial difficulty that it could not pay the rent on the modest building that housed the school. As a result, its promotors were seriously considering closure. Levy was so impressed by the work they were doing that he purchased the building for them. It was not that a very wealthy man helped them with a small part of his surplus money. Levy had to borrow money for the purchase and mortgaged several of his stores to guarantee the loan.

In later years, Levy contributed generously to the construction of a new building for Junkabal and created a foundation to support it. Although he died as a practicing Jew, in the foundation's articles of incorporation he expressly stipulated that the moral formation given in Junkabal would always be entrusted to Opus Dei. He did this, his son said, to guarantee that there would never be any discrimination in Junkabal. "If Opus Dei is there," the son said, "my father felt sure, there will be religious freedom."

On one occasion, Cofiño was able to introduce Levy to the Founder of Opus Dei, who thanked him warmly for his support. Levy responded, "Monsignor, I want to remind you in the first place that I am not Catholic and in the second place that I am Jewish."

"Come to my arms," Escrivá said as he gave him a warm embrace. From then on, Escrivá always sent him greetings for his birthday and other special occasions. Levy told his son that never in his life had anyone treated him with greater affection.

The New Ciudad Vieja Residence

By the mid-1960s, the residence no longer had difficulties finding students. Now its problem was finding room for all the qualified students who wanted to live there. At first, they installed bunkbeds and tried other measures to increase the capacity of the residence, but eventually it became clear they needed a bigger building. The board member who took care of the accounts thought the project was crazy but voted to move forward anyway. He said,

"I have learned one thing in Opus Dei: In apostolic undertakings, we cannot work only with economic logic, which teaches us that two plus two is four. We have to add a decisive third factor: God plus two plus two."

About this time, during a meeting in Rome with Escrivá, Father Rodriguez commented that Cofiño and his fellow board members were thinking of building a new residence for forty students. "Forty?" the Father asked with surprise. "Only forty?"

"Bigger than that, Father?" Fr. Rodriguez asked. "How many were you thinking of? Sixty?"

"Bigger!"

"A hundred?" Rodriguez asked hesitantly.

"Bigger, still," the Father responded with a chuckle.

The board members were shocked, but they decided to try. This, of course, required a major fundraising effort. Cofiño commented: "Everybody is embarrassed to ask for money. I'm not." Fr. Rodriguez, who knew him well, adds:

> I think that at the beginning he must have found it hard to ask for money, like everyone else. But his love of God made him overcome that sense of embarrassment, thinking about the good that would be done from that university center and contemplating daily with his own eyes so much poverty, so many people in need, so much forgetfulness of God. He saw Ciudad Vieja University Center as a powerful motor for human, professional, and spiritual progress in all of Central America. That center would form many professional men who would contribute decisively to peace, understanding among people, and development in all sectors of those countries.

Close friends of Cofiño donated a large tract of land, and an architect designed a building that was daring for its time but fit well with local taste and architectural traditions. The project moved forward quickly and opened in 1968 with 134 beds. From the beginning, a high percentage of the students received scholarships. The residents included young men from indigenous families who had never been outside their small towns, boys of mixed race whose families were often poor, and students from prosperous families of Guatemala and other countries of Central America. Dr. Cofiño and the staff of the residence worked hard to ensure that they all lived together in harmony, following the insistent teaching of St. Josemaría, "There is only one race: the race of the children of God."

Cofiño was named the first rector of Ciudad Vieja, a position he held virtually to the end of his life. He did not consider rector an honorary position. He spent much of his time in an office in the residence. In 1959, he retired from both the hospital and his teaching position at the university, partly to make way for younger colleagues, but in large part because he wanted to dedicate more time to Ciudad Vieja. He worked untiringly to develop educational programs, form new members of the board, raise money, and above all mentor individual residents. He urged them all to pursue professional excellence and encouraged many of them to go abroad to complete their studies.

Ernesto was extraordinarily cordial, and the residents soon learned that they could count on him not only for good advice but a sympathetic ear. He took a real interest in each of them, remembered their names, and prayed for them. Each student who approached him came away with the impression that he was someone special to him, a person, not just a resident or student.

A Tireless Fundraiser

Cofiño's dedication to raising money for scholarships and the operating expenses of Ciudad Vieja and other centers of Opus Dei was astounding. Even late in his life, he often approached five or six people in a single day for contributions. On one occasion when there was a particularly urgent need, he went with another member of the board of Ciudad Vieja to visit someone whose office was on the ninth floor. They discovered that the elevator was out of order but were told that it would probably be repaired that afternoon. His companion turned around to leave, but Cofiño, who was in his eighties, started up the stairs saying, "Don't worry about it. It's only nine stories." When they reached the landing on the third floor, Cofiño stopped to rest for a moment and reminded his companion of something they had heard in a day of recollection the previous day:

> We should take advantage of anything we find hard to offer it to God. . . . And we should ask him for vocations saying: "Lord, souls!

They are for You. They are for your glory!" Well, that's what we have to ask
for with each step. Souls! Let every step represent a soul for the Lord.

Cofiño reached the ninth floor exhausted and had to rest for about fifteen
minutes, but eventually he was able to ask for the help he had come to seek.

Although that visit was successful, not everyone was receptive to his
requests. On one occasion, a receptionist refused to let him see the person
he had come to visit and threw him out rudely. Far from taking offense,
Cofiño, who had noticed that the receptionist had symptoms of a serious
illness, gave her a slip of paper with the names of two doctors, saying, "I
have written down here the names of two physicians. I would advise you to
go see them as soon as possible." A few months later Cofiño proposed to the
person who had accompanied him on that visit to try again. When his companion objected, "Don't you remember how that fellow's receptionist treated
us?" he brushed it off and insisted on going back. When they arrived, they
encountered a new receptionist who said she would call the office manager.
The office manager turned out to be the former receptionist, but this time
she greeted Cofiño warmly: "Doctor! I'm so glad to see you again. You saved
my life. I went to see one of the doctors you suggested, and he told me that
I was suffering from a very serious illness, but now I have recovered." This
time they had no difficulty getting in.

As we have seen in talking about his work with Samuel Levy, Cofiño's
efforts were not limited to supporting Ciudad Vieja. At the end of the six-
ties, when pro-abortion groups were beginning to gain strength in Guatemala, Cofiño began collecting signatures for a pro-life petition. He also
founded an association for the defense of life and began to give talks and
conferences on the value of human life. He argued not only on scientific
and moral grounds but also from his experience as a pediatrician. His presentations were backed by the passion and experience of a man who had
fought for many years against poverty, injustice, social marginalization, and
the lamentable situation of many indigenous women. Not content with
making prepared remarks, he made a point of talking personally with any
participant who wanted to see him and tried to help them find solutions to
their situations. The Congress of Guatemala invited him to talk about life
issues at a plenary session.

He also worked diligently to support other centers of Opus Dei as well as charitable activities with no connection to the Work. For five years after his retirement, for instance, he served as the head of the Guatemalan branch of the German charity Caritas, which at the time was distributing food to some ninety thousand people. It is not possible to explore all Cofiño's charitable works here. Suffice it to say that they reflected the same generosity, spirit of service, and confidence in God as his activities at Ciudad Vieja.

A Guest in His Own Home

In 1979, Cofiño's youngest son, José Luis, announced that he had become engaged. Knowing how important it was to his father that his grandchildren be brought up as good Catholics, José Luis struggled to find the right moment to tell him that his fiancée was not Catholic. The first day he brought her home, they didn't talk about religion while the three of them were together. During a period when José Luis was out of the room, however, the topic did come up. The conversation went very smoothly and proved to be the first in a long series. The young woman later said she found their conversations seemed like those of a father with his daughter. After a while, she began to accompany Cofiño and his son to Sunday Mass, and eventually, she was baptized.

José Luis and his wife wanted to move in with Cofiño so that he would not be alone. Ernesto strongly opposed that plan, not for his own sake but for theirs. "You need to have your own house and solve your problems in peace. I would just get in the way." Eventually, however, his sister convinced him that the young couple really did want him to live with them, and he gave in.

The house had been Cofiño's home for fifty years, first with his wife and then as a widower. It cannot have been easy for him, but he quietly stepped back and treated the house as the home of his son and daughter-in-law in which he was a guest. The young woman had little experience with housekeeping, but he made her feel that it was her home in which she was free to change curtains, move furniture, and do—or undo—whatever else she wanted.

Cofiño was an excellent cook. When his young daughter-in-law took over the kitchen, she still had much to learn; but if a dish turned out poorly or was burned, he seemed not even to notice. Far from showing off his gifts as a chef or giving lessons, he treated her with great understanding and affection without saying a word about the burnt or spoiled dish. On the rare occasions when he saw something in the house that really did need to be corrected, Cofiño suggested something to his son but said nothing directly to his daughter-in-law.

Although some friends expected the arrangement to work out poorly, the young couple and the eighty-year-old lived together happily. His son, writing to his children about their grandfather, attributed their ability to get along so well to the fact that "he was not a little old man of eighty years of age, loaded with complaints, who needed to be taken out to sit in the sun in the morning. Rather he was a good father, amusing, likable, and optimistic. He was full of hopes and projects and was always finding new ways to help others." After his death, his daughter-in-law recalled, "He was always smiling. His smile is engraved deep in my heart."

Brushes with Violent Death

In 1987, when Cofiño was going with a friend to solicit money for scholarships, they were assaulted by two armed men who ordered them to get into the back seat. As they drove off at high speed, the bandits ordered them to hand over their wallets, watches, medals, and rings. Cofiño could not help crying as he handed over the wedding ring he had worn for more than fifty years. When the leader decided to kill them and throw them at the side of the road, Cofiño began to pray out loud. The bandits ordered him to "shut up once and for all, old man."

He responded calmly, "I always pray, and more now. I am praying that the Lord may give you his light because you are on a very bad path."

Hearing this, the leader shouted to his companion, "Let's get out of here."

When they pulled over to the side of the road, the man who had been covering them with his pistol opened the door and helped Cofiño get out of the car. As he did so he held out his hand and wished Cofiño good luck. Ernesto responded, "No. I won't shake your hand now, because you're on a very bad path. I will pray a lot for you that you may find God. And when you do, I will be very happy to shake hands with you." From then until the end of his life, Cofiño prayed regularly for the two bandits.

This was not the first time that Ernesto had had a close call with violent death. In 1971, he left an academic conference in the middle of a torrential rainstorm. When he got out of the car in a lonely spot to take a shortcut to his destination, someone grabbed him from behind, began to choke him, and threw him to the ground. As the robber was trying to pull the ring from Cofiño's finger, he suddenly jumped up and began to run away because a police officer was approaching.

Cofiño later wrote about the experience in the third person:

> Although at the moment the victim may not have invoked the name of God, he had undoubtedly had it in his heart throughout the day. As he usually did, that morning he had attended Holy Mass and had received the Body of our Lord. He had said his usual prayers, among them the Rosary. In the afternoon he had visited the Blessed Sacrament.

He concluded his account by reaffirming his confidence in God:

> A God whom he feels is very close, so close that he not only lives in his heart but gives himself to him as the only food. God our Lord had given that man a series of tasks to carry out. . . . But that man, who should have been fully mature, continuously exposed himself to many dangers. . . . The Lord must have thought that he needed to teach him a lesson that he would never forget again. For that man what happened has a very deep sense: to feel in his flesh the real loving presence of Our Father God, protecting him and saving him.

When he told relatives and friends about what had happened, he said he was convinced that the policeman had been his guardian angel.

Living with Cancer

At age eighty-two, Cofiño began to have pain in his jaw. At first, he gave it no importance, thinking that it was caused by his dentures, but eventually he consulted a dentist, who told him that he had jaw cancer. With characteristic decisiveness, Cofiño immediately flew to Houston for treatment. That night, he reported, "We slept very well." One of his biographers comments:

> The phrase in itself could not have more human content, the joy of being able to say one slept well. But coming at the end of the day in which he had been clearly told that he had cancer of the jaw, it seems rather the joyful prayer of a man who treats God as a friend and says to him "You know very well what you dispose and do. Why should I worry?" And he goes to bed and sleeps well.

Although the operation removed a large part of his lower jaw, Cofiño returned to normal life and continued working actively. A few years later, a student asked him how he was doing. He responded with a smile: "I feel well. The only thing is that I can't see or hear. I can't walk, and I have no sense of smell or taste." On his ninetieth birthday, he wrote, "I prepare for death, living each day as if it were the last day of my life. In this way, I carry out each activity as well as I can, offering it to the Lord."

Shortly after Cofiño turned ninety, the cancer reappeared in his jaw. Once again his first reaction was to seek aggressive treatment which might enable him to continue working for God and others for a few more years. His son-in-law tried to dissuade him, pointing out that he was ninety years old, that surgery would leave him disfigured, and that he might lose an eye. Ernesto was initially undeterred and went to Houston to consult the surgeon who had operated on him previously. The surgeon told him brusquely that radiation would do no good and that surgery was his only alternative. When Ernesto said that he wanted to go ahead with the surgery, his youngest son, who had accompanied him, suggested that they go to the Opus Dei center nearby to pray in the chapel. Eventually, Cofiño decided against aggressive therapy and returned home.

Although much weakened physically, Cofiño continued attending classes and other means of formation at the Opus Dei center in Guatemala, taking notes and showing great interest in what was said although he was familiar with much of the material. He also continued, for a time, giving weekly spiritual life classes in his home to small groups of friends and the people whom they invited. Although the subjects were ones that Ernesto had studied deeply, thought about at length, and prayed about, he continued to prepare each presentation carefully. He also made a point of meeting with each of the participants individually to talk about the practical implications of what they had gone over in class.

At first, Ernesto continued to take walks for exercise, but after a sudden fall, he decided to switch to a stationary bike and asked a friend who was an avid cyclist to teach him how to use it. When his friend suggested that they would need a few twenty-minute sessions, he replied, "Fine. But we will need forty minutes. For the first twenty, you instruct me on the bike. The second twenty, I instruct you on our Christian faith."

Eventually, Cofiño needed a full-time caregiver. The man was surprised at how well Ernesto treated him and at the interest Ernesto took in his life, his family, and his problems. Above all, he was impressed by the fact that Cofiño always seemed content. He later recounted: "The only thing that distressed [Ernesto] was not being able to help others. His illness did not make him sad. I was with him all day and all night, and he never, never, never complained."

During the final months of his life, Cofiño's principal concern was getting to Mass. Toward the end, the parish priest suggested that he come into the sacristy and take a seat near the altar to be able to follow Mass better. He also wanted to say the Rosary, even though his mind was failing. His caregiver describes in detail the Rosaries of his last few weeks:

> He could no longer coordinate his ideas. "The first mystery," he would say and begin the Hail Mary, but after the second or third Hail Mary, he would announce the Third Mystery and shortly thereafter the Fourth Mystery. Those Rosaries were very short. But it seems to me that it did not matter, that the Virgin understood him and that those Rosaries had special value in the eyes of Our Lord. . . . Those unusual and disorderly Rosaries were one of the prayers that I have seen prayed with the greatest devotion. I am sure that they made Our Lady especially happy because he prayed with immense faith when he was already failing and had no strength.

On October 16, 1991, the day before his death, the head of Opus Dei in Guatemala arrived with a letter from the successor of St. Josemaría as head of Opus Dei, Bishop Álvaro del Portillo:

I have been moved by your supernatural vision of the illness you are suffering. Continue to abandon yourself into the fatherly arms of God, convinced that the Lord always gives us what is best for each one of us, although at times it may be hard to understand. I count especially on you, my son, to move forward the apostolate of the Work in the whole world. Continue to offer your pains and sufferings for my intentions. May God reward you for it.

Early the next morning, October 17, 1991, Cofiño quietly slipped away. In the words of the caregiver who was with him,

His death was like a candle that had burned itself down completely, giving all the light of which it is capable. He left quietly, almost on tiptoe, without making noise, with the God he loved so much. I have always thought that the deaths of the saints should be like that, happy and serene. I have not the slightest doubt that Dr. Cofiño was a true saint.

The archbishop of Guatemala City opened Ernesto Cofiño's cause for canonization in 2000.

SOURCES AND SUGGESTIONS FOR FURTHER READING

The information in this book was taken largely from the publications listed below. A reader who wants to learn more about the subjects of these sketches might start with them.

Chapter One: Ruth Pakaluk

Pakaluk, Michael. *The Appalling Strangeness of the Mercy of God: The Story of Ruth Pakaluk, Convert, Mother, Pro-Life Activist.* San Francisco: Ignatius Press, 2011.

Chapter Two: Tomás and Paquita Alvira

Vázquez, Antonio. *Tomás Alvira y Paquita Domínguez. La aventura de un matrimonio feliz.* Madrid: Palabra, 2007.

Marlin, Olga Emily. *Our Lives in His Hands: An Ordinary Couple's Path to Holiness.* New York: Scepter, 2018.

Chapter Three: Carlos Martínez

Íniguez Herrero, José Antonio, and Pablo Alvarez Valbuena. *Carlos Martínez pescadero. Un revolucionario que se encontró con Dios.* Madrid: Palabra, 2011.

Chapter Four: Dora del Hoyo

Medina Bayo, Javier. *Dora del Hoyo: A Lighted Lamp.* Hounslow, UK: Scepter, 2017.

Chapter Five: Eduardo Ortiz de Landázuri

López-Escobar, Esteban, and Pedro Lozano Bartolozzi. *Eduardo Ortiz de Landázuri. El médico amigo.* Madrid: Rialp, 2003.

Narváez Sánchez, Juan Antonio. *El Doctor Ortiz de Landázuri. Un hombre de ciencia al encuentro con Dios.* 2nd ed. Madrid: Palabra, 1999.

Chapter Six: Father Joseph Múzquiz

Coverdale, John. *Putting Down Roots: Father Joseph Múzquiz and the Growth of Opus Dei.* New Rochelle, NY: Scepter, 2009.

Chapter Seven: Ana Gonzalo

Gonzalo Castellano, Blanca. *Una prolongada carta de familia. Mi hermana Ana—Un testimonio de coraje en las instituciones europeas.* Madrid: Ediciones de Buena Tinta, 2013.

Chapter Eight: Guadalupe Ortiz de Landázuri

Montero, Mercedes. *En vanguardia. Guadalupe Ortiz de Landázuri (1916–1975).* Madrid: Rialp, 2019.

Abad Cadenas, Cristina. *The Freedom of Loving.* New York: Scepter 2019.

Del Rincón, María, and María Teresa Escobar, eds. *Letters to a Saint: Guadalupe Ortiz de Landázuri.* Madrid: Letragrande, 2019.

Equibar Galarz, Mercedes. *Blessed Guadalupe Ortiz de Landázuri.* New York: Scepter, 2019.

Chapter Nine: Isidoro Zorzano

Pero-Sanz, José Miguel. *Isidoro Zorzano Ledesma.* 2nd ed. Madrid: Palabra, 1996.

Chapter Ten: Montserrat Grases

Cejas, José Miguel. *Like Any Other: A Girl Named Montse.* New York: Scepter, 2016.

Eguibar Galaraza, Mercedes. *Montserrat Grases. Una vida sencilla.* Madrid: Rialp, 2018.

Chapter Eleven: Pepe Serret

Raventos Artes, Lluis. *Pepe Serret. Himno a la vida.* Madrid: Palabra, 2000.

Rico, Octavio, and Juan Zandri, eds. *Pepe Serret. Recuerdos de sus amigos.* Lleida: Privately published, 1994.

Chapter Twelve: Toni Zweifel

López Kindler, Agustín. *Given to Others: The Life of Toni Zweifel.* New York: Scepter, 2016.

Chapter Thirteen: Ed Dillett

Dillett, Jim. *Love and Faithfulness: The Life Stories of Ed and Myra Dillett.* Milwaukee: Privately published, 2008.

Chapter Fourteen: Ernesto Cofiño

McDonough, Thomas A. *No Small Goals: The Life of Dr. Ernesto Cofiño—Guatemalan Physician, Humanitarian, Pioneer in Pediatric Medicine and Servant of God.* New York: Scepter, 2019.

Cofiño, José Luis, and José Miguel Cejas. *Ernesto Cofiño. Perfil de un hombre del Opus Dei, 1899–1991.* Madrid: Rialp, 2003.